T0294356

R M S
TITANIC

RMS
TITANIC
MADE IN THE MIDLANDS

ANDREW P.B. LOUND

The
History
Press

For Linda Waite

Cover illustrations
Front: *Titanic* ready for launch and fitting out. *Back*: *Titanic*'s central anchor outside Lloyds' testing house (both Avery Historical Museum)

First published 2017

The History Press
The Mill, Brimscombe Port
Stroud, Gloucestershire, GL5 2QG
www.thehistorypress.co.uk

British Library Cataloguing in Publication Data.
A catalogue record for this book is available from the British Library.

ISBN 978 0 7509 6705 1

Typesetting and origination by The History Press
Printed and bound in Great Britain by TJ International Ltd

CONTENTS

FOREWORD

Andrew Lound is an expert on astronomy and one of the world's leading authorities on the ill-fated liner, *Titanic*, which sank in April 1912 with many lives lost. In particular he has carried out extensive, pioneering and revealing research into the connections between the ship and the Midlands, showing that although Belfast and Southampton may claim *Titanic* as their own, over 70 per cent of the ship's interior was actually manufactured in the Midlands.

One of those firms was the famed anchor-makers of Netherton – Noah Hingley. For both *Titanic* and its sister ship *Olympic*, there were three anchors: the port and starboard bower anchors were 7.81 long tons and 7.89 long tons, whilst the centre anchor was a massive 15.8 long tons made of forged and cast steel. The cable chain was 165 fathoms long per anchor and 3⅜in in diameter produced in the traditional manner by a gang of sweating Black Country men without counterpart in the country, whose movements were as artistic and graceful as any seen in an Olympics gymnastics event.

There are several photographs in existence showing *Titanic*'s centre anchor as it was pulled by horses on a heavy cart from Netherton to Dudley, where it was put on a train to make its way eventually to Belfast to the Harland and Wolff shipyard where *Titanic* was built. Andrew explains that the railway company planned to use twelve horses to pull the cart with the anchor upon it. However, when the anchor came to be moved, Hingleys' management refused to use them, as they looked poor and their leathers were dirty. It was insisted upon using eight of the company's own horses. This infuriated the railway man, who demanded that his horses were also attached to the cart carrying the anchor, with the result that twenty horses pulled one of *Titanic*'s anchors through the streets of the Black Country.

Andrew's talent lies not only in his research but also in his ability to bring to life the relationship of *Titanic* with the Midlands through stories such as this. Importantly he has also brought to the fore the life of William E. Hipkins, managing director of W&T Avery Limited and the last managing director of the James Watt Company based at the Soho Foundry in Smethwick. Hipkins was from Birmingham and a first-class passenger on *Titanic* who died in the tragedy.

Interestingly, Commander E.J. Smith, the captain of *Titanic*, was also a Midlander, coming from Hanley in the Potteries. He was amongst the many who died when the ship sank in April 1912. In Beacon Park, Lichfield, there is a bronze statue of him. It was carved by Lady Kathleen Scott, the widow of the courageous Captain Robert Scott, the Antarctic explorer. Unveiled in 1914 the statue was paid for by a national subscription. Thanks to the important work of Andrew Lound we now understand that *Titanic* was not only captained by a Midlander but also that most of it was 'Made in the Midlands'.

Professor Carl Chinn MBE

ACKNOWLEDGEMENTS

This book would not have been possible without the assistance of a number of organisations and individuals who have given freely of their time and allowed me access to archives, private documents and specialist knowledge. I would like to acknowledge the assistance rendered to me by staff at thefollowing: Birmingham Archives and Heritage; Dudley Archives and Local History Centre; Coventry History Centre; Lichfield Record Office; Sandwell Community History and Archives Service at Sandwell Library; Staffordshire County Record Office; Stoke-on-Trent Archives; The Potteries Museum; Walsall Local History Centre; Warwick County Record Office; West Bromwich Library; Wolverhampton Archives and Local Studies Centre; Worcester Archive and Archaeology Service; Bristol Central Library; Ulster Folk and Transport Museum; Liverpool Maritime Museum and Archives; Birmingham Museums Trust; and The National Archives. I am grateful for access to the Avery Historical Museum Archive, and especially to the files of W.A. Benton, the Museum's first curator who amassed an enormous archive of industrial history. Benton's research included interviews, photographs and copies of documents from many local firms who supplied the shipping industry. Howard Green and John Doran, former curators of the Avery Historical Museum, assisted greatly in finding long-forgotten material. I am indebted to the late Peter Hingley, who gave me access to his research into the Hingley family and business, and to the United States Clydesdale Society, Felicity Smith and Dr Martin McCormack for their expertise in working horses. Engineering technical advice and railway working practices was provided by the late Michael Horne. The following organisations have provided assistance: Cradley Then and Now History Group, in particular Jill Guest, who arranged a special evening where research relating to Noah Hingley & Sons and Walter Somers was exchanged. I am especially thankful to Stuart McMaster (former Heavy Machine Shop Manager), Dr Rex Bayliss (former managing director) and John Layton (former forge manager) at Somers; Titanic Historical Society for their resources and published papers; Birmingham & Midland Society for Genealogy and Heraldry; The British Titanic Society; Colton History Society; Stourbridge History Society; West Bromwich History Society; and the Titanic Heritage Trust. I would like to express appreciation to the following individuals: Muriel Bennett, Ann Biggs, Brian Knowles, Mavis Whitehouse, Stuart Williams, Jeanette Woodward, Robert Woodward and the late Howard Nelson. I will be eternally grateful to John Willis and Cheryl Lewandowski, née Davies, for details of the Davies brothers and their family. I would like to mention my gratitude to James Cameron for imaging William Hipkins' cabin and the Pooley Weighing Machine in the Turkish bath, and thank Ken Marshall for his assistance in allowing me to see high-resolution images of these rooms. I would like to thank Janet and Christopher Pickard for their continued support. I would like to acknowledge the hard work of Linda Waite who has read the manuscript, assisted in research, offered advice and listened to endless stories about the Midlands' connections with *Titanic*. I would also like to thank Carl Chinn for agreeing to write the Foreword. Finally, I would like to mention the late Harry Seabourne, who in 1981 encouraged me to continue my research into that fateful night in April 1912. Without him this work would never have come to fruition.

INTRODUCTION

Titanic is easily the most famous ship in history. Regardless of nationality, culture and age, the name *Titanic* conjures up images of a starry night, wealthy passengers enjoying a meal in a sumptuous restaurant, third-class passengers enjoying their own entertainments deep down in the bowels of the ship, the largest ship in the world on its maiden voyage. What could be more romantic? Yet, with everyone enjoying themselves feeling that life was just fine, fate in the shape of an iceberg was to deal a fatal blow resulting in a story that has been told and retold a million times.

One would have thought that since 1912 all that could be written about the ship, its passengers and crew would have been written, that after all this time there could be no new stories or twists to the tale. Yet, that is not so. Over 2,000 people were on board, which naturally means there are at least 2,000 stories to tell! Add to these the stories of those who built her, aided in the rescue of the survivors, or took part in the two inquiries and one can see that there are countless opportunities to discover something new.

At the beginning of the twentieth century Birmingham and the Black Country was the region in the United Kingdom where almost anything that could be made was made. It was a region filled with workshops, factories, foundries, assembly lines and workmen (and women) of great skill; and as the many books and television documentaries lament of the workers of Belfast and of the crew from Southampton and Liverpool, no one has ever mentioned the role played by the Midlands in the fitting out of the world's most famous liner, save for one exhausted fact – when one mentions *Titanic* and the Midlands in the same sentence, one will often hear the comment, 'Did you know that the anchor was made in the Black Country?'

It is the one *Titanic* connection with the Midlands that everyone knows. For most of the nineteenth century and beginning of the twentieth century Birmingham and the Black Country was the centre of world manufacturing, so one would not be surprised if there were more connections with *Titanic* than just anchors. Birmingham, located in the centre of the Midlands, is a long way from the coast, and it is perhaps because the region did not supply the shipping industry that there is such a dearth of information regarding *Titanic*. My own research into the region's connections with the most famous of liners began not with the anchors but with a first-class passenger – William Edward Hipkins – a Birmingham man who was the managing director of the famous weighing-machine firm W&T Avery Limited. He died on the ship, and it was while I was researching his life that my attention turned to all possible industry connections. I had no lack of anecdotal information – following one of my lectures I would be contacted by people who had a relative who had worked on the ship, made components for it, or was destined to travel on it but cancelled at the last minute. Anecdotal information is interesting, but without documentary evidence to support it, it has to remain just an interesting story. The need to obtain firm, documented information has been a difficult and, at times, frustrating task, especially as ship's chandlers' carefully concealed details of their favoured suppliers.

The process has been rewarding – discovering hidden documents in libraries, personal collections, secondhand bookshops and even on Ebay, and unearthing information relating not only to several major suppliers, but also to a complex supply chain involving major companies and legions of outworkers, a string of passengers and crew, and the rather fascinating response by midlanders to the tragedy. It has been very gratifying to uncover an unspoken story of *Titanic*, a story that throws a new light onto Birmingham and the Black Country and its role in a rapidly developing industrial world, with the shipping industry playing a vital role. The information contained in these pages is not definitive, and no doubt new documents will surface in the years to come to add more pieces to a complicated puzzle. Even so, I am sure that by the end of this book you may be forgiven for thinking that *Titanic* was, in fact, a Birmingham and Black Country ship.

ONE SHIP – A THOUSAND TRADES

Titanic was built at a time when passenger shipbuilding was reaching a new level, both in quantity of ships built and in size of construction. This increase in size was driven by three forces. Firstly, the need to transport goods and emigrants across the Atlantic. The increase in skilled labour leaving the Old World for a better life in the New required better transport to carry them, with shipping companies vying with each other to attract passengers. This boom in emigration from Europe to the United States had fuelled the need to build larger ships with more accommodation for emigrant passengers, or 'third class' as they were now to be called. This new class was to improve on-board conditions for the passengers, bringing them up to the level of second-class accommodation on smaller ships. The second force was the rivalry between Germany and Great Britain at sea. Kaiser Wilhelm wanted a navy as powerful as the Royal Navy and wanted his merchant fleet to challenge Britain's global domination. Global trade was a big feature in both of these forces, with British government policy favouring free trade with limited, if any, tariffs on imported goods from the United States and European countries. The United States and most European countries, however, charged strict tariffs on British goods and this had placed a great strain on industry. Joseph Chamberlain, an MP for Birmingham and a former president of the Board of Trade, was keen to see tariff reforms protecting British industry from what he saw as unfair foreign competition.

The demand for shipping was immense and around the UK shipbuilders were hard at work with full order books. This was due, in part, to the third force, which was not known to many people at the time. The great shipbuilders were large employers in a variety of trades, and these builders also supported a vast quantity of suppliers of parts, equipment, sundries and men from all over the country. The motor car and the rail industries of the mid- to late twentieth century supported a chain of manufacturers, and the shipping industry operated in the same manner. It was important that the shipyards had full order books, and the shipbuilders conspired to encourage their customers to build bigger and better – in essence creating their own market. This was assisted by the cosy relationship the shipbuilders had with the shipping companies. For example, Harland and Wolff was the sole builder for the White Star Line, an arrangement guaranteed by the chairman of Harland and Wolff, Lord Pirrie, having a seat on the White Star board. It was in this climate that the two rival shipping companies, Cunard and White Star, vied to attract passengers to their ships, and to attract them they had to build larger and more luxurious vessels.

In 1907 Cunard had two new ships crossing the Atlantic: *Mauritania* and *Lusitania*, the largest, most luxurious and fastest ships afloat. These ships were built with the aid of a government loan of £2.6 million at 2.75 per cent interest, payable over twenty years through an arrangement entered into by Cunard in order to help prevent them from being taken over by the International Mercantile Marine (IMM), an American company headed by the famous and somewhat ruthless businessman J. Pierpoint Morgan. Morgan wanted to control the cost of shipping across the Atlantic. He took control of the US shipping companies International Navigation Company (operating the Atlantic Line and Red Star Line) and the Atlantic Transport Line. Morgan then turned to Britain, taking control of the Leyland Line, Dominion Line and, most remarkably, the White Star Line. He then entered into partnership with the German shipping companies Norddeutscher Lloyd and the Hamburg-Amerika Line*, agreeing to conditions protecting German shipping. Morgan's new company IMM seemed destined to dominate world shipping when he turned his attention to the other great British Atlantic carrier – Cunard. Cunard's chairman, Lord Inverclyde, decided to play Morgan off against the British government in order to get the best deal for his shareholders. After his stint at the Board of Trade, Joseph Chamberlain became Secretary of State for the Colonies and his concern turned to the shipping industry, as shipping was critical to Britain and its empire. Chamberlain was anxious that Morgan's domination of the shipping industry would threaten Britain's security, as, by prior arrangement in a time of crises, passenger liners were used by the Royal Navy as auxiliary cruisers, hospital ships and troop carriers at a preferred rate. If Britain's passenger and cargo fleets fell into the hands of foreign ownership Britain might find itself in jeopardy. Chamberlain met with Morgan to discuss the issue, but the two could not reach an agreement. Chamberlain suggested that government subsidies should be given to Cunard in order to protect British shipping. This led to the loan to Cunard of £2.6 million, plus an annual subsidy of £150,000, and put Cunard and IMM on a collision course.

Mauritania and *Lusitania* were constructed in line with Admiralty specifications, as they may, in the future, have had to face attack from warships. This specification dictated the nature of the power plant for the ships – six Parsons turbine engines (four forward, two reverse) that would enable the Cunarders to easily outpace any rival ship.

Morgan's aim had been to dominate the Atlantic shipping industry, thus controlling the cost of cargo transport, which would give him control of supplies to and from the United States. His failure to secure the takeover of Cunard was a blow to his plans, one which led to an even greater rivalry between his White Star Line and Cunard. What's more, due to Chamberlain's intervention, the French shipping company of Compagnie Générale Transatlantique found it could stand up against Morgan and his dreams of domination came to an end.

The putting to sea of the Cunarders *Mauretania* and *Lusitania* in 1907 raised the stakes: White Star Line would have to compete with these new ships. J. Bruce Ismay was the son of the founder of White Star and had remained as managing director after the takeover by IMM. In 1904 he became president of IMM, giving him almost unlimited power and resources to increase the White Star fleet.

Lord Pirrie put forward a proposal for a new class of ship – a third larger than the Cunarders and far more luxurious. This appealed greatly to Ismay, as White Star prided itself on the prestige of having the most luxurious of liners; speed was not his priority for he wanted to attract the cream of society. To compete with the two high-speed Cunarders, White Star needed three ships – three near-identical sisters that would be the finest in the world. He named them *Olympic* (the class ship), *Titanic* and *Gigantic* (later to be renamed *Britannic*). Thomas Andrews, Lord Pirrie's nephew, was managing director of the design department at Harland and Wolff and would supervise every aspect of the design.

The building of a ship of even moderate size requires a staggering amount of organisation; the project planning alone may take over a year before even the first steel plate has been cast. Work began on *Olympic* in 1908, *Titanic* in 1909 and *Britannic* in 1911. *Olympic* and *Titanic* would be side by side during construction, with *Olympic* being four months ahead of her sister. Any design issues with *Olympic* would be designed out of *Titanic* and thus they were not identical sisters. Indeed, *Titanic* was 3in longer and over 1,000 tons heavier than her sibling. The two ships rose from the keel, the largest moving objects ever built up to that time. The people of Belfast – the home of Harland and Wolff – were justifiably proud of the new ships. For this reason *Titanic* is often referred to as a Belfast ship or an Irish ship. Yet, although the ships were constructed in Belfast, it is clear that every component could not be made in Ireland. These huge ships with hundreds of rooms required millions of components, many of which had to be manufactured and shipped into Belfast from elsewhere. A large number of shipping-associated trades were located near to the shipbuilders themselves, usually Glasgow, Newcastle, Belfast, Hull, Bristol etc.

However, the large quantity of material required for ships meant the supply chain had to be spread over the entire country, with the majority of firms being located in Birmingham and the Black Country. Thus, the construction of a ship entailed the mobilisation of a large quantity of manufacturers. To control this, Harland and Wolff managed the design and assembly of the ship, ensuring that it met the requirements of the customer and regulations of the Board of Trade. The ship's plate, structure and heavy engineering – such as the engines and boilers – were managed by the builders, and in many cases built on site. Much of the ship's interior was sourced by ships' chandlers who would issue contracts to fit out the vessel. Large companies would apply for contracts and would then subcontract some of the work to smaller firms. This led to a complicated supply chain, yet in an age of no electronic computers it was a system that worked well.

The biggest issue was, of course, delivery. In the twenty-first century there is much talk of just-in-time deliveries and expensive computer software is used to schedule the delivery of products. At the turn of the last century, 'just-in-time' was the standard in the shipping industry, but instead of computers the process was controlled by teams of clerks with card indexes. Each firm that secured a contract allocated a manager to oversee it. Some firms may have had five or six different contracts for three or four shipping companies located at different yards, so project management was critical. This process was slightly easier if two or more ships of the same class were to be built. The follow-on contracts would adhere to what went before, with all the kinks ironed out – in theory. *Olympic* being four months in front of *Titanic* did not give much leeway, especially as some of the interiors were different on *Titanic*.

The Olympic Class contract was signed on 31 July 1908. *Olympic*'s keel was laid on 16 December 1908 and *Titanic*'s on 31 March 1909. Detailed design work then went on at a pace as the ships' structures rose.

Table 1: Shipbuilding development 1858–1911

Name	Country	Year	Length (ft)	Tonnage
Great Eastern	UK	1858	680	24,360
Paris / New York	UK	1888	528	10,499
Teutonic / Majestic	UK	1890	565	9,686
Fürst Bismark	Germany	1891	503	8,000
Campania / Lucania	UK	1893	600	12,500
St Louis / St. Paul	USA	1895	536	11,629
Kaiser Wilhelm der Grosse	Germany	1897	625	14,349
Oceanic	UK	1899	685	17,274
Deutschland	Germany	1900	662.9	16,502
Kronprinz Wilhelm	Germany	1901	663	14,908
Kaiser Wilhelm II	Germany	1903	678	19,361
La Provence	France	1906	597	13,750
Kronprinzessin Cecilie	Germany	1907	678	19,400
Adriatic	UK	1907	709	24,541
Lusitania	UK	1907	760	30,822
Mauritania	UK	1907	760	31,938
Olympic / Titanic	UK	1911	882.6	45,000

The Hull

One of the great myths regarding the Midlands and *Titanic* is that the rivets were supplied by Nettlefolds. This is untrue. All the 3 million rivets for the ship were produced from metal bar on site at Harland and Wolff.

Propelling Machinery

It may seem surprising, with Birmingham being so far from the coast, that marine engines were produced nearby. The famous Soho Foundry opened in 1796 by Matthew Boulton and James Watt became a major supplier of marine engines to both the merchant and Royal Navy. The most famous marine engine supplied was that of the screw engine for Brunel's *Great Eastern*. This ship was ahead of its time when launched in 1858 and remained the heaviest ship ever built until 1907 when White Star's *Adriatic* was completed. Cunard's *Mauritania* and *Lusitania* would surpass *Adriatic* the same year, and it was in response to those that *Olympic* and *Titanic* were constructed. By this period, marine engines were becoming so large it was more cost-effective to have them constructed on site. Even so, components for marine engines were still purchased from Birmingham and Black Country firms by the shipbuilders.

The power plant for *Titanic* was a mixed reciprocating and turbine combination. Two four-cylinder triple-expansion reciprocating engines were fitted. Each engine stood four storeys tall and weighed 1,000 tons – the largest engines of their type fitted to an ocean-going vessel. The main steam and exhaust pipes for *Titanic* were produced in Birmingham by Thomas Piggott & Company of Western Road, Spring Hill. The firm dates from 1822 when 21-year-old Thomas Piggott took over from the boiler and gas holder maker Joshua Horton at the Swallow Foundry, Spring Hill, situated at Taylor's Dock. Piggotts expanded in 1854 with the purchase of land located between Swallow Foundry and the Birmingham Workhouse (now the City Hospital on Dudley Road). Although a successful firm, it was the involvement of the Lloyd family that turned Piggott's into a powerful engineering company. George Herbert Lloyd joined the company in 1871 and his improvements led to the development of a wrought-iron lifeboat called *Petrel*. Continued expansion led to the purchase of the Atlas Works in Oozells Street in 1881. Soon thereafter Piggotts started to produce large-diameter steel pipes by water and gas welding. With lengths of 12–15ft, with expanded or riveted transverse joints, these pipes were cutting-edge technology that continued to develop. For Piggotts the growing steamship industry was ideal, as Piggotts could produce the piping to the standards required for high-pressure engines. It is not surprising that they received the contract to supply the exhaust pipes for *Olympic* and *Titanic*, having previously supplied piping for other liners as well as the Admiralty.

Piggotts set to work to produce the two main steam pipes that carried steam from the boilers to the engines. These were of welded steel with a butt-strap riveted over the weld from which branches were carried to the various boilers, and which gradually increased in diameter as they approached the engine room forward bulkhead. Through a series of stop-valves the steam passed to the reciprocating engines and, after expanding through the various stages, was led to the low-pressure cylinders by a 61in pipe to a huge changeover valve. By means of these change-valves the exhaust steam was deflected downwards to the turbine. These exhaust pipes were steel lap-welded with a strap riveted over the weld and were provided with concertina or bellow joints between each rigid connection to allow for expansion without endangering the air-tightness of the pipes leading to the condensers. The joints consisted of two thin steel discs riveted together at their periphery through a steel ring and were about 2ft 6in larger in diameter than the pipes to which they were connected by flanges. In addition to these pipes Piggott's supplied the Auxiliary Steam-Pipe System. The five single-ended boilers in No. 1 Boiler Room were arranged for running the auxiliary machinery when in port, while two boilers in each of the other compartments had separate steam pipes leading to the auxiliary machinery, which included the very large dynamo engines.

Piggotts were naturally proud of their contract with Harland and Wolff to supply the world's largest liners, thus they took out advertisements in the marine press to show off their prowess. It does seem a surprise to find that the main power plant only had one major subcontractor from Birmingham and the Black Country, especially as the region had several firms who had already supplied equipment to the shipping industry. One of the biggest names was Bellis and Morcom – cited by several people as a 'definite supplier of electrical machinery to the *Titanic*'. Research, however, contradicts this view. Bellis and Morcom did not supply anything for *Titanic*, or *Olympic*. A firm with which they were to merge decades later, W.H. Allen Limited of Bedford, did have the contract for the electrical power plant for the new liners.

Titanic (left) and *Olympic* under construction in 1909. (Avery Historical Museum)

Thomas Piggott & Co. Ltd advertisement. (Author's collection)

THE
MAIN STEAM
AND EXHAUST PIPES
FOR THE
"OLYMPIC"
"TITANIC"
AND THE
HAVE BEEN SUPPLIED BY
THOS. PIGGOTT & CO. LTD.
BIRMINGHAM.
WHO ALSO MAKE
CORRUGATED BOILER FURNACES
(FOX, DEIGHTON OR MORISON SUSPENSION PIPES)
WELDED & RIVETED STEEL PIPES,
TO ADMIRALTY, BOARD OF TRADE AND
OTHER SURVEYS.
Prompt attention given to enquiries.
SEND FOR LISTS.
ESTABLISHED 1822.

Thomas Piggott
& Co. Ltd
advertisement,
1911. (Author's
collection)

The Welin Davit
and Engineering
Co. Ltd
advertisement,
1911. (Author's
collection)

THE
"WELIN QUADRANT" DAVIT
OVER
4000
FITTED or FITTING on vessels of all Nationalities.

TYPE DA²
As fitted on S.S's "OLYMPIC" & "TITANIC" (White Star Line),
and many others.
Manufactured in 30 Distinct Sizes.
THE WELIN DAVIT AND ENGINEERING CO. Ltd.,
5 LLOYD'S AVENUE, E.C.
Telegrams: "QUADAVIT, LONDON."   Telephone 2422 Central.

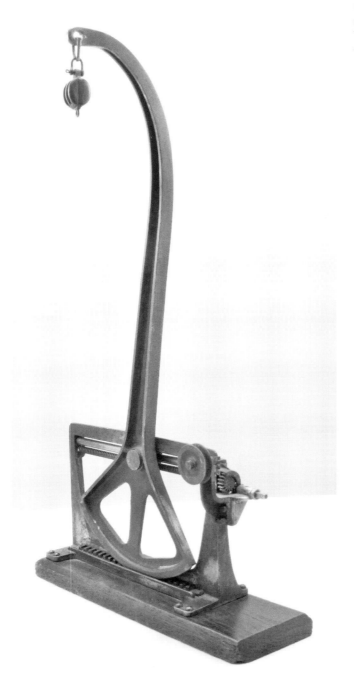

Demonstration
model of a
Welin Davit.
(Welin-Lambie)

2

ANCHORS AWEIGH!

The most commonly known Midland connection with *Titanic* was the anchors, which were produced by Noah Hingley & Sons of Netherton. Yet, this fact is so often distorted by a variety of myths and tall stories. It is true, however, that the famous firm of anchor and chain makers rose from obscurity to become the world's leading wrought-iron producers supplying some of the most famous ships in history with anchors and cable chain.

Noah Hingley was born in 1796 and worked for his father, Isaac, as a journeyman ironworker in a factory on the banks of the River Stour in Cradley, North Worcestershire, making nails and small chains. In 1820 following one of his regular trips to Liverpool, he accepted an order to make ships' cables even though he knew nothing about the ships' cable business. This first cable was only 1½in diameter and made from wrought iron, yet from this small beginning there grew a great business. In 1838 Noah re-formed the enterprise into his own business as Noah Hingley & Sons, and ten years later Hingleys became the first firm in the Black Country to make anchors. Hingleys did well and expanded in 1852 by opening a new purpose-built works at Netherton on the banks of the Birmingham canal where the firm began producing pig iron. Within half a century, the Netherton area had developed a worldwide reputation for producing quality anchors and cables. Hingleys had got into the market at the right time – John Brown and Company of Sheffield stopped producing wrought iron in around 1859, thus preventing them from making large anchors and cable chain. Hingleys' wrought iron, known as Netherton iron, was ideal for large anchors and cable chain as it was resistant to rusting, had high durability and enormous tensile strength. The process employed by Hingleys in its manufacture produced a very high-quality iron.

After his death in 1877, Noah was succeeded by his son Benjamin (from Noah's first wife) who, in 1890, turned the firm into a private limited company. Benjamin, acting more as a chairman than managing director (due to his other interests), along with his brother Hezekiah's two sons George Benjamin and Henry Montagu, ran the firm, developing its products and reaching out for new markets. George Hingley's main responsibility was setting up agents worldwide and he travelled all over the Orient, Australasia and Italy. He was, essentially, the managing director, always being involved in the day-to-day activities of the firm. His brother Henry travelled across Europe and South Africa. Henry was a brilliant technical innovator; it is due to him that Hingleys developed the new techniques that were to propel the firm to global recognition. The Hingleys were ably assisted by Alfred Hilton Legge, who became the company secretary in 1890; he had been with Hingleys since 1860 and knew virtually everything about the business.

Benjamin, like many family firm MDs, had other interests that would be used to boost the image of the firm. He was a Justice of the Peace in Worcestershire, Staffordshire and Dudley, and he was mayor of Dudley in 1887 and 1888, became high sheriff of Worcestershire in 1900 and became deputy lieutenant of Worcestershire. He was MP for North Worcestershire from 1885–95 and was created a baronet by William Gladstone in 1893. Much of the running of the firm would have been down to his nephews and, of course, the company secretary. Benjamin retired in 1895 due to ill health, leaving George and Henry in full control.

George and Henry's travels had brought great success in setting up agents abroad. These agents were all Sheffield based and it seems it is this Sheffield connection that led to the rise of Hingleys as a world power in anchors and cables. The most important Sheffield connection would be the engineer and inventor John Francis Hall. Hall was manager at the Jessop and Sons Limited steel works in Sheffield; it was with John Verity in 1886 that he patented a new type of anchor to equip the new larger ships being planned. With the rapid growth in weight of passenger liners and warships, existing anchors were too rigid, leading to the rolling movement of vessels causing cables to twist and break. Hall and Verity's design allowed the flukes (arms on the head) to pivot, and this radial movement prevented the shank and cable from twisting. Additional improvements were made in 1888 and 1889. In 1891 Hingleys entered into an agreement with Hall and Verity to be the sole manufacturers of the Hall's patent stockless anchor. A year later, Hall and Verity formed Hall's Patent Anchor Company Limited (HPAC) to act as a holding company for the patents. The design called for the heads of the anchors to be cast steel. Hingleys, having no facility to create such large steel castings, turned to Charles Cammell and Company of Sheffield. Hingleys were, therefore, well positioned when, in 1899, the Anchor and Chain Cables Act came into force. This Act, controlled by the Board of Trade, enforced a standard onto shipbuilders, stating:

> The maker or dealer in anchors and cables may not sell or contract to sell – nor shall any person purchase or contract to purchase – for the use in any British ship any anchor or cable exceeding in weight 168lb which has not been previously tested and stamped in accordance with the Cables and Anchors Act.

Anchors and cable chain now had to carry test marks to prove they had met a standard – an important development that would keep non-British-produced anchors and cable chain out of the British market. Testing of cable in Britain dates back to 1816 when Samuel Brown developed a testing machine to examine the quality of cable he and his cousin, Samuel Lennox, were manufacturing. It was Lloyds Register that, in 1853, introduced a regulation that cable chain on ships had to be tested, and this was followed by the setting up of a committee to discuss the issue of testing of cable chain and anchors for the Royal Navy. Since 1864, Hingleys had a Proof House in the Black Country. The Staffordshire Public Chain and Anchor Testing Company was initially located at Bloomfield in Tipton, with a second testing house being built at the top of Primrose Hill in Cradley Heath. The driving forces behind these facilities were Noah Hingley and Henry Perhouse Parkes. The new Act of 1899 was produced following the experience gained through Hingley and Parkes' work, leading to the formation of Lloyds British Testing Company Limited (LBTC), which absorbed the Staffordshire testing company. The chairman of the new company was Sir Benjamin Hingley. Anchors and cable chain for shipping now had to meet strict standards to be approved by Lloyds Register of British and Foreign Shipping, with the LBTC carrying out the testing on behalf of the Board of Trade.

Hingleys were the pre-eminent anchor and cable chain manufacturer in the UK. Even so, they still had to rely on good castings from Sheffield. In the case of anchors for the Admiralty, Hingleys found that all was not as it should be. An Admiralty inspector condemned three castings in 1903, which led to a rift between Hingleys and the Admiralty. The problem appeared to be the general design of the anchor; the cast head was hollow in places and this was not to the satisfaction of the Admiralty, due to the fact that water could fill the voids. Although the patentees always knew there would be hollow elements to the head they did not inform Hingleys of this fact. The Admiralty decided it would not order Hall's designs, but instead would use the Wasteneys Smith design (manufactured by Spencer & Sons of Newcastle upon Tyne). The quarrel, which became public and very acrimonious, was not settled until 1915.

In response to yet larger ship designs and the Admiralty's complaints about the anchor, Hall's original design of 1886 was modified again in 1904 by HPAC. Hingleys were heavily dependent on this anchor design and thus it was decided that Hingleys' own engineer Joseph Earnest Fletcher would work on yet another redesign of Hall's anchor. Fletcher had been the steel works manager at Charles Cammell and was an expert on the steel casting of anchor heads. He joined Hingleys in January 1906 as engineer and works manager and set to work on the new design. In his development Fletcher essentially created a whole new concept of deliberately forming voids in steel castings that would not undermine the design. This, along with several other modifications, became the 1906 patent for the most advanced anchor design in the world.

Yet, even with the redesign, the Admiralty would not relent and would not accept Hall's anchors on their ships. However, Hingleys still supplied anchors and cable chain to the merchant marine and to foreign navies. In the case of the merchant marine a race was ensuing between Germany and Britain for domination of the North Atlantic routes. The loss of potential Admiralty contracts was offset by an upsurge in passenger ship construction, with Cunard ordering 3½in cable for their new 19,500-ton ship *Caronia*. Sir Benjamin Hingley was naturally pleased by this order, especially as Lloyds carried out the testing, but he would not live to see just how quickly passenger ship development would thrust Hingleys into legend. Sir Benjamin died in May 1905 and the mantel was passed to George (by then Sir George) Hingley, who found himself faced with an incredible influx of orders. So dramatic were the developments that he arranged a meeting with other cable makers to form a sort of cartel to deal with the impending work. The Cable and Anchor Makers' Association was formed in June 1905. Hingleys had always formed alliances with other firms across the country as well as in Europe. This was common practice as it stabilised the market and prevented a spiralling price war. The association co-operated reasonably well until the slump of 1908.

Hingleys also worked with shipbuilders directly and collaborated with John Brown Shipbuilders on the Clyde. They also had, since 1897, Alexander Carlisle acting as their agent promoting their equipment; he was the managing director of Site Operations at Harland and Wolff in Belfast. Carlisle was a major figure in shipping circles, and it was he who suggested that passenger ships such as *Olympic* and *Titanic* should be fitted with more lifeboat capacity than required by law. Hingleys paid Carlisle 2.5 per cent on the value of all outfits (a complete package of anchors and cable) supplied to Harland and Wolff – the highest commission paid to an agent by Hingleys. Belfast was well catered for, as acting as an agent for Hingleys was B.J. Ackerley, who also covered Liverpool and all the shipyards on the Mersey. The Clyde shipyards in Glasgow were serviced by Captain T.G. Hardie, and along with their association with John Brown Shipbuilders, all the bases of the big shipping companies in the UK were covered. Hingleys also had agents around the world covering the major shipbuilders in Germany, Japan, South Africa, Sweden, Norway, France, Belgium, Italy, USA and even Russia and China.

The Admiralty may not have been buying Hingley anchors and cable, but other navies were. Hingleys had good arrangements with German shipbuilders, as well as supplying anchors for foreign naval vessels built in the UK. The brief boom period of 1905–07 saw Hingleys and their collaborators supplying merchant ships built to Admiralty specifications. Cunard and White Star Line's rivalry was good news for the shipping industry. With shipbuilders and subcontractors having common directors, it became standard practice to play Cunard and White Star off each other. Cunard's first new build, under a lucrative agreement with the British government, was for *Mauretania* and *Lusitania*. Two shipping companies received the build contracts: Swan, Hunter & Wigham Richardson for *Mauretania* and John Brown for *Lusitania*. Both ships were to be fitted with Hall's patent stockless anchors, and with the ships weighing in around 30,000 tons the anchors and cable chain had to be large. The anchors for the two Cunarders brought with them a number of problems. At over 10 tons each, the size of the shank was too big for Hingleys; the shanks were therefore sub-contracted under a long-standing agreement to Walter Somers of Halesowen.

The lull between the laying down of a ship's hull and its fitting out tended to create a boom and slump pattern in orders. Therefore, following the maiden voyages of *Lusitania* and *Mauretania*, there was a slump in orders. The continued dispute with the Admiralty, as well as a global financial downturn, placed Hingleys and its collaborators in some financial difficulties. Hingleys looked to make cost savings, even considering new methods of manufacturing cable chain using automatic machines rather than traditional methods. The slump was fortunately short-lived; a global boom was about to begin. Orders would start to pour in from around the world as merchant fleets increased and naval expansion grew. The putting to sea of *Lusitania* and *Mauretania* prompted the White Star Line to place an order with Harland and Wolff for *Olympic, Titanic*, and *Gigantic*, plus two tenders to support them – *Nomadic* and *Traffic*. The concept design-plan meeting was held on 28 July 1908 with the first two ships starting in 1908 and 1909, and complete outfits of anchors, cable chain and fittings required in 1910 and 1911. Alexander Carlisle at Harland and Wolff first notified Hingleys of the new ships at the beginning of 1909. It was the practice of Carlisle to confidentially inform Hingleys of the shipyard's plans for the forthcoming year. This would have included the building plans for *Olympic* (No. 400) and *Titanic* (No. 401) and White Star tenders *Nomadic* (No. 422) and *Traffic* (No. 423). This advance notice enabled Hingleys to look at material and manpower schedules, vital in such an industry. In some instances Hingleys would ask Carlisle for an advanced look at specifications.

The new White Star liners would have three principal anchors and two Trotman's iron kedge anchors. One Trotmans was fitted to the poop deck at the stern (stream anchor), weighing just over 1¼ tons, and one on the deck at the bow, weighing just over ½ ton. The Trotmans were taken from stock as they were of standard supply. The two bower anchors were Hall's patent stockless anchors with cast-steel heads, weighing just over 7¾ tons each. The third central anchor was of the same design as the bowers but larger at 17ft long by 10ft 3in wide and weighing just over 15¾ tons, making it the largest anchor in the world at that time.

The cable chains for the bower anchors were 165 fathoms long per anchor and 3⅜ in diameter – the whole package weighing 96 tons. The central anchor did not have cable chain; it was raised and lowered with steel cable produced by Bullivants of Millwall.

One can infer from correspondence between Alexander Carlisle and George Hingley that since the beginning of 1909 discussions had taken place about the supply of cable chain to Harland and Wolff. Hingleys were concerned about costs, and as early as 1904 a great debate had been raging in the cable industry over the practicality of machine-made cable. Hingleys and John Brown had entered into an alliance to produce machine-made cable chain using two methods: the Girlot process by L'Homogène Société Anonyme Internationale and the Maison process by La Société Générale du Laminage. The two firms formed the British Machine-Made Cable Company Limited (BMMC) with a capital of over £3 million. The big downturn of 1908 led Hingleys to examine ways of reducing the workforce and thus overheads; the machine-made cable seemed an ideal solution. Initially, the prospects regarding orders were good, with Carlisle's advance notice and foreign orders looking particularly advantageous. Hingleys' alliance with John Brown was not an easy one, as they were also competing for the same orders. For example Hingleys had supplied cable chain and anchors to the Brazilian government for thirty years and was shocked when a large order for the cable went to John Brown.

To stop the rivalry the firms agreed to construct a BMMC-specific works in Netherton equipped with machines for both methods of manufacture. On 5 July 1909 Hingley and John Brown suggested setting a price for the machine-made cable at a rate of £32 per ton with a discount of £2 per ton, and possibly a consideration of 2.5 per cent on some orders. It was thought that this figure would offset the high cost of installing the new machinery. This information had been forwarded to Carlisle, who duly responded on 24 August asking about consideration for the cables for the new White Star liners. Seven days later Hingleys responded, stating that BMMC representative William H. Ellis would call on him to discuss the order. William Ellis was the managing director of John Brown and Company at the Atlas Works in Sheffield, having taken over from his father John Devonshire Ellis. J.D. Ellis came from Birmingham and was educated at King Edward VI School, after which he worked in his father's successful brass foundry. J.D. (along with another Birmingham engineer William Bragge) became a partner with John Brown in 1855, setting up a steel works in Sheffield. Among his many accomplishments he developed armoured plate for warships. He became managing director of the firm in 1864, leading them to much loftier heights culminating in 1899 when he bought J&G Thomson shipbuilders on the Clyde, thus forming John Brown Shipbuilders. The mantel had now passed to his son William Henry who, with his brother Charles Edward, had continued the success of the firm seen as one of the world's leading steel forging and shipbuilding producers. William Henry's specialism was in heavy forging; he had set up a 4,000-ton forging press at the Atlas Works. As a major partner in the BMMC business he entered into discussions with potential customers. Then with the orders for the new

White Star liners being issued, John Brown (for BMMC) picked up the cable order. This did not please George Hingley, who may have wondered if Ellis was putting his company ahead of BMMC. Nonetheless, in the spirit of co-operation with BMMC, discussions with Harland and Wolff continued. There did seem to be some confusion at Harland and Wolff as Carlisle wrote to George Hingley regarding the price for the cable, which seemed to offer a different consideration than was usual with Hingleys. George wrote to Carlisle explaining that although the contract was via BMMC it was John Brown and Company's own conditions that applied. Even so, George Hingley attended a board meeting of BMMC where he raised the issue of a consideration, suggesting that he thought he had said a 5 per cent discount as opposed to 2.5 per cent. He duly communicated this to Carlisle. Looking at previous communications it does seem George Hingley was trying to make John Brown and Company look less attractive and co-operative than Noah Hingley & Sons.

William Ellis had bigger problems. The machines to manufacture the cable were not living up to their potential and it seems that the required quality of cable could not be met in time to meet the contract. In fact, the problems were affecting other contracts too. The situation grew worse when the Admiralty, a major customer of John Brown, refused to place orders for machine-made cable. This had a knock-on effect with other countries. Spain refused to buy machine-made cable and Brazil cancelled its original order. To top it all, Hingleys' workforce had refused to co-operate with the running of the machines installed at Netherton and to carry out the hand finishing that was required. Ellis, Hingley and the BMMC were in a fix; if the orders were to be met there was only one solution. Cyril E. Lloyd, assistant to George Hingley and de facto general manager, had been instrumental in the setting up of BMMC, but as a professional manager he was a pragmatist. He decided that the only way to meet the contract was to have the cable manufactured at Netherton in the traditional manner. George Hingley wrote to Alexander Carlisle in February 1910:

> With reference to No 400 (*Olympic*) I am pretty sure that W.H. Ellis has told you what arrangement we have made with the British Machine Made Cable Co. In reference to these Cables and that we are now proceeding with the work, the formal order having been handed over to us and I do not think you need trouble to confirm to us direct unless you wish to do so, because I perfectly understand the position and am personally attending to this important matter.

In view of our heavy work which is coming forward I am rather anxious to get these cables completed as early as possible, and presume that if we can deliver in the month of June there would be no objection on your part to receive them. I propose to invoice them under the Schedule conditions – which I hope will be all right.

It is perhaps fitting that the cable for the largest ships in the world should be fashioned from the blood, sweat and tears of Black Country working men. The physical act of smithing has to be seen to be appreciated; demonstrations at the Black Country Living Museum illustrate the effort that is required to fashion the enormous cable chain, with big men hammering away, furnaces belching out heat and white-hot metal glowing. The old hands at Hingleys were no doubt pleased with the contract.

Benjamin Hodgetts had worked at Hingleys since he was a boy – slowly climbing his way up. He did much to improve the conditions of chain makers, becoming a founder member (and eventually an executive board member) of the Chain Makers' & Strikers' Association in 1889. The association was responsible for significant improvement in the conditions of employment in the chain trade, especially relating to pay and conditions, sickness and accident benefit, as well as fair trade. He was not only an old hand at chain-making but a well-known figure in the community. He was a member of the Cradley Parish Council and acted as an overseer for the Parish for seventeen years. He owned a number of properties in Cradley, one of which he converted into a butcher's shop. As was traditional in the region, several members of a family would work for the same company. Hodgetts' family was no exception, with three of Benjamin's five sons following him into chain-making, the other two sons being butchers. He had worked on some of the most important chains to leave the old firm including the chain for *Lusitania*, but he was not alone. The great skilled workforce, all of whom had trod a similar path as Benjamin, had sweated blood alongside him. Ben Woodhouse, George Bridgwater, Albert Hodgetts, Theophulos Dunn, Jacob Bloome, Samuel Wishwood, to mention a few, contributed to the making of a chain that would be legendary.

The shackles and fittings for the anchors were also produced by traditional methods with a team of specialist workmen. This team included the Jones brothers George and John, who had learned their trade from their father Edwin. Alongside them were two other families of workers: the Denholms – Walter, Robert and William – all blacksmiths and strikers; and the French family – William (shackle maker), Stanley (a striker) and Claude (labourer).

The foreman in charge was William Brimson, a long-standing anchorsmith with his brother Robert. William's son (also Robert) worked at Hingleys as an anchorsmith labourer.

The two Trotman's anchors would be supplied from stock but would have been manufactured by the anchorsmiths at Hingleys – again, the type of work that the Denholms could produce along with Edwin Jones and Elijah Biggs.

The three Hall's patent stockless anchors would require mechanical construction. The heads of the anchors were cast by John Rogerson and Company, Walingsham, County Durham. The move from their regular supplier of Charles Cammell and Company was due to the merging in 1903 of Charles Cammell with Laird Brothers shipbuilders, forming Cammell–Laird. Cammell–Laird would concentrate on the construction of warships and thus Hingleys lost their regular casting contractor. This initially presented Hingleys with a problem. Fletcher's 1906 patent specified that a high quality of casting was required for the anchor head, limiting the number of firms that could produce it. Darlington Forge Limited were snowed under with orders, including orders for components for the new White Star ships, which left the German firm of Friedrich Krupp AG and John Rogerson and Company. As usual, Hingleys subcontracted the shanks to another famous Black Country firm – Walter Somers in Halesowen.

Walter Somers was born at Repton near Derby in 1839. In 1866 he set up a firm making wrought-iron forgings, taking over the Haywood Ironworks located near the canal in Halesowen that had been run by George Homfray making cable chain and anchors. The works was well equipped with a 30cwt Nasmyth steam hammer, two coal-fired reverberatory furnaces, two swivelling wooden jib cranes, a 40hp steam engine, two egg-ended boilers and a 16in rolling mill. Work began producing general forgings for steam engine components and other machine parts. Within two years Somers was producing forgings for the rail industry. In 1870 Somers entered into partnership with W.R. Colbourn, forming Colbourn and Somers. The partnership was successful, with the firm developing a reputation for quality forgings, especially for the shipping industry. In 1881 Walter Somers, using a loan of £1,600 from Jeston Homfray of Homfray and Halberton, bought out the Colbourns. Once again the firm was called Walter Somers.

Heavier plant, including steam hammers and lathes, was purchased, enabling Somers to produce bigger forgings. Following approval by the Admiralty for the use of steel in certain manufactures Somers began purchasing steel ingots. Firstly, from the New British Iron Company in Cradley and then from various companies in Sheffield. The quality of work improved, as, with a growing market in forgings, testing of materials was becoming the norm – especially in the shipping industry. In 1895 Somers purchased a tensile testing machine from Tangyes of Smethwick giving a degree of independence from external testing companies. By the end of the nineteenth century the shipping industry was playing a large role in supporting the iron industry of the Black Country. Somers produced wrought-iron and steel forgings for anchor components. Marine cranes or catheads, used to raise and secure anchors, were also manufactured. In 1888 Hall's patent stockless anchor made the cathead virtually obsolete, as the new design had swivelling flukes that enabled it to lock into the hawser holes after it was hauled up. The Hall's anchor was slowly phased into the shipping industry with the main manufacturer of these anchors being Noah Hingley & Sons, with whom Somers had a good working relationship. The increase in the use of steel in forgings meant a change in manufacturing processes. Wrought-iron products were often built up using small pieces; however, steel required new techniques, as the product would have to be forged from a single piece of metal. Somers was using a 7-ton steam hammer, but this was too small for steel work. Sir George Hingley had purchased a 12-ton steam hammer from Thwaites and Carbutt of Bradford with the intention of making heavy forgings. Sir George, however, had a change of mind, probably thinking that the need for the hammer would be limited compared to the cost of running it. Somers bought the hammer complete with two Cornish boilers and two steam cranes for £1,000. In order to pay for the new equipment the firm became a limited company in 1897 with Walter Somers as managing director, his son Seth as manager, E.N. Carter as financial director and C.E. Bloomer as company secretary.

The change to a limited company brought in much-needed capital that was used to build a new site on the opposite side of the canal. Somers needed access to the Great Western Railway (GWR), the line of which ran on the opposite side of the canal to their works. Halesowen Station had been opened in 1878, but following lengthy negotiations a branch line was opened to the new site in the summer of 1901. Somers could now handle heavier materials and bring in large quantities of coal to fuel the new machinery. Like all engineering companies, Somers had to keep pace with changing technology. In forging, the change from steam hammer to hydraulic press would improve the size and quality of products. German companies were leading the way with new technology, a development fuelled by the growing German navy and merchant marine. In 1905, Somers purchased a 3,600-ton hydraulic press from Haniel and Lueg of Düsseldorf at a cost of £8,500. The installation of the hydraulic press, along with all the necessary ancillary equipment and a building to house it, cost Somers in excess of £24,000.

Somers had a good mix of steam and hydraulic equipment to produce high-quality forgings of all sizes. Hingleys placing the order for the anchor shanks with Somers was par for the course. Following the sale of the Thwaites and Carbutt press Hingleys used Somers for all of their major shank work. The shanks for the anchors for *Mauretania* and *Lusitania* as well as many others were produced at Somers.

The bower anchor shanks for *Olympic* and *Titanic* – ordered on 8 August 1910 (completed 22 August) and 4 January 1911 (completed 25 January) respectively – were of Siemens steel, forged and annealed, measuring 13ft long. The central anchor shanks were also of Siemens steel, measuring 15ft 10in long for *Olympic* – ordered in July 1910 and completed on 12 August – and 15ft 7in long for *Titanic* – ordered on 27 January 1911 and completed on 18 March.

The shanks for the anchors for *Olympic* and *Titanic* (and eventually *Britannic*) were not the only connection between Somers and the White Star ships. Stothert and Pitt of Bath had the contract to supply the ships with cargo cranes. The high-quality forged-steel axle bars required for these cranes were produced by Somers, along with miscellaneous forged steel pins for Thomas Piggott and Sons for their steam pipes.

The anchors were assembled under the supervision of Head Fitter William Norman from Handsworth. Hydraulic jacks were used to assist in the assembly – one of the workers assisting this operation was William G. Edwards, who sixty years later recalled in a newspaper article the hard work involved of assembling the largest anchor in the world. The *Titanic* work made a big impression on Edwards. He tried to book passage on the ship, but due to personal reasons he sailed on a later ship heading to Quebec, Canada.

All parts of the anchors and cable chain had to be tested. The cable chain had to undergo tensile testing and sample links were sent to Lloyds' testing house. The test machines had been supplied by George Tangye, located at the Cornwall Works in Smethwick. Henry Green was the proof house supervisor but the testing was left in charge of Job Garrett, and it is here that another myth can be dispelled. It is often said that *Titanic*'s cable was so strong that it was unable to be broken during testing. However, the tests on links of chain were destructive tests aimed at determining the actual breaking strength, and although the cable exceeded the required specification by some way, it was indeed broken.

Once all the testing was complete and the cable and the anchors had received their certification they could be delivered to Harland and Wolff in Belfast. Distribution was made as soon as the items were ready. This is where the rail link became vital. As was usual, Hingleys sent out letters to various carriers to quote for the collection and delivery of the anchors and cables to Belfast. For some years Hingleys had used the Belfast Steamship Company to transport their anchors and cable chain to Belfast via Liverpool. However, Hingleys and the Belfast SSC had fallen out over charges, with Hingleys complaining of the high rate of transport. At a meeting between Sir George Hingley and James McDowell of Belfast SSC they agreed a rate of 6s per ton from Liverpool to Belfast. Two years later Hingley was again complaining about the cost of shipping, suggesting that shipping should be charged at 5s per ton. James McDowell responded initially by telegram and then by letter, tersely stating they had to make a profit! In fact, the cost of carriage was a constant problem for Hingleys, with railway and steamship companies changing their rates monthly as a rule (although they could adjust the price at any time), due mainly to the changing price of coal and changing cost of dock facilities such as cranes. Hingleys' reply emphasised that they had been using 'another route' and suggested that unless Belfast SSC gave the matter serious consideration then Hingleys would no longer use them, expressing it rather politely: 'We never like to desert our old friends because we know it is not a good policy in the long run, and hope you will take the same view, and when trade improves it will no doubt be a different matter …' The letter ends with a statement that if the company's manager would like to call in at Hingleys then the matter could be discussed. McDowell responded on 2 November sticking to his position.

Hingleys' alternative route was shipping from Fleetwood to Belfast via the Lancashire & Yorkshire and London North Western railways' Belfast & Fleetwood Royal Mail route. The shipping to Belfast was cheaper than from Liverpool and had an added bonus that the London North Western Railway (LNWR) had stations in Dudley that served the north-west. The LNWR was very keen to get the contract, as it offered publicity and had strong links with the White Star Line (Bruce Ismay was a member of their board). LNWR and London South Western Railway (LSWR) acted as the overland link to the ports for White Star's passengers and cargo. LNWR's joint venture with the Lancashire & Yorkshire Railway to operate a steam-packet service to Belfast from Fleetwood began in 1849 with the purchase of the Preston and Wyre Railway and Fleetwood harbour. The harbour and the rail link developed quickly, and in 1892 the old paddle steamers started to be replaced by twin-screw steamers, improving crossing times and the amount of cargo carried. With more people wanting to cross to Belfast (and from Belfast to England) and the need for greater cargo capacity, larger and faster ships were introduced to the route including *Duke of Connaught*, *Duke of Cornwall* and *Duke of Albany*. LNWR connected Fleetwood to London and the main towns by regular services, and by 1909 two turbine steamers were added. For LNWR this was an important commercial venture for, although the romance of the railways sees passenger travel as the key, it was in fact the movement of goods that was the lifeblood of the railways, with routes from Birmingham and the Black Country being seen as essential. LNWR and GWR were competitors for the goods traffic in the region, with the LNWR seeing themselves as the front runners, as can be read in their own publication:

> For the North Western not only claims pre-eminence as the standard mail and passenger line of the United Kingdom, but likewise maintains a reputation for dealing with a higher tonnage of merchandise than that of any other railway of Great Britain … especially with the agricultural, mining and manufacturing centres of England, Wales, Scotland and Ireland.

Three-fifths of LNWR's revenue came from goods traffic, and with Birmingham and the Black Country being the manufacturing centre of the world, it was vital to be the prime mover of the region. Thus, *Olympic*'s and *Titanic*'s cable chains were sent via LNWR to Fleetwood and onto Belfast in eight lengths as they were completed between June and October 1910. At Belfast, Harland and Wolff arranged for John Harkness and Company to collect the material from the dock.

The movement of the anchors would be a different affair, mainly because of their size. Hingleys' traditional route using the GWR to Liverpool and then to Belfast was still denied them by the dispute with Belfast SSC. For Hingleys, GWR offered the most convenient method of transport, as the anchors could be moved from the testing house to the GWR Withymoor Goods Station, which was only a short cart haulage from Hingleys. Instead, the anchors would have to be hauled to the LNWR Goods Station on the Tipton Road in Dudley. Then came an added complication when it was decided that *Olympic*'s central anchor (the largest in the world) was to be put on display at the Naval & Mercantile Marine & General Engineering & Machinery Exhibition at Olympia in London (1–26 September 1910). The anchor was to be 'unveiled' as part of the White Star Line's publicity for its new liners. Following completion of tests, *Olympic*'s anchor was transported to GWR's Withymore Goods Station, from thence it travelled to London's Paddington Station. GWR's own haulage team consisting of twelve horses conveyed the anchor to Olympia through the chaotic London traffic.

It was to be the LNWR that would have the honour of taking *Titanic*'s anchors to Belfast via Fleetwood. The hauling of the nearly 8-ton bower anchors had been routine, being shipped out in April 1911 (*Olympic*'s had been shipped out in October 1910 in time for the launch on 20 October). The central anchor was large and heavy and required a crane with a larger lifting capacity than was usual for a single item. This meant that the LNWR Goods Station had to ensure a suitable crane was in place. Contrary to many modern commentators' views, the moving of such weights was not as uncommon as one might imagine. W&T Avery at Soho Foundry often moved weighbridge assemblies weighing up to 20 tons per load by horse-drawn carts or drays. Motor and steam road transport was not, in this period, reliable enough to carry such heavy loads and it was a common sight to see large drays with teams of six, eight and even twelve horses pass through a town. Even so, the 15¾-ton anchor posed a problem due to its shape – the lashing down was critical to the move, but the LNWR had expert draymen.

The story of the movement of *Titanic*'s central anchor has become one of legend and the number of myths grown around it has been extraordinary. Following completion of the anchor's shaft on 18 March and delivery to Hingleys, the whole anchor was fitted up and transferred to Lloyd's Proof House by Hingleys' own dray team. The anchor had been painted light grey with the words 'Hingley, Netherton' picked out in black to improve the contrast in photographs. Once 'proofed', the anchor was placed on LNWR's cart that had been sent to Lloyd's. The contract to ship the anchor included the condition for LNWR to collect the anchor from Lloyd's. LNWR had a specialist dray team to collect heavy consignments; the heavy-duty cart bears the name of the railway company and that of W.A. Ree. Ree is Walter Alexander Ree, the district goods manager for the LNWR based in Wolverhampton. He is the forgotten man of the anchor story, as many have assumed that he was instead a haulage contractor. Ree was born in Holland and educated at Rossall School in Fleetwood, joining the LNWR in 1892. He worked his way up through the ranks of the goods division, subsequently being promoted to the Wolverhampton post in 1909. Cyril Lloyd had been disappointed that Hingleys had not received any publicity for *Olympic*'s anchor when it was sent to London. Bruce Ismay at the White Star Line had been keen for a special unveiling at the Olympia Exhibition. Both George Hingley and Cyril Lloyd had felt aggrieved at this – after all they had supplied it. Cyril wanted to at least get a mention in the local newspapers and arranged for Vert and Company to photograph the anchor outside the Test House. Local newspapers would then receive basic information about the anchor along with the contact details of Vert and Company should they want a photograph.

The day for moving the anchor was May Day 1910: a Monday. As part of the route to the goods station the cart needed to enter the marketplace in Dudley town centre. This was only free for access on Mondays, Wednesdays and Fridays, which were non-market days. George Hingley, along with other family members, and Cyril Lloyd wanted to see off the great anchor. Members of the workforce also gathered to watch the anchor leave the Test House – this was not an uncommon event, especially as those who had worked on the anchor would bring their children to see it before they went to school. William Finch was 39 and had moved heavy goods for the LNWR for many years, so many in fact that the anchor was just another day's work. Draymen in the region all knew each other, as when major haulage was required a number of draymen might be called in to assist. When he was told that *Titanic*'s 15¾-ton anchor was to be hauled to Dudley Goods Depot, he needed to work out the number of horses he needed for the pull. The Clydesdale horses that were used for such work in towns could pull deadweight equal to double their bodyweight over a short distance. With a wheeled cart they could pull even more; horses working in tandem could pull even better, pulling three times their body weight. Nonetheless, with a distance of about 3 miles and an incline, he worked out he needed twelve horses (six pairs) – the same number GWR's drayman used for the pull from Paddington Station to Olympia. Yet, it is clear from a well-known photograph that twenty horses (ten pairs) were used, which was certainly overkill. The story regarding why there was so many varies from person to person, but in essence the premise is the same.

William turned up with twelve horses. The management of Hingleys (perhaps Cyril Lloyd) or, according to Peter Hingley, a member of the Hingley family, asked, 'What do you expect to do with those nags?'

'I've come for the anchor,' responded the drayman, rather put out.

'Not with those you're not!' came the response from the Hingley entourage.

In due course, Cyril Lloyd sent a runner to James Grosvenor (Hingleys' groom) with a message to bring their own horses.

'What do you expect me to do with mine?' complained the drayman.

One can imagine the reply from the hardy Black Country workers! Hingleys' team of eight horses, led by a pair of greys, hauled the anchor onto the Cradley Road where after some wrangling, and to the irritation of some of Hingleys' men, the railwayman's horses were attached and the anchor had a twenty-horse team! William Edwards in his account in 1976 tells a similar story. In a private, handwritten communication between Cyril Lloyd and George Hingley, dated 2 May 1911, he wrote:

> After some delay the anchor was carried to the station. I enlisted the aid of Grosvenor to use our beasts, which are of superior quality. The carman protested but agreed to include our animals in the haulage.

It is the fact that twenty horses were used that drew attention in the streets, as eight- and twelve-horse pulls were quite common. A local photographer, Edwin Beech, who ran the Imperial Studios at 192 High Street, Dudley, set up his camera on the Cradley Road to photograph the anchor. He was noted for selling postcards of local scenes and no doubt saw an opportunity. He took the most well-known image, which shows the anchor after it had just passed the disused Saltwells Colliery Pit No. 29, with the windows of Lloyd's Proof House behind it. Children on their way to St Andrew's Boys and Girls School walk alongside. The run to the station was not a straight run and the various turns required a lot of work unhitching some of the horses, turning the cart to the correct direction and then re-hitching. When the anchor reached the marketplace, the horses were rested as the cart was repositioned. One can imagine the slow progress of the haul having to work its way through the town, although it must have been easy compared to the hauling of *Olympic*'s anchor through London. Once the anchor had arrived at the station it was booked in as received and sometime later it was crane-loaded onto a 40-ton platform goods wagon with a destination board added that said 'FLEETWOOD'.

LNWR's line did not go directly to Fleetwood from Dudley, so the wagon was placed in a siding awaiting the evening shunter to take a number of wagons via the Sedgley loop to Albion Goods Depot near Greets Green.

It was here that a train would be put together carrying goods from Black Country firms heading to the west coast. The anchor set off on 2 May working through Wolverhampton, Stafford and thence on to Crewe. After negotiating the multiple junctions the anchor would pass through Wigan, finally reaching the Christian Road Goods Depot at Preston where the wagon with the anchor would be attached to a train for Fleetwood. Due to the size of the anchor it was here that special working was required to get the wagon through three junctions before heading up the line to Fleetwood, eventually arriving at the goods siding late on 3 May. The anchor was loaded onboard the aft cargo section of *Duke of Albany* on 5 May, sailing at 10.53 a.m. in dry weather and arriving in Belfast at 5.48 p.m. where, following the landing of the mails and parcels, the 186 tons of cargo was unloaded. The anchor needed the services of a 25-ton crane, which ran up an unexpected bill to the shipping company. The anchor was collected by John Harkness and Company on behalf of Harland and Wolff using a cart with six horses.

While the anchor was en route to Fleetwood, the press were singing the praises of Hingleys and their anchor. The dramatic sight of the anchor passing through Dudley caused a stir. The *Express and Star* made a major feature of it in 1 May evening newspaper:

THE BIGGEST ANCHOR IN THE WORLD

It was an exile from Erin who on being told that he could not be accommodated with a job at a Black Country works craved permission to be allowed to remain in the yard till he could see the man who worked 'that almighty great pic'. The implement to which the Irishman pointed was nothing but a ship's anchor, a species of commodity which are made in many sites in several works in Dudley and Tipton districts. Paddy's 'pick' was probably a little thing compared to that which was sent out to-day (Monday) from the works of Messrs. N. Hingley and Son, Netherton. The latter is the biggest anchor in the world, and it has been made for the biggest ship in the world. It required twenty horses to draw it on a wagon from the works at Primrose Hill to the London and North Western station at Dudley. It has been made for the *Titanic* the ocean liner built by Messrs. Harland and Wolff, Belfast. Our illustration shows the anchor as it lay in Lloyd's Proof House. It was again photographed by Messrs. Vert and Company when it was loaded upon the wagon with the horses yoked all ready to start. This colossal anchor weighs 16 tons, and occupied a dozen men three weeks in the making. The head is of cast steel, and the other part of forged steel. Its breaking strain is incalculable. The head weighs 9 tons, the shank

5½ tons and the shackle ½ ton. The firm have also made two smaller anchors for the *Titanic* each weighing eight tons. The cable made by Messrs. Hingley for the monster anchor consists of 22 lengths of 15 fathoms each of chain, the links of which are 3⅜ inches in diameter. Naturally, the removal of this big anchor and its transference to the railway wagon attracted a considerable amount of public attention.

The *Birmingham Daily Mail*'s evening edition carried a similar article (although without a photograph). The news spread wide, which does suggest a concerted effort. The *Dundee Evening Telegraph* put the story on their front page:

ANCHOR FOR THE LATEST WHITE STAR LINER
Requires 20 Horses to Take to Station
This afternoon the largest anchor in the world was dispatched from the chain works of Messrs. Hingley & Sons, Netherton, Dudley.

The morning dailies published the story on 2 May, with *The Times* simply mentioning that the 'largest anchor in the world has been dispatched yesterday from Dudley'. The 2 May edition of the *Sheffield Telegraph* went into more detail:

WORLD'S LARGEST ANCHOR
DISPATCHED FROM THE MIDLANDS TO BELFAST
The world's largest anchor passed through Dudley yesterday, lashed to a heavy wagon drawn by a team of 20 horses. It was being conveyed from the proving house, Netherton to the London and North Western Railway Station at Dudley en route to Belfast, where it is intended for the steamship *Titanic* …

The story even appeared in the weeklies published on Saturday 6 May; the *Derbyshire Times* and the *Leicester Chronicle* were just two of the many newspapers that reported the dispatch of the anchor. George Hingley and Cyril Lloyd were both happy that the firm had received national recognition, but Bruce Ismay at White Star was not. His grievance was that the name White Star Line had not appeared in any of the reports. He wrote to Harland and Wolff (probably Lord Pirrie himself) to complain. Harland and Wolff in turn wrote to Hingley to express Ismay's annoyance and to find out who had told the press. On 24 May, Hingleys contacted Walter A. Ree at the

LNWR asking if anyone there had informed the press about the dispatch of the anchor. Ree duly responded on 17 June commenting that no one at LNWR was responsible, adding that given the special arrangements made for the dispatch, it was likely to have attracted public interest. Hingleys wrote to Harland and Wolff to clarify the situation, stating:

> May we add that we ourselves have done our utmost to ensure that any notices about which we were consulted should emphasize particularly the name of the White Star Line as owners of the s/s 'Titanic', and of your own same as builders of the vessel, and we believe that in all the chief notices which have appeared these notices have been properly emphasized.

Hingleys were clearly admitting they had issued press notices but had mentioned both White Star and Harland and Wolff. Essentially it was the media's fault!

Frontispiece to the N. Hingley & Sons catalogue, 1910. (Author's collection)

Noah Hingley.
(Avery
Historical
Museum)

Chain-making
workshop
at Hingleys.
(Avery
Historical
Museum)

Benjamin Hodgetts working a chain cable. (Avery Historical Museum)

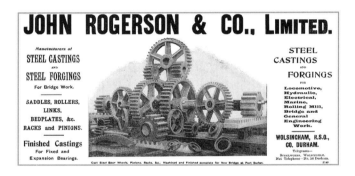

John Rogerson & Co. advertisement. (Author's collection)

Opposite:

Top: Drawing for shanks for *Titanic*'s bower anchors. (Dudley Archives)

Centre: Drawing for shank for *Titanic*'s central anchor. (Dudley Archives)

Bottom: *Titanic*'s central anchor loaded onto LNWR dray, 30 April 1911. (Avery Historical Museum)

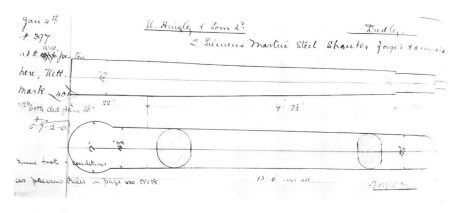

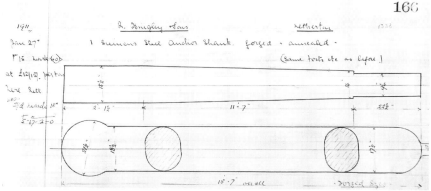

166

James Grosvenor organises Hingleys' horses at Lloyd's Test House. Cyril Lloyd and members of the Hingley family stand near the dray. (Avery Historical Museum)

James Grosvenor prepares the horses to pull the anchor out of Lloyd's Test House, 1 May 1911. (Author's collection)

'The Great Pull' of the central anchor through Netherton and Dudley. (Avery Historical Museum)

Progression of the anchor towards Dudley. (Avery Historical Museum)

SS *Duke of Albany* leaving Fleetwood for Belfast. (Author's collection)

Titanic's central anchor heading to Harland and Wolff in Belfast. (Avery Historical Museum)

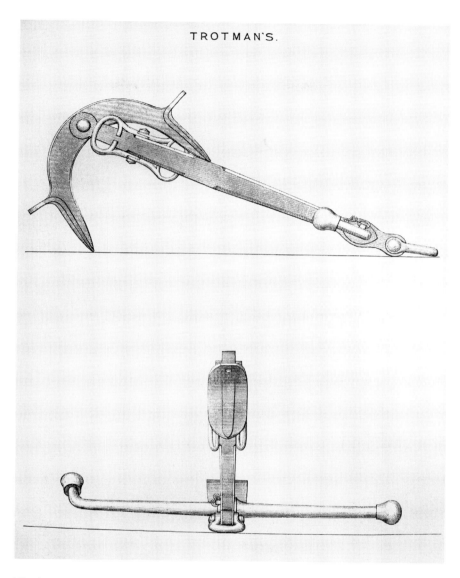

TROTMAN'S.

Hingleys' Trotman anchor. (Dudley Archives)

49

11 [401]
2 Halls Stockless.   156.0.14
157.3.8.   S/s TITANIC
313.3.22.

	Anchor Heads + Blocks.	187.3.4	12/3	112.2.10
	Shanks.	107.2.0	12/9	68.10.8.
	Gudgeons.	6.3.0	8/6	2.17.4
	Back Pins.	4.2.0	7/6	1.13.9
	Nuts.	1.1.14	24/.	1.13.0
	Shackles.	12.0.0	10/.	10.16.0
	Shee Pins.	2.3.0	7/6	1.0.8.
	Wages - Machining			11.16.3
	Machinery.	533	@	13.6
	Testing	313.3.22	9ˢ	11.15.6.
	Labour + Haulage.			2.10.0
	Carriage.			

Drilling 13½   34.1
Sawing   9   3.6
Turning 100   50.0
Facing   30½   25.6
Cutting 15ˣ   62.6
Shaping 59   22.4
Fitting 90   30.1
         11.16.3

---

[401]
1 Halls Stockless.   15.16   S/s White Star — Titanic — 14

(Robinson)   Anchor Head + Blocks.   183.3.8   12/3   112.11.10
(Somers)   Shank.   117.0.0   12/9   74.11.9.
              Gudgeon.   5.3.0   8/6   2.8.10.
              Back Pins.   5.0.0   7/6   1.17.6
              Nuts.   .3.0   24/.   .18.0
              Shackle.   11.3.8.3 27/6   16.5.0.
                    pin   .18.9
              Wages - Machining   2.2.0.3   7/6   13.16.10.
              Machinery.   450½   6ˢ   11.5.8
              Testing   316.0.0   9ˢ   11.17.0.
              Labour + Haulage.   3.0.0.
              Carriage.   316.0.0   11.17.0
                                                          261.7.9

Drilling 103
Sawing   7
Turning   114½
Facing   90½
Cutting   131½
Shaping   60
Fitting   177

Titanic's anchors' entry in Hingleys' anchor cost book. (Dudley Archives)

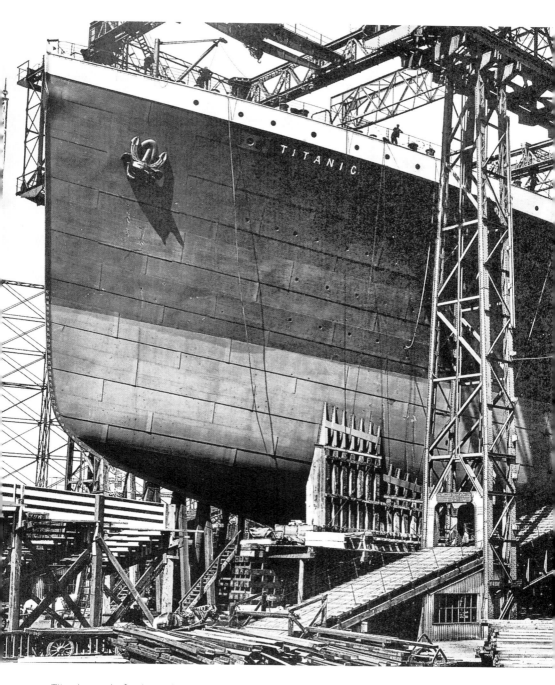

Titanic ready for launch and fitting out. (Avery Historical Museum)

3

FITTING OUT

The Midlands is famous for ironwork, and as early as the sixteenth century the region was known for its smiths. Brasswork became a major part of regional manufacturing from the eighteenth century, leading to Birmingham setting up its first brasshouse in Coleshill Street in 1740. Development in the brass trade grew rapidly, due to the high level of skilled workers in the region and not due to access to copper and zinc, which had to be imported from other areas. Sand was plentiful and a large pit was created in what would become Warstone Lane cemetery following sand extraction. Just forty years after the first brasshouse Birmingham had nineteen brassfounders, and these formed a group that led to the building of a new brasshouse in Broad Street (commemorated by Brasshouse Passage). The industry continued to grow, with Birmingham being seen as the centre of brassfoundry in Britain, if not the world, with upwards of 30,000 people employed in the trade by 1895. Brassfoundry divided into a number of distinct branches: cabinet brassfoundry covered items for the carpentry trade and cabinetmakers, bell brassfoundry covered all items required for the bell industry, and general brassfoundry covered anything that did not readily come under cabinet or bell brassfoundry, including railings, balustrades, picture and hat rods, screen poles and anything of a special nature requiring low quantities. In the early days of the trade the quality of the items was not of the best grade and, in effect, mass production was more important.

By the nineteenth century, however, high-quality items, even mass-produced items, were the hallmark of brass goods from Birmingham. Manufacturers in Birmingham also developed new design and manufacturing techniques. High-quality decorative styles of cabinet brassfoundry were in great demand throughout the nineteenth and early twentieth centuries, as large houses owned by wealthy industrialists were being decorated to meet a variety of tastes. Large hotels were also demanding a wider range of styles and these naturally were translated to the interior decor of the new passenger ships. Ship, marine or naval brassfoundry was developed with one particularly important special requirement: the metal fittings had to withstand the rigour of a saltwater environment.

The Midlands had a long tradition of manufacturing for the shipping industry. In 1779, James Keir, a member of the famous Lunar Society, patented a metal that was capable of being forged or wrought when red hot or cold, which was suitable for making bolts, nails and sheathing for ships. In 1790 William Collins patented a sheathing process, but it was George Frederick Muntz who gained the greatest reputation for metal sheathing of ships with his patent of 1832. Muntz's Metal, as it became known, was produced at his premises in Water Street, Birmingham, before moving to Swansea and later opening a manufactory in Smethwick. In 1844, James Marrian set up a manufactory in Slaney Street, Birmingham, dedicated to naval brassfoundry, which greatly extended the range of articles for use on ships manufactured in Birmingham, including receptacles for binnacles and compasses, port lights, deck lights, lashing and rope eyes, ring bolts, pulleys, hinges, rowlocks, belaying pins and candle and oil lamps with gimbal joints. The adaptation of Midlands' industries was remarkable, and when lighting changed from oil to gas and then to electric, local industries were able to adapt manufacturing light fittings in high-quality brass, including the combination of cut glass and brass to produce chandeliers and ceiling-mounted lights.

Birmingham firms such as Thomas Westley and Company supplied marine brassfoundry as subcontractors to firms like William McGeoch of Glasgow. The shipbuilding industry operated using a complex supply chain, with shipbuilders contracting out various elements of a build to interior design companies, who in turn would use their preferred suppliers for parts. Ships' chandlers were used to source specific material and these chandlers had their own preferred suppliers. Birmingham and Black Country firms allied themselves to various chandlers, interior designers and shipping companies; thus, when the boom in shipbuilding began Birmingham industry was well placed to take advantage.

Passenger and Crew Accommodation

The size of the new White Star liners, accommodating up to 3,300 passengers and crew, required a vast quantity of interior fittings, including door furniture, cabinet furniture, fixings of every size and type, light fittings, brackets, vent grills, curtain rails, door hooks, coat hoots, mirror fittings, toilet fittings and luggage racks. The list is almost endless, with first, second and third class having a standard superior to all rival vessels. The range and quality would rewrite the book on the interior design of ships. First-class accommodation stretched over five decks amidships, with access via two grand staircases in the style of William and Mary with Louis XIV style of wrought-iron balustrade. The special staterooms located on B and C decks amidships, between the two grand staircases, demonstrated the level of quality. The rooms were decorated in varying styles: Louis XIV to XVI, Adam, Italian Renaissance, Georgian, Regency, Queen Anne, Empire, modern Dutch and old Dutch. The first-class staterooms contained sofas, dressing tables, wardrobes and washbasins, with ninety-six of them being single berths. The first-class dining saloon adopted a Jacobean style, with Haddon Hall in Derbyshire serving as the inspiration. The restaurant was 60ft by 45ft and the decor was reminiscient of Louis XVI's style, panelled in French walnut with mouldings richly carved and gilded. Verandah cafés and palm courts were situated on either side of the deck house; there was also a reception room, reading and writing room, lounge and smoking room designed to resemble the finest gentlemen's clubs. For entertainment and leisure there was a swimming pool, squash court, gymnasium and even a Turkish bath.

Second-class accommodation stretched over seven decks and the quality easily matched, and in many cases surpassed, first class in many other ships crossing the Atlantic at that time. Second class had its own grand staircase entrance, a dining saloon equal to many first-class dining saloons on other ships, a library and smoking room. The second-class staterooms were not too dissimilar to the ordinary first-class rooms, although they could accommodate up to four persons rather than three.

Third class was an important part of the new liners' design in that the standard of accommodation was equal to second class on most ships crossing the Atlantic. This was a deliberate effort to attract a better quality of emigrant – a skilled or professional worker. Large public rooms and a smoking room were also provided. Staterooms and berths, all with running water, offered in many ways better accommodation than cabin passengers had thirty years previously.

Interior Fittings

Harland and Wolff's contract for the new ships would require a phenomenal amount of material. *Olympic*, as the class ship, would serve as the principal design and *Titanic* would be an improvement based on the experience of the class ship. *Gigantic* would incorporate all the development and improvements of the two previous ships. Much of the ships' interior was designed by Aldam Heaton and Company (from 1911 part of the IMM group). The founder of the company, John Aldam Heaton, was acquainted with the artist Dante Gabriel Rossetti, and the influence of the pre-Raphaelite artist movement can be seen in some of the interior designs of the ships. Birmingham-born Sir Edward Burne-Jones was one of the artists of this movement who would transform interior design. Heatons had developed close ties with a number of suppliers and were, like all companies, keen to reduce costs and would from time to time request catalogues and ask for discounts or consideration on bulk orders. For the brassfounders, costs were also a problem, especially in raw materials and transport. It was these pressures that led to smaller companies merging to form larger companies or to specialise on a narrow front.

George Field and Company was formed in Birmingham in 1900 in order to meet the specific need of naval and marine interior designers. George Field had spent his working life in the hardware business, starting out as a hardware merchants clerk before setting up his own business at 56 Holloway Head, advertising his firm as a specialist in high-class ship furnishings. His introduction to cabinet furniture most likely originated with his father, Thomas, who was a carpenter. The Holloway Head site incorporated offices, a sales department and a manufactory producing cabin, stateroom, saloon and fittings in brass, bronze, silveroid and white metal. To emphasise his speciality, the firm's telegram address was 'Nautical, Birmingham'. Field's catalogue illustrates the large range of interior fittings supplied for the new ships, from hat and coat hooks to toilet-roll holders. Harland and Wolff's own cabinetmakers produced a large quantity of cabinets and furniture, but the brass fittings for these were supplied, in the main, by George Field. These fittings included drawer pulls, door latches, corner plates, knobs and a host of small brass parts. Guest, Keen and Nettlefold Limited of Broad Street, Birmingham, supplied general fixings, such as woodscrews and bolts, to Belfast. The famous screw manufacturers had been producing marine-grade fixings for many years and supplied copious quantities directly to all the shipyards across the country. Between 1909 and 1911 Harland and Wolff received 1,000 tons of fixings, which equates to over 170 million screws.

Other designers of interiors included H.P. Mutters and Zoon of The Hague, who was commissioned to decorate twenty-four staterooms. The Dutch interior designers had been formed in 1816 and developed a reputation for designing the interiors of lavish houses and hotels in various period designs. They had a strong connection with the Birmingham firm of Tonks Limited of 201 Moseley Street. Tonks' origins date back to the eighteenth century when George Tonks formed a partnership with William Beddington. Although the partnership was dissolved in 1811, William Tonks remained with Beddington, forming another partnership that traded as Beddington, Tonks and Company. William died in 1836, but his son (also William) continued the partnership until it was dissolved in 1851 and began trading as William Tonks and Sons. The company continued to prosper in family hands and by 1881 they had a workforce of 450. John Edgar Tonks ran the business into the twentieth century. Tonks' became a private limited company in 1891, investing in new machinery targeting the expanding marine and hotel trades. With *Olympic* and *Titanic* incorporating interior designs from many different periods, all would require matching brass fittings, thus, the experience of Birmingham firms in manufacturing these styles was invaluable.

Stamped brassfoundry of all kinds was supplied to the ship including brass signs that indicated 'First Class', 'Second Class' and 'Crew Only'. These along with others were produced by Vaughton Brothers of the Gothic Works, Livery Street, Birmingham. The family firm was founded by Philip Vaughton in 1819 as P. Vaughton and Sons, a silversmiths, goldsmiths and general manufacturer that developed over the course of the nineteenth century and adding a wide range of products, including medals, badges, chains of office and memorials to its repetoire. One of the 'sons' was Howard Vaughton who played professional football for Aston Villa. It was through his connections with the company that Vaughtons got the contract to produce a replacement FA Cup after the original was stolen from a shop window in Birmingham. The company also produced quality pin badges depicting ships, company ensignia and steward's badges for a number of shipping companies. A specialist die-sinking and stamping workshop was set up at the Gothic Works to cater for the growing shipping industry and it is here that they produced a wide range of signage for numerous ships via orders with chandlers.

Lighting

The principal suppliers for the interior decorative lights were the London-based Perry and Company of Grafton Street and N. Burt and Company Limited of Wardour Street. Like most manufacturing companies they had connections with Midland firms.

Perry and Company was a famous London chandelier maker that had a manufactory in Birmingham. The firm started when William Perry entered into partnership with William Collins at 227 The Strand, London. In 1803 he joined William Parker as Parker and Perry. William Parker was the leading chandelier maker of the late eighteenth century, supplying fashionable households and royalty. Parker was an expert in flint glass who supplied many scientific instrument makers, with connections to the Lunar Society members Matthew Boulton, James Keir, James Watt and William Small. On the death of William Parker in 1817, William Perry continued establishing himself at 72 New Bond Street as 'Glass Manufacturer to the Prince Regent'. The firm moved to Grafton Street, London, in 1890, operating a manufactory at Avery Road, London, and working with Perry and Grinsell in Birmingham.

Perry and Grinsell was an electrical engineering company specialising in cooking and heating apparatus located at 1–2 Leopold Street. It was at these premises that electrical radiators for Perry and Company were produced for the liners. Although Perrys was expert in cut-glass chandeliers, the scale of the order for the new liners meant obtaining cut-glass segments from other suppliers such as Thomas Webb and Sons at the Stourbridge Glassworks. The cut-glass segments used in ceiling lights and small chandeliers were of a standard design being of pear, diamond, cube or pyramid shape. Perrys also ordered glass light globes and covers in a variety of shapes from Webb, as well as Stevens and Williams Limited at the Brierley Hill Works. Certain types of brasswork was also ordered from Birmingham, with William Tonks being requested to supply various cast brasswork that was then sent to the Avery Road premises.

The development of the electrical trade had given Birmingham brass firms an additional range of products. Many electrical components could be stamped out on mass and Birmingham firms readily adapted their machinery. Traditional lighting firms such as Perrys had lived through the changes from candle to oil, to gas and then to electric. They ordered numerous small stamped components from Midland firms to be used in their light fittings. There was also a change made by firms that specialised in shipping such as William McGeoch and

Company Limited. The well-known Birmingham manufacturer began life as a hardware company at 113 Argyle Street, Glasgow. It was William McGeoch's visits to the River Clyde and the ships' chandlers that led him to enter the shipping trade, supplying lamps, marlinspikes, coir mats and deck and cabin stores of every kind. He brought his sons William, Andrew and Alexander into the business and became an agent for Nettlefold and Chamberlain. William identified a problem with lock mechanisms used on ships, noticing how they often became rusty and had to be changed out on a regular basis. As a result, the company sought out more durable lock suppliers, settling on two firms in Willenhall as their principal suppliers: T. Benton and Son of Newhall Street and Beddow and Sturmey Limited of Clemson Street.

Thomas Benton was born in 1835 and along with his brother Joseph, eleven years his junior, went to the United States to work in the coal mines. With the money they made there, they returned to Willenhall where they set up as lock makers – Thomas in premises in Newhall Street and Joseph as a mortice-lock maker at 31 Doctor's Piece, Willenhall. In about 1900, Thomas built a family house with workshops at the back in Victoria Street.

Beddow and Sturmey was a company formed by two dynasties of locksmiths. Silas Beddow was born in 1835 in Willenhall where his father James was a locksmith. Silas married Sarah Sturmey and went into partnership with his brother-in-law William Sturmey. William's grandfather, John, was a locksmith in Little London and his father Thomas ran a locksmith business in Willenhall employing, in 1861, two men and two boys. By 1881, as Beddow and Sturmey, the business employed thirty-six men and boys. McGeochs agreed with suppliers not to stamp their own name on the goods supplied, a move that was done in order to establish the name McGeoch and to deny the ships' chandlers and shipping companies from knowing the name of their suppliers for fear that the lock makers may be approached directly. McGeochs' suppliers were agreeable to this arrangement, as they would have a regular customer for their products – yet another example of the co-operation between Birmingham and Black Country firms.

McGeochs also worked with the Birmingham firm of Thomas Westley and Company based at the Warwick Works, Coventry Road, who provided quality cabin brassfoundry, lamps etc. In 1887, William McGeoch (II) purchased Westley's works in order to have control of the brassfoundry production. This move was timed to meet the new demand for electric lights in ships. Two years later McGeochs had the contract to supply the SS *City of Paris* with electric light fittings. Alexander McGeoch was the works manager in

Birmingham, Andrew the salesman, with William (II) in charge in Glasgow. Between them they grew the company's reputation for high-quality marine fittings, meeting the high Admiralty standards as well as the Board of Trade regulations. As the shipping industry grew so too did McGeochs. In 1900 McGeochs was restructured into a limited company to meet the demands of the growing shipping industry, being a prime contractor for all the big ships supplying Cunard's *Mauretania* and *Lusitania*.

For *Olympic* and *Titanic* McGeochs was a natural choice, but as they were contracted to supply virtually every ship being produced in a British shipyard their relationship with their suppliers was critical. For mortice and cabin locks virtually the entire output of Beddow and Sturmey Limited was required, along with locks from Thomas Benton and Son, Joseph Benton and W. Vaughan and Sons, all based in Willenhall. Watertight lighting supplied by McGeochs included oyster bulkhead lights, portable lamps, cargo cluster lights and arc lamps, along with wiring and light bulbs (supplied by Edison & Swan United Electric Light Company Limited, Edmund Street, Birmingham). Other watertight electrical items included plugs, sockets and switches. McGeochs' watertight bulkhead lights were used all over the ship on the exterior as well as the interior. For the exterior lights, high-quality glass was required to enable the lights to be seen at a distance. McGeochs purchased their glass fittings from James Stevens and Son of the Victoria Glassworks, Dartmouth Street, Birmingham. Prior to forming his own company James Stevens had worked for Rice Harris at the Islington Glassworks, Birmingham. It was there in 1836 he made the first pressed glass moulds, having gained experience making such moulds for an American glassmaker. He set up his own business by 1841 at the Victoria Glassworks, specialising in high-quality lenses for ship sidelights, masthead lamps, anchor lamps, deck-light glass, bent and bevelled glass for hand-signal lamps, skylight reflectors and flint-glass signal lantern globes. Stevens supplied numerous ships' lamp and light suppliers across the country, in most cases never knowing in which ships their glass would be used.

James retired to Newton Abbott in Devon prior to 1881 when his son (also James) took over. James (II) sold the business around 1890 and it continued to prosper; in fact, it grew with the booming shipping industry – McGeochs was a regular customer who kept the works busy. Another customer of Stevens was W.H. Allen & Company of the Queen's Engineering Works, Bedford, who supplied navigation lights to *Olympic* and *Titanic*. Allens supplied a number of ships with electrical equipment and had a stock of navigation lights to be fitted to masts and to the sides of ships. Stevens supplied dioptric lenses to Allens. Other marine brassfoundry supplied by McGeochs included gimbled table lamps, sprung door hinges, saloon pendants and hundreds of small brass items used throughout the ship.

McGeochs' sprung door hinges were fitted to many of the cabin doors to help keep them closed, although a more robust way to keep doors closed was to use a door-closing valve known as a 'door check'. The Blount System of door checks was fitted throughout the ship and these were supplied by Charles Winn and Company of Granville Street Birmingham. The firm, famous for valves, sanitary appliances, fire-fighting equipment and pressure indicators was formed in 1859 by Charles Winn, the son of a metal-tray maker. He trained as a brassfounder, and it is following his marriage to Emma Webley, of the famous gun-making family, that Charles set up his business.

George Field and Company catalogue. (Author's collection)

Although he manufactured a variety of brassfoundry-related products he specialised in sanitary equipment with an emphasis on valves, which led to manufacturing valves of all types. The business rapidly grew, with his St Thomas works on Granville Street expanding to meet demand.

Charles was aware of the growing shipbuilding trade and began manufacturing valves adapted for the marine industry, some of which were patented designs produced under license. Winns supplied a whole range of valves, pressure gauges and sanitary equipment as a primary contractor and as a subcontractor. Through a chandler they received an order to supply Blount door checks described as 'noiseless, strong and durable. Never require lubrication.' Winns also supplied, as a subcontractor, a number of pressure gauges and valve assemblies to W.H. Allen in Bedford, which were rebadged.

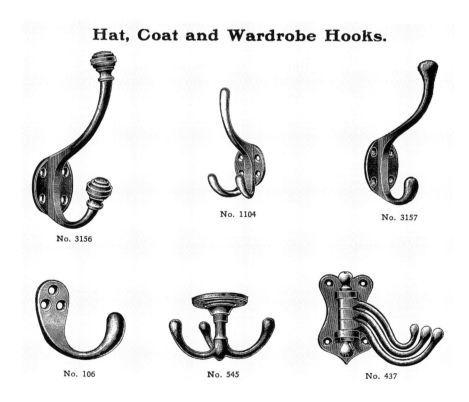

Hat, coat and wardrobe hooks. (Author's collection)

Storm Rail Brackets.

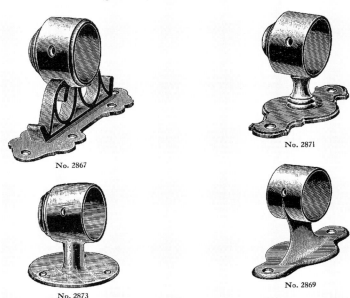

Storm rail brackets. (Author's collection)

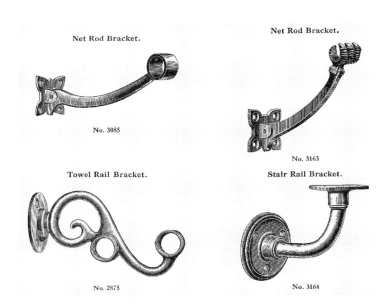

Miscellaneous brackets. (Author's collection)

Drawer Pulls.

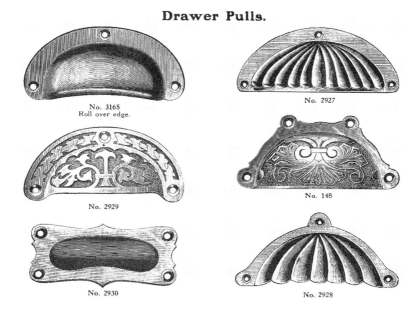

Cabinet furniture. (Author's collection)

Curtain Fittings.

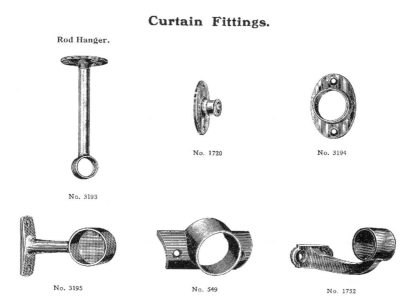

Curtain fittings. (Author's collection)

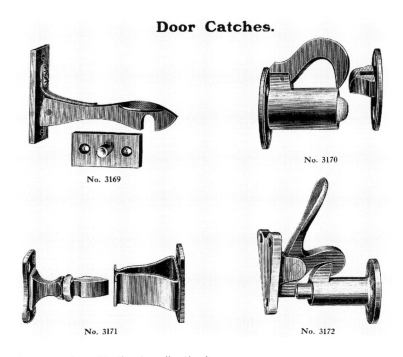

Door Catches.

No. 3169

No. 3170

No. 3171

No. 3172

Door catches. (Author's collection)

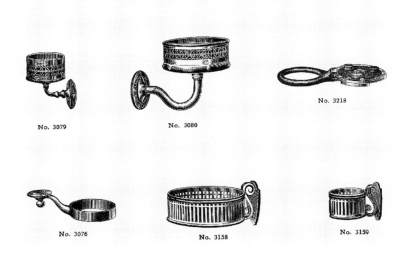

Water Bottle and Tumbler Holders.

No. 3079

No. 3080

No. 3218

No. 3076

No. 3158

No. 3159

Water bottle and tumbler holders. (Author's collection)

Sponge Baskets.

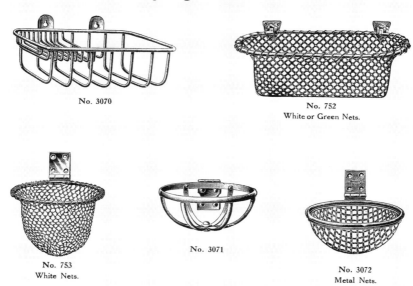

Sponge baskets. (Author's collection)

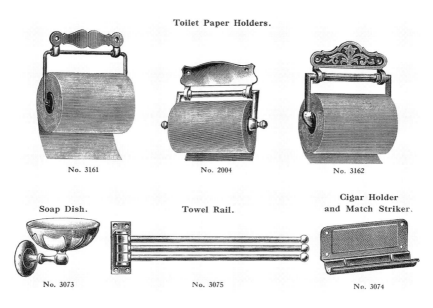

Toilet paper holders. (Author's collection)

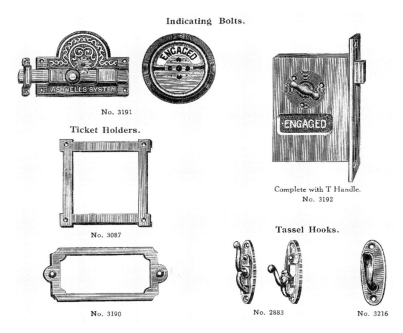

Indicating bolts, ticket holders and tassel hooks. (Author's collection)

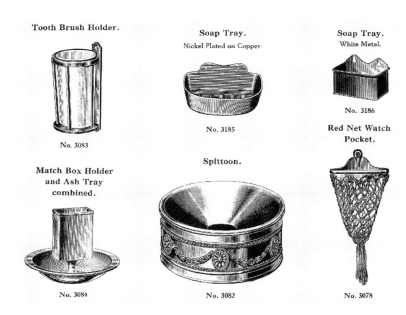

Trays and holders. (Author's collection)

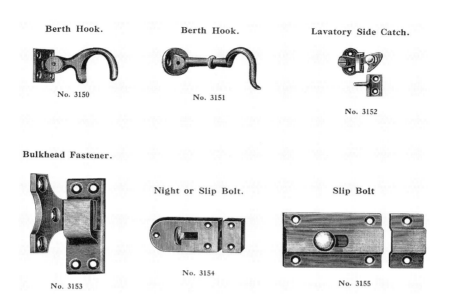

Hooks and fasteners. (Author's collection)

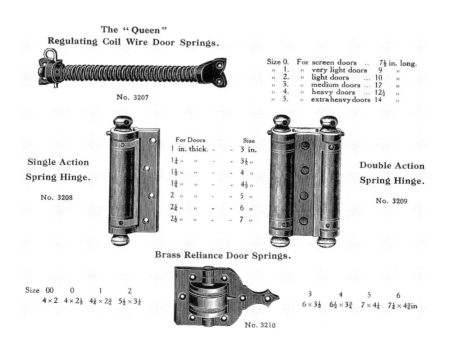

Door springs and hinges. (Author's collection)

Mirror Fittings.

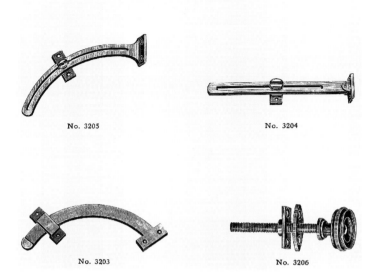

No. 3205   No. 3204

No. 3203   No. 3206

Mirror fittings. (Author's collection)

Spring and Flush Latches and Knobs.

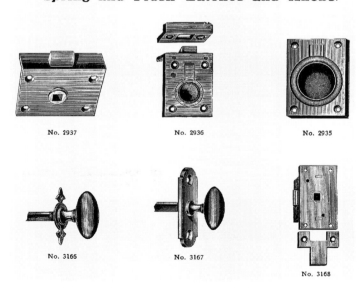

No. 2937   No. 2936   No. 2935

No. 3166   No. 3167   No. 3168

Spring and flush latches and knobs. (Author's collection)

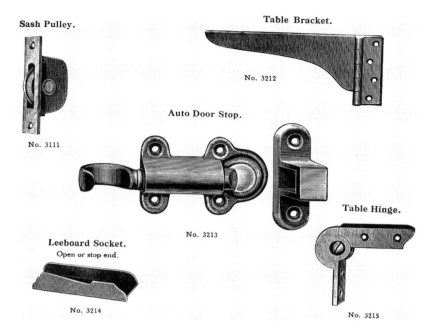

Cabinet fittings. (Author's collection)

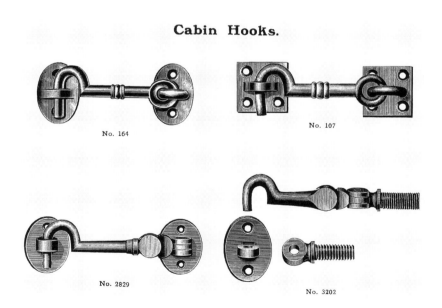

Cabin hooks. (Author's collection)

Drawer Knobs.

Drawer
knobs.
(Author's
collection)

No. 3198

No. 3199

No. 3200

No. 3201

Door Furniture and Finger Plates en suite.

Door
furniture.
(Author's
collection)

No. 3217
Door Furniture and Finger Plates, en suite.

No. 3119
Door Furniture and Finger Plates en suite.

Door furniture. (Author's collection)

George Field's
Patent Ball-joint Silent Cabin Door Hook.
(Patent No. 13530/07)

The great advantage of this Hook is that it is so constructed that it cannot touch the wood when not in use; it is therefore impossible for it to mark the paint or enamel, a defect common to most hooks.

These hooks have been officially tested and have withstood a strain of over 7 cwt. without in any way affecting the joint.

PRICES:

	2½	3	3½	4	5	6	7in.
Polished Brass - - -	31/-	33/-	36/-	41/-	45/-	51/-	60/- per doz.
Polished White Metal or Burnt Bronze on Real Bronze Metal	36/-	40/-	43/-	48/-	52/-	58/-	66/- ,,

SIZES MEASURED BETWEEN PLATES.

George Field's ball-joint silent cabin door hook. (Author's collection)

BLOUNT DOOR CHECKS
Fixed throughout the "OLYMPIC" and "TITANIC"
NOISELESS - STRONG AND DURABLE
HAVE AN OIL CHECK.   NEVER REQUIRE LUBRICATION
NO PACKING LEATHERS
EASILY FIXED - LATCH THE DOORS
THERE ARE OTHERS
BUT NONE SO GOOD
CHARLES WINN & CO
(Dept. S.)   **BIRMINGHAM**

Above: Charles Winn and Company advertisement,1911. (Author's collection)

Right: Charles Winn's works at Granville Street, Birmingham. (Author's collection)

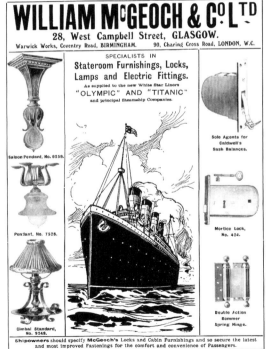

Left: William McGeoch and Company Ltd advertisement, 1911, showing Willenhall-made locks. (Author's collection)

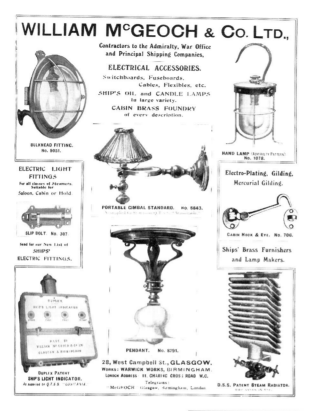

William McGeoch and Company Ltd advertisement, 1911. (Author's collection)

The Electric & Ordnance Accessories Co. advertisement, 1911. (Author's collection)

Turkish Bath

The Turkish bath was situated on F Deck containing rooms for steam, hot temperature, shampooing and cooling. The cooling room was decorated in the Arabic style of the seventeenth century with walls tiled in large panels of blue and green. The ceiling cornice and beams were gilt with the intervening panels picked out in dull red. From the panels were suspended bronze Arab lamps. Turkish baths had been introduced to the United Kingdom by David Urquhart, a diplomat and sometime Member of Parliament for Stafford from 1847 to 1852. The first passenger ship to be fitted with a Turkish bath was RMS *Adriatic*, built for the White Star Line by Harland and Wolff. A personal weighing machine was installed in the cooling room of the Turkish bath to enable passengers to monitor how much weight they had lost by using the baths. The weighing machine on *Adriatic* was supplied by W&T Avery Limited in Smethwick. The Model 1054 chair weighing machine, complete with patent recording steelyard, enabled passengers to receive a ticket with their weight recorded on it for posterity. The weighing machines for *Olympic* and *Titanic* were ordered from Averys' bitter rival Henry Pooley and Son of Birmingham and London and were custom machines based around a standard design.

Following a couple of disastrous partnerships, Henry Pooley started a grate manufacturers, ironmongers and general smiths business in around 1815 located at Dale Street, Liverpool. His son (Henry II) joined him as an apprentice in 1817, and after working with his father for twenty-three years he set up on his own in the Old Haymarket, Liverpool. Henry Pooley (II) prospered and constructed a foundry he named the Albion Foundry and soon thereafter his father's business merged with his to form Henry Pooley and Son. In 1834 the company began manufacturing a platform weighing machine of the Fairbanks design. Pooleys had become so successful as a weighing-machine company that in some product lines they dominated the market and in others began challenging older established companies such as W&T Avery, with whom a trade war ensued.

In 1813 William and Thomas Avery had taken control of a business that could trace its history back to 1728 in the Digbeth area of Birmingham. The Averys manufactured steelyards, beam scales, dead weighers and platform machines. Initially, relations between the firms Averys and Pooleys had been amicable, with under-the-table agreements to keep out of each other's hometowns (Liverpool and Birmingham). In 1881, William Beilby and Henry Johnson Avery took over the Birmingham firm and began a policy of expansion setting up branches in towns and cities across the country. Pooleys' home city of Liverpool found itself as a target when Averys supplied a weighbridge to the Hide and Skin Market. Pooleys responded by opening a branch in Birmingham located in Heath Lane in 1885, and two years later Pooleys began producing scales of the type normally associated with the Averys. It was open commercial warfare. In 1894 Henry Avery died suddenly at the young age of 34; Averys became a public limited company and appointed a new managing director, William Edward Hipkins, who oversaw the redevelopment of the famous Soho Foundry in Smethwick, creating the largest weighing-machine manufactory on earth.

Pooleys restructured to meet the competition and attempted to match Averys' expansion and set their sights on a new large foundry at Kidsgrove in Staffordshire. A year later they moved their headquarters from Liverpool to Birmingham. Pooleys' Liverpool connections had always enabled them to have a good relationship with shipping companies, although as the liners became larger the manner of construction changed, with interior-design companies settling on who should supply them. Pooleys had been unhappy that Averys supplied weighing equipment to Harland and Wolff in Belfast, but Pooleys' managing director, Laurence Jacob, was very pleased when he received an enquiry from Aldam Heaton and Company to supply weighing machines for the Turkish bath.

Personal weighing was very much in vogue, with many machines installed in gentlemen's clubs, officers' mess, sports clubs, hotels and large private homes. Both Averys and Pooleys produced examples. The one chosen for the Turkish bath was Pooleys' Model S133 – the seat weighing machine was equipped with a patent steelyard that could print the weight onto loose tickets. The standard machine was made in polished mahogany or oak case, with the seat upholstered in best quality American cloth or upholstered Morocco leather. Maximum weight was 24 stone and it had a standard price of £90–£100 plus carriage. For the Turkish bath, however, the model would require customising to match the decor, with the printing box and pillar finished in gold. The tickets would also have the name of the ship printed on the front; a rather nice if unusual souvenir of the ship. The cost was £120.

Turkish bath on *Titanic*. (Avery Historical Museum)

No. S 133

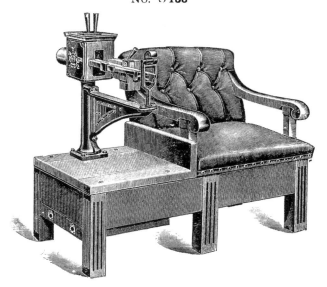

Pooley Model S133 personal weigh chair. (Avery Historical Museum)

Pooley Model S133 customised for the Turkish bath. (Avery Historical Museum)

STONES	LBS.	S. S. TITANIC
		DATE
		T1272

HENRY POOLEY & SON, LTD.,

SOLE MAKERS,

BIRMINGHAM & LONDON.

Weighing machine ticket from *Titanic* (front/back). (Author's collection)

Mail Room

Averys may have missed out on the Turkish bath but they did supply weighing equipment to the mailroom. The Royal Mail and W&T Avery Limited have a long association. The introduction in 1840 of the uniform 'penny post' in Great Britain led to the establishment of post offices around the country, all of which required weighing machines. In 1876 W&T Avery and De Grave received the contract to supply all post offices with weighing equipment; by 1885 Averys was the sole supplier. This arrangement extended to post offices on board passenger ships. The carrying of mail from Britain to other nations was important, and ships that could carry it under contract had the designation 'RMS' (Royal Mail Ship) prefixed to the ships' name. Averys supplied a number of scales and weights to the mailrooms of all passenger ships designated RMS. For *Olympic* and *Titanic* the order from Royal Mail was for:

Model 364 Letter and Parcel Scale. A well-finished brass scale on a polished oak slab with brass handles and ivory plate with postal rates complete with brass weights down to 1/4oz. Capacity 7lb. cost 70*s*. (x2).

Model 365 Improved Lever Parcel Balance. With copper scale and brass steelyard and slide, graduated by one ounce divisions. Capacity 14lb. Cost 45*s* (x2).

Model 118 Parcel Weigher. Gun metal steelyard finished in black complete with proportional weights. Capacity 2cwt. Cost 80*s*.

The three machines were pretty standard for postal work but interestingly the order also includes two Model 900 Pocket Sovereign Balances at 15*s* each, and two Model 908 Averys improved coin testers at 10*s* each. Averys also had an order for three weighing machines for the ships' hospitals:

Model 1076 Personal Weighing Machine fitted with improved steelyard dispensing entirely with loose weights. Highly sensitive and accurate, with best hardened steel knife edges and bearings. With nickel-plated measuring standard graduated from 3ft 6in to 6ft 6in. To weigh 24 stone by single ounces. Painted white with *White Star Line* insignia on platform. Cost 200*s*.

This model had been developed by Averys specifically for ships as it had no loose weights that could be lost. The machine was, however, popular with clinics, doctors' surgeries, schools etc. and was thus rolled out as a standard catalogue item. As the order does not specify where the machines were to be used it can be assumed that these machines were for the doctor's surgery, hospital and infectious diseases hospital. All the weighing machines were manufactured at Soho Foundry in Smethwick.

Elevators and Hoists

The increase in size of passenger vessels enabled or even required the fitting of elevators. *Olympic* and *Titanic* had three first-class and one second-class passenger elevators. These were supplied by R. Waygood and Company of Falmouth Road, Great Dover Street, London. They had an ironworks at the Vulcan Works, The Burges, Coventry. Richard Waygood founded the company in Beaminster in Dorset in 1833, starting out as an ironmonger and then manufacturing farm-related machinery, which included hoists. With a desire to expand, in 1840 he moved to London where he started a foundry and carried on a trade of general engineering, including waterwheels and sawing machinery.

In 1863 the Newington Works on Falmouth Road was built, thereby increasing his manufacturing capability. In 1868 a market was perceived for hydraulic lifts and the firm's first was sold to Hobbs, Hart and Company. Richard Waygood sold the business in 1875 to John Marsh Day (his foreman in Beaminster who had followed him to London), William Robert Green (his nephew who had joined him in 1863) and Henry C. Walker. Miscellaneous work was given up for the development of cranes, hoists and lifts, the simplest of which was the hand-powered type for private homes, hotels and restaurants. Steam and gas engines were soon utilised to take power to larger, higher lifts by means of belts.

With the need to develop higher-quality products to meet the needs of electrically powered lifts, Waygoods looked to set up a works in the skill-filled region of the Midlands, settling on Coventry. Waygoods became a private limited company in 1900 and two years later it absorbed the Otis Elevator Company. With works in London and Coventry and branches in Glasgow, Bombay, St Petersburg and Mexico they were the largest elevator manufacturer in the UK. They had the contract to install elevators in *Lusitania* and *Mauritania*; thus, they were the only company likely to get the contract for *Olympic* and *Titanic*. The Coventry works manufactured a variety of components for the passenger elevators. Waygoods also supplied and installed four service hoists.

Safes

Like all liners and hotels, a safe was available for passengers to keep their valuables in. The principal safe was located in the purser's office and was manufactured by the Ratner Safe Company of London. The Bilston firm of Thomas Perry and Son supplied safes for use in other parts of the ship and were ordered by the interior design chandlers. Dating back to 1806, Thomas Perry founded the business as an ironfounders located at Church Street, manufacturing fencing, hurdles and general ironwork. Thomas Perry was known as 'Gentleman Perry'; he was highly esteemed and loved by all and one of the founders of the Bilston District Bank, remaining a director until his death. Charles T., the eldest son, married Harriet, the third daughter of the late G.B. Thorneycroft, the first Mayor of Wolverhampton and the founder of the firm of G.B. Thorneycroft and Company. His second son,

Faceplate from a Thomas Perry safe. (Author's collection)

Thomas Perry, took over the business on his father's death. By the end of the nineteenth century the firm was producing more heavy engineering products, with heavy-duty fireproof safes being produced from 1883 using their armoured metal. Located at the Highfield Works, Bilston, Perrys had an enviable reputation for manufacturing, so it is a surprise they did not produce more for the shipping industry. They had an agent in Glasgow yet it seems they produced material for other suppliers to the shipping industry. The order for safes used in the restaurants came through a chandler and Perrys were not aware of their final use.

4

RESTING ON SEA BEDS

For the greater part of history a sea voyage had been fraught with discomfort, and in many cases, danger. Many people were unable to sleep due to the rolling of the ship, water ingress, or even the fear of fellow passengers (or crew). Sleeping conditions for passengers varied widely between the classes. Cabin passengers had the best conditions, but even their beds were simple wooden bunks with a thin mattress. Steerage passengers would get nothing at all and had to sleep on the floor or a long table; any bed linen was their own that they had to bring on board. In the better ships, steerage passengers lived below deck in what looked like stables that were insanitary with slop buckets. Even when wooden sailing ships were slowly replaced by iron steamships, bed comfort left a lot to be desired. There were exceptions like Brunel's SS *Great Britain* and then his enormous *Great Eastern*, but in the main passenger bed comfort was far from comfortable. Cunard's SS *Britannia* in 1840 was the first of a small fleet of ships to offer more comfortable conditions; although even these left a lot to be desired, as experienced by Charles Dickens and his wife who travelled from Liverpool to Boston in 1842:

> … the two berths, one above the other (the top one a most inaccessible shelf) than which nothing smaller for sleeping in was ever made except coffins, it was no bigger than one of those hackney cabriolets which have the door behind and soot their fares out, like sacks of coals, upon the pavement.

One ocean traveller took more than a casual interest in the beds on ships. William Parish Hoskins was the son of Ebenezer Hoskins, a metallic bedstead manufacturer in Birmingham. Ebenezer had left his home town of Exeter in Devon to obtain a trade in the Midlands, possibly due to the connections of his mother Elizabeth who came from Birmingham. In 1839 he was indentured as an apprentice coachsmith with Matthew Hawkins in Wednesbury. In 1851 he was working as a smith in Deritend before teaming up with John Key to manufacture metallic bedsteads at High Street, Bordesley. Key and Hoskins had an outlet in London and acting as their agent was Edward Henry Sewell. Sewell became a full partner in 1864, eventually making sole partner when Key left in 1872. As Hoskins and Sewell the firm developed a reputation for quality bedsteads, and they continued to expand.

Ebenezer's large family was involved in the business with his sons Frederick, Herbert and John Ebenezer taking actives roles. Another son, William Parish, was more wayward, being described in an anonymous account as a 'ne'er-do-well'. He was educated at King Edwards' School and progressed to the family business working as a clerk, but that did not satisfy his needs. His father felt that William should travel abroad and gain some experience of life – in essence, find out what he wanted to do. It was trips abroad that would lead him to his success. While travelling on ships he was curious as to why ships' bunks and berths were made of wood. Steerage passengers' conditions were particularly poor and he saw an opportunity to improve the quality of sleeping conditions for all those on board ships.

He designed metal bedsteads of various types: high quality for cabin passengers, slightly lesser for second class, and in third class tubular-constructed bunks that could be dismantled or adapted to the various spaces on board. The metal bedsteads would be coated to protect them from the salt-water environment and have fittings to the legs to enable them to be bolted to the floor. With a series of specially designed fittings, a variety of tubular designs could be made up, enabling the beds to be easily distributed to the shipbuilders and erected on ships. He took his idea to his father, Ebenezer, who helped him to form a manufacturing company, Hoskins and Son, the son being William Marrian Hoskins. The company, which would specialise in the manufacture of ships' beds, bunks, cots and berths of all types, was formed in 1887 and located at the Neptune Works in Bordesley.

Hoskins and Son made an immediate impact. Cunard and White Star were looking to improve the quality of steerage, thus creating 'third class', driven by the upsurge in demand for emigrant passengers. The Inman liner *City Of Paris*, built in 1888–89 by J&G Thompson at Clydebank, incorporated many new features, including William Hoskins' metal bedsteads. That was just the beginning; it was not long before shipbuilders and interior designers were adopting the new sleeping arrangements for their passengers. Harland

and Wolff in Belfast incorporated metal bedsteads in the new White Star Liners *Teutonic*, *Majestic* and *Cufic*. It may seem odd that Hoskins and Sewell and Hoskins and Son were in competition with each other yet were of the same family, but it is also true that Hoskins and Son concentrated on the shipping industry (expanding into the rail industry with berths for sleeper trains), whereas Hoskins and Sewell concentrated more on hotels and domestic market.

For William Parish Hoskins and his son William Marrian it was a very successful enterprise employing around 200 men, but such drive and energy takes its toll. William Parish's health deteriorated and he was diagnosed with a heart condition that would require more rest and a healthier environment on the south coast. Thus, in 1897, Hoskins and Son was sold to a member of another family of Birmingham businessmen: A. Neville Chamberlain. The Chamberlains dominated Birmingham in industry and politics. Neville's father, Joseph, was the Birmingham MP who was largely responsible for building Birmingham into the greatest and best-governed city in the world. Neville had returned from managing his father's plantation in the Bahamas and he was looking for a new project. With the support of his family he purchased Hoskins and Son. William and his son stayed with the old firm while Chamberlain formed a limited company. The firm's managing director, William Langley Hall, had over the years built up the confidence of the various shipbuilders, but initially he was suspicious of the new arrangement and it would take time for Chamberlain to get into the swing of the new business, and although William Parish Hoskins owned preferential shares in the company he founded, he did not take any active part in the business.

Times were also changing for Hoskins and Sewell. Ebenezer died in 1897 and his sons John and Frederick took over. John and Frederick wanted to take the company into the ships' berth trade, especially as shipbuilding was increasing, and although Hoskins and Son had a great share of the market it was envisioned that there would be plenty of work to go round. The following year saw Frederick's son, Charles, celebrate his coming of age, thus taking on more responsibility in the company. Soon thereafter Frederick died, thus placing the company in a slight difficulty, which the sale of Hoskins and Son to Chamberlain solved. William Marrian Hoskins moved to the original family business bringing with him agreements, patents and the good will of many shipbuilders and design houses – something that would cause a dispute with Chamberlain. In October 1898 William Parish Hoskins was made a director at Hoskins and Sewell and with his son would oversee the new Ships' Berth Department. In 1900, John further secured the firm's position by taking over Hoskins Brothers, a mattress manufacturer that had been run by his brother William P.; this move denied Hoskins and Son an important supplier. When William Parish resigned due to ill health he transferred all his shares to his son, who headed the Ships' Berth Department in a dynamic fashion, obtaining orders by personally following up quotations. The momentum of setting up the department seemed unstoppable when a maritime disaster struck the firm. In November 1901 Charles Hoskins was drowned when the schooner *Christie Campbell*, sailing between St. Peter's and Sydney in Nova Scotia, was involved in a collision and sank on the Bras d'Or Lake. The loss of two generations of Hoskins in quick succession was a blow but Hoskins adjusted to the loss. In February 1902, John Hoskins was optimistic: 'The Ships' Berth Department is still in its infancy but is working in a manner promising a good return in the near future.'

The key to obtaining orders at the shipyards was in finding reliable agents. In 1904 Hoskins and Sewell entered into an agreement with William Wilson of Belfast to act as agent for the sale of their ships' berths in Northern Ireland. The move paid off. Within a month John Hoskins reported to the board that he had received an enquiry through Wilson and a specification from Harland and Wolff, although Neville Chamberlain was concerned by this move as it put pressure on his company. In 1904 the directors considered expanding their operations to the regular bedstead trade, challenging Hoskins and Sewell on their turf. There was also concern that Hoskins and Sewell was infringing Hoskins and Son patents, although Chamberlain had been notified by his agent on the Clyde that Hoskins and Sewell considered that their patents were being infringed.

Hoskins and Son was still getting the bulk of the orders for the new ships, but with insider knowledge of how they operated, Hoskins and Sewell began to catch up. The key moment came in 1906. Harland and Wolff was building White Star's new liner *Adriatic*; Hoskins and Son got the bulk of the order for metallic beds in first and second class, but Hoskins and Sewell picked up orders for third class. Then the designers for Cunard's new ships, *Mauretania* and *Lusitania*, split the first-class orders. The interior designers of both ships chose a mix of designs from both companies, with Hoskins and Sewell supplying third-class berths as well as their 'Hoskwell' portable cabins. This development was not lost on Chamberlain, who noted in his chairman's report:

The Directors are pleased to be able to report a further large increase in the Company's turnover though the profits have not increased in the same proportions owing to the growing severity of competition.

Hoskins and Sewell made the most of their order to supply the new Cunarders, taking out advertisements in *The Shipbuilder* magazine. Orders began to flow at the expense of Hoskins and Son. It seems that the shipbuilders and agents felt they were dealing with the same individuals (William P. and William M. Hoskins) who had given such exemplary service in the past regardless of the company change; indeed, both of them had their names on patents. The two now had a more powerful enterprise behind them capable of greater production levels and thus able to reduce price. The growth of Hoskins and Sewell's Ships' Berth work can be seen from their trading figures:

Date	Ship's berths orders £s
1905	7,076
1906	35,434
1907	73,400
1908	19,557
1909	15,500
1910	32,400
1911	49,450
1912	97,270

The slump of 1908–09 can be clearly seen, but following the slump came the sudden and enormous growth in shipbuilding. Hoskins and Sewell overtook their rivals and became the dominant force in ships' berths. Sadly, one man would not see the pinnacle of Hoskins and Sewell's success; William Parish Hoskins collapsed and died on his way to Birmingham from his home in Eastbourne. He was the man who transformed the lives of those on board passenger ships, especially for those who travelled in third class. His greatest triumph would be the utilisation of his patents for the designs of beds and berths used on *Olympic* and *Titanic*.

The contracts for *Olympic* and *Titanic* came via Wilson in Belfast, with Aldam Heaton and Company and H.P. Mutters and Zoon sending designers to Birmingham to discuss the design brief with William Marrian and John Ebenezer Hoskins. The contract (initially for *Olympic* and then repeated for

Titanic) was for brass cot berths for the Empire, Adams and Sheraton Cabines De Luxe and metallic berths and mattresses for the first, second and third class and crew's accommodation, including the third-class patent portable cabins. A number of beds for the hospital were also ordered; these were divided into metallic bunks and operating table-cum-cots. Children's folding cots were also ordered, which would be stored on the ship and used as required. One of the reasons for Hoskins and Sewell receiving the contract was for their patented finish on metallic berths – they offered a highly polished finish in silver known as 'Silvex' and brass known as 'Varnoid'. In artwork prepared by Hoskins and Sewell the satin brass finish can be seen to compliment the decorative fittings of the Empire Suite room on *Olympic*. The satin brass was an excellent finish and looked stunning, but the finish highlighted fingermarks and took a while to clean, which was noted by the White Star Line. A comparison could be made with the enamelled finish on the beds supplied to *Adriatic*. In an interview with W.A. Benton, William Marrian Hoskins (chairman at the time of the interview) commented about the order for the big ships:

> The orders for the *Adriatic, Mauretania* and *Lusitania* raised the profile of the company in the eyes of *Cunard* and *White Star*, and we impressed them not only with the quality of the beds but also with the lower price compared to Hoskins and Son, with which they could compare side by side on those ships. [Neville] Chamberlain was not pleased and threatened to take us to court over patent infringements, but the patents were in my father's and my name and I had a legal right to use the designs. With *Olympic*, John [his uncle] and I made the decision to offer specially designed beds which enabled us to avoid any patent infringement problems and it allowed us to match the decorative elements of the beds with the interior design. Mr Ismay at *White Star* insisted on the satin brass finish as it gave an air of opulence. He was impressed with the Palace of Versailles and wanted to have the gold effect everywhere. He was obsessed with his ships bettering the Cundarders. The stewardesses were not as happy, as it took them a long time to clean and polish them. Unlike in a hotel the beds on a ship suffer more from the air and require more attention. The solution was to have the beds in white enamel (as we supplied to the *Adriatic*), which is easier to maintain.

Thus, on *Titanic*, enamelled white replaced the satin brass finish, which although did not look as spectacular, was easier to clean. During refits of *Olympic* enamelled white was fitted as well.

Models 550, 551, 554, 590 and 650 were fitted to the Adams Suite with a variation of detailed decoration. The 550, 551 and 590 were brass cot beds with 1in round reeded pillars with square tops; the 554 and 650 had square-tube pillars. In the Sheraton suites the Model 552 was supplied. This was a brass cot bed with 1½in square-tube pillars, reeded down the centre, with moulded and square-tube rails. The key part to a bed is the mattress and the bed frame mattress on the beds supplied was a new design for *Olympic* called the 'Olympex'. The frame was painted with anti-corrosive, surrounding a close-spaced galvanized lath mattress with 2in mesh. This design was to negate the vibration from the ship's engines that on very soft beds could be felt by the passenger. On top of the frame was the main mattress, the 'Nesta' patent sanitary mattress, which was a spring mattress covered with wool and hair.

The child's cots supplied were Model 638, which were portable and could be folded away. Finished in white enamel with brass knobs the cot was fixed to the side of a berth by two leather straps. In the hospital, the Model 635 operating table and cot was fitted. These metal framework cots were enamelled in white and could be adjusted if a patient needed to be placed in a particular position, or the sides could be added and it could be used as a standard hospital bed. A number of metallic bunks were also supplied for the hospital and used for patients who needed rest. In third class, Hoskins and Sewell supplied their patented 'Hoskwell' portable cabins. These became very popular with shipping companies, as they could provide reasonable accommodation to meet the ever-changing regulations for third-class passengers. The system was, essentially, two- or four-berth metal bunks surrounded by wooden partitions, which enabled a shipping company to provide additional passenger accommodation in spaces such as holds or between decks. The metal bunks were also supplied separately for use by crew and in third-class cabins; the type chosen was Model 145 with extra-strong lee rails.

The contract for *Titanic* was administered by William George Coleman, a 33-year-old from Sparkbrook. His principal task was to ensure the contract was delivered on time and to specification – a task made easier because of the strong relationship between Hoskins and Sewell and the interior designers. William Marrian Hoskins commented:

I had really good working relationship with *Heaton's* that dated back to when I was at the Neptune Works [*Hoskins and Son*], they gave clear guidance to what they wanted and essentially left me to it. The Dutch [*H.P. Mutters and*

Zoon] gave me fully prepared designs and said 'this is what we want', so I gave them what they wanted. Will Coleman was responsible for ensuring it all went smoothly and he did a good job. I felt very sorry for Will, he took the *Titanic* sinking to heart, you see we take a deep personal interest in the ships we supply. His wife [Sarah Ann] died a couple of years later [1914]. He was never the same again. He passed away two years ago [1924].

The beds were delivered via rail and ship to Belfast in the most part, but additional beds for *Titanic*, to be fitted in third class, were shipped to Southampton for installation before sailing.

The comfort on board the new luxurious liners owed much to William Parish Hoskins and the two companies with which he was associated. So comfortable were the beds in first class that it was often hard to stir the passengers – something that would prove to be dangerous on *Titanic*.

John Hoskins of
Hoskins & Sewell.
(Author's collection)

Left: William Coleman of Hoskins & Sewell. (Courtesy of Glen Westwood)

Right: Design artwork for *Olympic*. (Author's collection)

Right: Model 990 'Olympex' close-spaced galvanised lath mattress. (Author's collection)

"NESTA" PATENT SANITARY MATTRESS.

"NESTA" MATTRESS open, showing arrangement of springs with covering of wool and hair turned back. The springs are so arranged that it is impossible for them to get out of place, and both for resiliency and life it is far superior to the ordinary hair mattress.

"NESTA" MATTRESS ready for use.
THE MOST COMFORTABLE SANITARY MATTRESS.

The 'Nesta' sanitary mattress. (Author's collection)

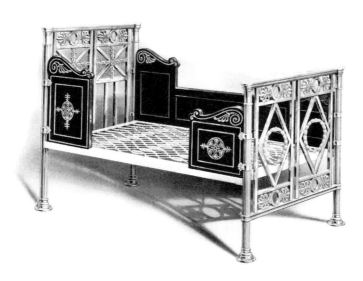

Model 595 cot bed designed for the Empire Suite. (Author's collection)

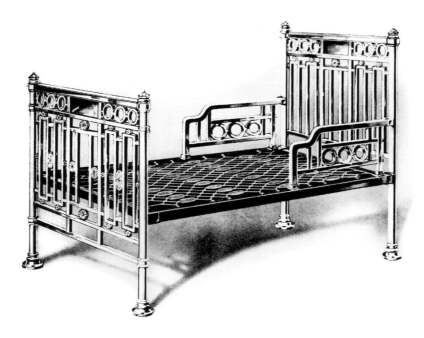

Cot bed designed for the Adams Suite. (Author's collection)

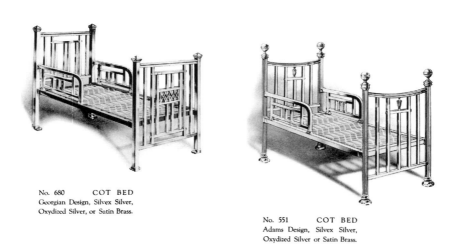

No. 680   COT BED
Georgian Design, Silvex Silver,
Oxydized Silver, or Satin Brass.

No. 551   COT BED
Adams Design, Silvex Silver,
Oxydized Silver or Satin Brass.

Models 680 and 551 cot beds. (Author's collection)

No. 638 CHILD'S COT. This is a portable folding Child's Cot, with galvanized steel woven wire mattress. It is attached to the Berth by two straps. The Lee Rail on one side of the Cot is about the same height as the Berth Lee Rail, so that the occupant of the Berth can easily attend to the child. The one illustration shows the Cot ready for use and the other folded for stowing away.

Above: Model 638 child's cot. (Author's collection)

Left: Parlour suite B-38 with enamelled bed. (Avery Historical Museum)

Right: Hospital bed. (Author's collection)

Hoskwell portable cabin. (Author's collection)

5

CRYSTAL, CHINA AND PLATE

The White Star Line prided itself on being the most luxurious shipping line in the world. Apart from the spacious and well-appointed state rooms, and amenities such as a gymnasium and library, the one feature a shipping line took pride in was the restaurants. Just as the best hotels are judged by the quality of their restaurants, so too were the big ships. Although it was the German passenger ships that introduced the à la carte restaurants, the idea that big ships should have excellent dining dates back to the middle of the nineteenth century, but then it was at an extra cost and for cabin passengers only. The great exception was Brunel's SS *Great Eastern* of 1858. The quality of the restaurant on board Brunel's steamship was to set a standard that would not be matched for fifty years.

As with the majority of interior components, the dining room and restaurant material was ordered via agents. The various china and glass manufacturers allied themselves with the principal agents of the shipping industry. The largest agent was John Stonier who was originally from Hanley, Stoke-on-Trent. Stonier started out as an earthenware manufacturer and dealer supplying earthenware to the public, hotels, boarding houses and shipping industry via the agent Ronald Livingston at 78 Lord Street, Liverpool. Ronald Livingston was a glass manufacturer and dealer who was in partnership with James Jackson, a specialist in earthenware, trading as Livingston and Jackson. After splitting up from Jackson, Livingston traded on his own until joining with Stonier in 1861 forming Livingston and Stonier, operating a shop and warehouse at Lord Street with their showroom known as the Dresden Rooms. Their long-standing working relationship was highly successful, acting as agents for numerous firms including Spode and Copeland, Stevenson and Hancock, Wedgwood and Mills and Webb and Stuart to name but a few.

Ronald Livingston retired and left the partnership in 1866, giving notice in the local press thanking everyone for their support. John Stonier continued alone operating a large warehouse and employing over 400 people, dominating the supply of glass and china to the shipping industry. In 1876 Stonier sold the business to one of his suppliers, Stuart and Sons, glass manufacturers of Stourbridge. The business reformed as Stonier and Company continued to supply the shipping industry. With Stoniers' being owned by Stuart and Sons, Stuart's glassware became the preferred supply to most ships. Two years later John Stonier entered into partnership with Edwin Powell and Frederick Bishop, forming Powell, Bishop and Stonier in Hanley.

The story of Stuart's began in 1827 when 11-year-old Frederick Stuart was sent to work as an office boy at the Red House Glassworks, working for Richard Bradley Ensell and later becoming a traveller for John Parish & Company. This glassworks was on the 'crystal mile', an area just outside Stourbridge where generations of local craftsmen had already made this the centre of English glass-making. Twenty-six years later, Frederick – with Richard Mills and Edward and Thomas Webb – formed Mills, Webb and Stuart. Richard Mills bought and updated the Wordsley Iron Foundry behind the Red House Glassworks, changing the name to Albert Glassworks. Thomas Webb had his own business at the Platts Glassworks, and just a year later he left the partnership to develop his own business building the Dennis Glassworks in Amblecote. The firm became Stuart and Mills in 1868 following the end of the term of the partnership. Stuarts' 1876 expansion, absorbing Stoniers, enabled them to supply more cut glass to the shipping industry, and not just tableware. They also supplied cut glass for chandeliers, wall lights, hall lamps and all forms of engraved and etched glass.

During one of *Great Eastern*'s many refits, Stuart and Mills supplied copious amounts of glass. It was this order that established the company as *the* supplier to the shipping industry. Even though things were moving well, a falling out between Frederick Stuart and George Mills led to them ending their partnership and going their separate ways. In 1883 Frederick formed a new partnership with his sons William Henry, Frederick (II) and Robert, having already taken the lease of the Red House Glassworks in Wordsley. The new firm was known as Stuart and Sons, and the sons became the dominant partners, with their father retiring in 1897 and passing away in 1900. Stoniers had remained aloof from the changes at Stuarts, mainly because it operated independently from a managerial aspect.

As the shipping industry expanded, so too did Stoniers' fortunes and therefore that of their suppliers'. One of the reasons for their success was their warehouse at Lord Street, which carried a large quantity of standard material required by the various shipping companies. Plain white earthenware plates, bowls and the like carrying the shipping companies' emblems were placed in racks ready to be distributed as required. More ornate patterned china, which also carried emblems, was kept in smaller quantities to replace breakages or be issued for new ships. Glassware, with the shipping companies' emblems etched to the sides of decanters, glasses, tumblers etc., was stored in delivery crates. Stoniers kept copies of pattern books from their various suppliers and could easily request more quantities to replace stock that had left the warehouse. With so many suppliers on their books Stoniers could always meet demand. Thus, when the orders began to appear for *Olympic* and then a repeat order for *Titanic*, Stoniers could easily provide the required material. For *Olympic* the glass order comprised the following:

8,000 cut tumblers	300 claret jugs
2,500 water bottles	2,000 salt cellars
1,500 crystal dishes	500 salad bowls
300 celery glasses	1,500 soufflé dishes
500 flower vases	1,200 pudding dishes
5,500 ice-cream plates	1,500 cocktail glasses
2,000 wine glasses	1,200 liquor glasses
2,500 champagne glasses	

A repeat order for *Titanic* was similar, although it seems Stuart and Sons found themselves with a problem when a sudden extra order appeared for 200 'Champagne Glasses, White Star'. Whether this was for actually sending to the ship or to restock Stoniers' warehouse is unknown. Nonetheless, the order had to be filled and this offers another demonstration of the close co-operation between Black Country firms. Stuart and Sons sub-contracted the order to Thomas Webb and Sons Limited in order to make the deadline. Webb's delivered the case of glasses to Stuarts' who then sent the consignment to Stoniers' warehouse in Southampton.

As previously noted, Thomas Webb had been a partner in Mills, Webb and Stuart before leaving to concentrate on his own glassworks. Thomas inherited his father's glass-making business, eventually selling the glassworks in 1842, and concentrated on his own business, winning a medal for cut glass at the 1851 Great Exhibition. His sons Thomas Wilkes Webb and Charles became partners in 1850 and 1869 respectively, forming Thomas Webb and Sons. The company went from strength to strength, being hailed as 'the best makers of glass in the world' at the 1878 Paris International Exhibition, with the Dennis Glassworks being awarded the Grand Prix in 1878 and 1889. One by one the Webb family began to leave the old firm. When the elder son Charles retired in 1900 it was left to a new managing director, Congreve William Jackson, to reinvigorate the company. In 1907 Thomas Webb and Sons Limited supplied lead crystal glass to HMS *Dreadnought*, replacing poorer-quality glass that tended to shatter when the battleship fired its guns. Webb's fame came from their development of Rock Crystal engraving introduced at the Dennis Glassworks by William Fritsche in 1868. This deep-cut engraving, using a copper wheel, offered stunning quality and was ideal for specialist material. Perrys, McGeochs and a number of other firms ordered cut-crystal light fittings from Webb – the deep cut on thick glass being ideal for such fittings.

First-class China

The first-class restaurants, the Café Parisien and staterooms would all be serviced with quality bone china. The à la carte restaurant was supplied with service from the Royal Crown Derby Company Limited. The firm was established in 1876 by Edward Phillips, a manufacturer from the North Staffordshire potteries, and William Litherland, the proprietor of a porcelain and glass retailer in Liverpool, both of whom had been associated with the Worcester Royal Porcelain Company. Phillips, joint managing director at Worcester with Richard Binns, was sacked by the Worcester Board of Directors, and in June 1875 the pair purchased land adjacent to the Derby Workhouse for a new factory. In December 1876 they were the successful bidders for the workhouse itself and its extensive grounds on Omaston Road. The term Royal Crown Derby was introduced in 1890 when the Royal Arms was granted by Queen Victoria. The order for *Titanic* was delivered in December 1911 and comprised:

600 dinner plates	100 breakfast cups and saucers
180 soup plates	100 teacups and saucers
180 breakfast plates	25 cream jugs
100 salad plates	25 slop basins

The interior designers had specified that the design of the china had to compliment the interior design of the restaurant, and Royal Crown Derby was specifically asked to have a pattern that closely matched. The china pattern consisted of a band of encrusted gold work with painted ornament of chaplets and festoons in the Louis XVI style, delicately finished in tints of green.

The special order through Stoniers for the à la carte china was exceptional. The first-class dining saloon on *Titanic* was located on D Deck; this was the traditional White Star first-class restaurant utilising established designs of china. For this reason a pottery firm may not have been aware that their china had been issued to *Titanic* or any other ship. This was the case for Copeland who supplied the Spode trademark.

Josiah Spode senior established a business in 1767 after working for a number of potters. While Josiah ran and developed the pottery works in Stoke, his son Josiah Spode (II) trained as a potter and ran the firm's warehouse in London. He took over the pottery factory from his father in 1797 taking on William Copeland as a partner and together they led the development of bone china, which became the standard English porcelain body from about 1800. The business eventually passed to William's son William Taylor Copeland and after a brief partnership with Thomas Garrett he passed the business through the family. Stoniers' warehouse contained many Spode patterns, which were used on White Star Line ships. New orders were placed to stock up for use on *Olympic* and *Titanic*. Spode's stunning cobalt blue decorated in gold-on-white bone china was a favourite of the company, with pattern numbers 1/9608, R.416, R.3717, R.4331 and R.4332 being supplied to Liverpool (and then forwarded to Southampton). Other patterns supplied to first class included a variation of William Brownfield and Sons Crown pattern, often erroneously referred to as the 'Gothic pattern'; this china was supplied by any number of companies supplying Stoniers, with many of these taken from stock. The A Deck service of plain white with gold rim was used on the ship; again, any one of Stoniers' suppliers from the Potteries could have supplied this service.

Second-class China

Second class on *Olympic* and *Titanic* was the equivalent of first class on most ships crossing the Atlantic, and this was easily demonstrated in the quality of the tableware. Blue and white delftware china was chosen for second class. This was a standard pattern stocked by Stoniers'. The main suppliers of this style were Bishop and Stonier, Wileman and Company and Minton.

Bishop and Stoniers' origins date back to 1845 when William Livesley, Edwin Powell and Frederick Bishop formed a new undertaking at Old Hall Lane and Miles Bank in Hanley, Stoke-on-Trent. When Livesley retired in 1866 the partnership became known as Powell and Bishop. Twelve years later, John Stonier joined the partnership. In 1891 the firm was renamed Bishop and Stonier, registering a new trademark – 'Bisto'. As would be expected, Bishop and Stonier supplied Stoniers.

Wileman and Company traded as the Foley Potteries, and the Foley China Company was established by Henry Wileman in around 1857, building the Foley China Works at Fenton. His two sons James and Charles succeeded him. In 1872 Joseph Ball Shelley entered the partnership, followed nine years later by his son Percy who took control when his father died in 1896. In 1910 Percy decided to try to register the Foley name as its trade name, as the china was still marked Foley China. E. Brain and Company Limited of Fenton, who also used the Foley name on its backstamp, objected, resulting in a court case where it was judged that Wileman's could not have the exclusive claim to use the name.

Thomas Minton, the founder of Thomas Minton and Sons, established his pottery factory in Stoke-on-Trent in 1793 producing earthenware. He formed a partnership, Minton & Poulson, in around 1796 with Joseph Poulson, who made bone china from around 1798 onwards in his nearby china pottery. From the mid 1890s onwards, Mintons made major contributions to art nouveau ceramics with a fine range of slip-trailed majolicaware. Minton developed the Secessionist range covering both practical and ornamental wares including cheese dishes, plates, teapots, jugs and comports, vases and large jardinières. Early Secessionist patterns featured realistic renderings of natural emblems – flowers, birds and human figures. The blue and white delftware plates clearly demonstrate the style that was popular with the public.

Third-class Earthenware

Third-class passengers had an excellent dining saloon located on F Deck divided into two rooms: one for single men and the other for families. The earthenware plates supplied were made for durability rather than style, being plain white with the White Star Line emblem in red in the centre. Being a basic design the stockpiles of these plates at Stoniers' warehouses in Liverpool and Southampton were enormous and they would simply restock as required. Numerous companies would have supplied the third-class plates; one of their main suppliers was John Maddock and Sons Limited. The firm was established in the 1830s at premises in Newcastle Street, Burslem. John Maddock was in partnership with Seddon from 1839 to 1842, and then traded on his own until 1855 when the firm became John Maddock and Sons. The firm became a limited company in 1896. Apart from the plain earthenware, Maddocks also produced the blue and white delftware that was seen in second class and could easily have been a supplier of that too.

Plateware

The service of plate, which number around 10,000 pieces, was supplied by the Goldsmiths and Silversmiths Company of London, although they contacted a number of companies allied to them to supply a quantity of material to the standard pattern for the White Star Line. The bulk of these orders went to Elkington and Company of Birmingham.

George Richards Elkington and his cousin Henry began as silversmiths in 1836 devising a method of electroplating and improving gilding techniques. The Elkingtons received financial support from Josiah Mason, a pen manufacturer, forming Elkington, Mason and Company. The new enterprise was a tremendous success, introducing electrotyping as a new method of production for silver-plated items. In 1843 Elkingtons acquired the English patent for Werner Siemens' process of electrogilding. The company's reputation was sealed at the Great Exhibition at the Crystal Palace in 1851 when their process and products impressed attendees. By this time the firm employed 500 workers at its Birmingham works in Newhall Street. In 1885 Elkington and Company registered designs by Christopher Dresser for tea services, sugar bowls, claret jugs, kettles, cruet stands, baskets, a tureen and a tankard. Two years later, Elkingtons became a limited company and was reconstituted in 1907.

The firm had an enviable reputation, producing high-quality silver plate and nickel plate of every kind of article, both practical and ornamental. Gilding techniques that they developed led the company to carry out gilding work on many architectural projects. Elkingtons supplied major hotels and railway companies (for the first-class dining cars) and prepared special silverware for civic events. The shipping industry was a natural extension of their work, requiring quality metal that could survive the rigours of many ocean voyages. Elkingtons was often on a list of approved suppliers for the shipping companies due to the high quality of the work, and because the finish on their silver and nickel plate cleaned easily and looked excellent. The factory had a large collection of dies that carried the emblems of various shipping lines, which included Cunard, White Star, Dominion, Blue Star, Leyland, P&O, Ellerman, Royal Mail Line and Red Star Line.

The quantity of silver plate for *Titanic* was immense and consisted of:

8,000 dinner forks	100 grape scissors
1,500 fruit forks	400 asparagus tongs
1,500 fish forks	400 sugar tongs
1,000 oyster forks	400 toast racks
400 butter knives	400 sugar basins
1,500 fruit knives	400 fruit dishes
1,500 fish knives	1,000 finger bowls
8,000 table and dessert knives	400 butter dishes
5,000 dinner spoons	400 vegetable dishes
3,000 dessert spoons	400 entrée dishes
1,500 mustard spoons	400 meat dishes
400 nut crackers	

Apart from these items Elkingtons also supplied 1,500 napkin rings, 3,000 tureens, metal dishes, chocolate pots etc. On behalf of Goldsmiths and Silversmiths Company they supplied 200 matchbox holders and ashtrays, 500 menu holders and 200 flower vases. For third class, Elkingtons was contracted to supply plateware made of nickel plate comprising a full range of cutlery and other plate:

2,500 Forks	1,000 ashtrays
2,500 dinner knives	200 meat dishes
2,500 dessert spoons	1,500 tureens/assorted dishes
2,500 dinner spoons	3,000 serving spoons ladles etc.
400 butter knives	

Elkingtons supplied cutlery with the 'Dubarry' and 'Panel Reed' patterns, with the White Star Line house flag emblem added to handles. Tureens, bowls etc. were standard catalogue items with the house flag emblem added. The menu holders featured a plinth with a silver star-shaped upright.

W.A. Benton discussed orders for shipping companies with Hyla Garrett Elkington, who commented:

> The shipping companies' orders always came in at the last minute, and the agents always wanted delivery yesterday. We [Elkingtons] can always produce and deliver large quantities due to our network of out-workers. Before the [first world] war we had something like 2,000 outworkers and at times of high demand we would send work around the region.

The outworkers referred to were mostly women who had a press or stamping machine in their homes, often in a shed at the bottom of their gardens. These workers would receive material and work through the night if required. The next day the material would be collected or, if they lived close enough to the factory, they would take the completed work to Elkingtons themselves. It was common in Birmingham (and the Black Country) to see women pushing prams of completed work into factories.

Although Elkingtons was known for their plateware business, they were also experts in all forms of plating, coating and gilding, and workers from Elkingtons were sent to Belfast to carry out special gilding work on metal adornments, ironwork and plaster.

Another Birmingham firm that supplied cutlery was Arthur Price Limited. The founder's father, Thomas Price, had worked as a diesinker and patternmaker for a number of Birmingham firms making flatware and hollowware, and his son Arthur followed in his stead, becoming a toolmaker and diesinker for forks and spoons. Arthur worked his way through the industry spending time at Hands and Company in Suffolk Street, the Potosi Silver Company in Newhall Street, and finally becoming works manager at

John Yates and Son in Prittchet Street. After twenty years in the trade, Arthur Price founded his own business at the back of a tenement, number 16½ Gem Street, Aston, employing twelve workmen. Small businesses like Prices were important in the metal trade; large firms used them to take up the extra production when times were booming – as long as the small business could match the quality. In 1907, Henry Talbot Bikker joined Price and became joint managing director, putting £700 into the business. This influx of capital enabled Prices to purchase a German electric press, the only one of its kind in the country at the time. The press replaced two men to cut thick nickel–silver sheet. This development increased production levels and enabled them to take on additional work. Prices became one of the suppliers of cutlery to the shipping industry, producing the Panel Reed pattern for the White Star Line.

Elkingtons Works in Newhall Street, Birmingham. (Author's collection)

White Star Line Reed and Dubarry pattern cutlery. (Author's collection)

Elkingtons jug and menu holder. (Author's collection)

Elkingtons matchbox holder and ashtray. (Author's collection)

Stuart and Sons carafe with deep-cut pattern (Author's collection).

Stuart and Sons glasses with deep-cut pattern. (Author's collection)

First-, second- and third-class plates. (Author's collection)

BUTTONS, WHISTLES AND GUNS

There is something about a naval uniform that has always attracted attention. The navy-blue jacket with brass or gilt buttons looks smart and gives the wearer an air of superiority. British merchant ships were noted for their officers' demeanour and the White Star Line went to great pains to ensure that in qualifications and behaviour their officers demonstrated the best of British Merchant Naval tradition. Their uniforms had the usual brass buttons, highly polished, depicting the White Star Line burgee. The principal supplier of these uniform buttons was a Birmingham firm – Firmin and Sons Limited in Villa Street.

Firmin and Sons' origins date to 1655 when Thomas Firmin traded as a button maker in London. Thomas came from Ipswich and in 1632 was apprenticed to The Girdlers Company (makers of quality belts). After completing his apprenticeship he set up as a button maker at Three Kings Court, off Lombard Street in London. During the Great Fire of London (1666) his Lombard Street premises were severely damaged. He secured temporary accommodation in Leadenhall Street and in a few years was able to rebuild in Lombard Street and carry on his business with increased success. In 1676 he left the management of the business in the hands of his nephew and partner, Jonathan James (son of his sister Prudence), who had been his apprentice. From modest beginnings as button makers Firmin became the leading supplier of every form of uniform, livery or badge and the accessories and accoutrements to go with them. By 1754, the company's ledgers and order books recorded purchases by King George II and various other members of the British royal family.

The first known royal warrant for a button maker was granted by King George III in 1796. Firmin's products were present at the battles of the Nile, Trafalgar and Waterloo. This achievement was recognised when Firmin exhibited at the 1851 Great Exhibition in London. Firmin's renown was international; in the American Civil War both sides wore Firmin buttons! The business name changed over the years as different partners came and went, becoming a limited company in 1876. Six years later Firmins worked with Bryant Brothers and Company who ran a button-making manufactory in a town famous for button-making – Birmingham. Since the eighteenth century Birmingham had produced high-quality buttons, with the most famous name being Matthew Boulton, who took over his father's works at Snow Hill in 1759. By the middle of the nineteenth century, Birmingham had a number of well-established brass button makers such as G.H. Bullivant, Edward Armfield, J.R. Gaunt, Smith and Wright, and William Dowler, all of whom manufactured quality military buttons. In 1881 Firmins took over Bryants at St Paul's Square, Birmingham, following a trend by many companies taking advantage of a skilled workforce and excellent transport. The company soon established itself producing quality insignia and buttons for military, civil and merchant marine uniforms. Although providing for uniform suppliers, they also provided buttons and badges on a personal basis with officers ordering spare cap badges.

Whistles

Another essential item for an officer was a whistle. The official merchant marine whistle was the Acme Thunderer manufactured by J. Hudson and Company located at Barr Street, Hockley. The most famous whistlemaker in the world was founded by Joseph Hudson, a farm worker from Derbyshire who moved to Birmingham during the Industrial Revolution and trained as a toolmaker working at Bent and Parker of Harper's Hill Works, Northwood Street, where they made military ornaments, badges, buckles and whistles. He left in 1870 to work on his own, converting the washhouse at the side of his end-of-terrace back-to-back home in St Mark's Street into a workshop, where he made many things such as snuff boxes, corkscrews and whistles. In 1882 he moved to larger premises in Buckingham Street where a year later came the event that would make the name Hudson synonymous around the world with whistles.

When the London Metropolitan Police advertised for an idea to replace the policeman's rattle, which was seen as a cumbersome means of communication for the bobby on his beat, Joseph Hudson invented a novel whistle for the purpose. It could be held in the mouth leaving the hands free – a clear advantage over the rattle. The whistle became known as the 'Metropolitan' and the police, military and other civil authorities put thousands into service. Over the next 135 years Hudsons developed and patented over forty different whistle designs and produced whistles of exceptional quality. The merchant and royal navies used the bosun's whistle to signal instructions – the high-pitched tone was easily heard over the sound of waves. The whistle was also used to pipe aboard officers. The Royal Navy used the bosun's whistle as a standard signalling device; the merchant navy used it mainly for ceremonial activities. However, both navies wanted another whistle that was distinct from the bosun's that could be used as an emergency call. A whistle that was popular was known as the 'Escargot' (snail) due to its shape of a round chamber from which protruded a small mouthpiece with a pea.

From 1880 this type of whistle went through a variety of changes and in 1900 Hudsons registered the Acme Thunderer. It was ideal and these were ordered by shipping companies (or rather their agents) to go on the bridge of a new ship. A box of ten was standard supply to a vessel, with each whistle carrying the name of the ship stamped on the side. These disappeared quickly as officers of a new vessel ensured they grabbed theirs as a souvenir. Each officer was expected to have his own personal whistle, which could be purchased directly from Hudsons and could have the name of a particular ship stamped on them at an additional charge. Bosun's whistles were not supplied to *Titanic*, as the chief quartermaster, boatswain, boatswain's mate and the quatermaster were expected to have their own.

Whistles were not the only form of communication on board a ship. *Olympic* and *Titanic* had a telephone system that connected the bridge with all parts of the ship including the crow's nest. This electric telephone system replaced the old speaking tubes that were still prevalent on many merchant ships and were still being fitted to Royal Navy vessels. Interestingly, these speaking tubes had whistles fitted into the mouthpiece that were blown to draw the attention of those at the other end – these whistles were also manufactured by Hudsons. The old-fashioned megaphone was, however, still used. Hudsons were the sole manufacturers of the Acme stetnor megaphone, two of which were each delivered to *Olympic* and *Titanic*.

Guns

Firearms were always carried on British merchant vessels. Initially, they were carried to ensure that the rough members of the crew (usually the black gangs in the boiler rooms and the more dubious seaman) could be kept in order, and to prevent mutinies. The firearms were also useful when ferrying steerage passengers who were kept below in very poor conditions and could themselves become very mutinous. It was also a necessity as many of those leaving Europe to immigrate to the USA were radicals, political agitators or simply criminals who were themselves armed. As ships improved and in essence the quality of the passengers improved, the need for firearms seemed less likely; however, in an emergency it may have been necessary to support the officers' arguments with a little force. The number of weapons supplied was minimal and unlikely to be enough to defend the ship from pirates or a major attack, although they could be used in such an event. A merchant ship, therefore, carried a number of revolvers. The quantity did vary depending on the shipping line, but approximately six to twelve guns with ammunition were stored in a locked metal cabinet under the control of the first officer. The guns issued to senior officers were the Webley Mk.IV .455 calibre short-barrelled revolvers, which were nickelplated and came supplied with a lanyard. The revolving chamber carried six rounds.

The Webley & Scott Revolver and Small Arms Company was established in 1790 by William Davies who made bullet, shot and fishing net moulds, as well as gun implements and gunmakers' tools. Philip Webley was apprenticed to Parker and Timmins as a gun lock filer in 1827 and eight years later joined his brother James' business as makers of percussioners, gun locks etc. in Weaman Street. In 1838 Philip married William Davies' daughter Caroline, and the business was styled as 'Philip Webley (successor to the late William Davies) original Bullet and Shot Mould manufacturers'. Webley slowly increased the type of items manufactured and sold, adding gun and pistol locks, gun furniture and rifle sights, expanding by 1849 to making guns and components. Webley manufactured their first production revolver in 1853 – a muzzle-loaded percussion cap and ball pistol called the Longspur. It was in 1867 that Webley made their mark when the Royal Irish Constabulary adopted one of their designs which became known as the RIC, a pistol that would be used by a number of police forces. A famous user of the gun was Brevet Major General George Armstrong Custer, who was given a pair by Lord Berkley in 1869. Two of Philip's sons, Thomas William and Henry, joined the company and the firm became P. Webley and Sons; Thomas ran the gun and rifle department and Henry ran the revolver department.

Webley supplied large quantities of material to merchant ships. A page in their catalogue is headed 'Merchant's Ships' Stores' and lists the items Webley supplied to shipping companies: leg irons, handcuffs, cutlasses, boarding pikes, tomahawks, revolvers, ships' pistol, ships' musket and bayonet and the best plain WD mould. Even when the revolver had become available, the old-fashioned muskets and pistols were still being supplied – the type of weapon that Webley had been supplying merchant ships since about 1840. These weapons were tough and made to survive difficult conditions, and it is a credit to Webley that many of these firearms were still in service forty years later.

In 1886 Webley developed a rugged and powerful revolver for the British military, the Webley Mk I. This was their first revolver built on the principles of interchangeability. In July of 1887, the British War Office issued a contract

WEBLEY'S "MARK IV" ·455. (Service Model).
AUTOMATIC EJECTOR.

4in. Barrel. 2lb. 3 oz.
6in. ,, 2 ,, 4 ,,

"This Revolver has been adopted by a Joint War Office and Admiralty Committee for the exclusive use of His Majesty's Army, Navy, Indian and Colonial Forces, and is described by the First Lord of the Admiralty as being "the most efficient weapon of the kind."—Vide "*Times*," Feb. 28th, 1893.

Webley Mk IV .455 revolver (service model). (Cornell Publications)

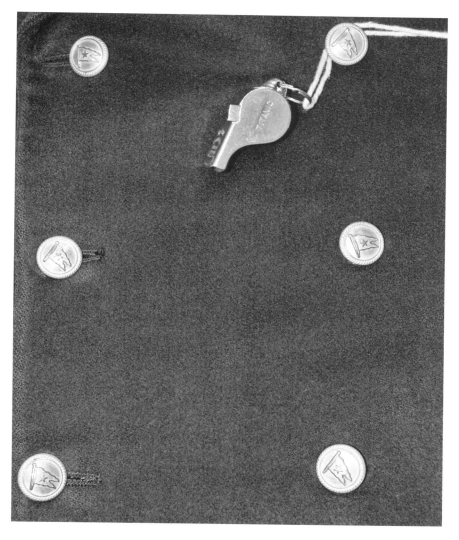

White Star buttons by Firmins and whistle by Hudsons. (Author's collection)

to Webley for 10,000 calibre .455 Mk I revolvers. They were the first of six models of Webleys that would see continual service until well past their final production run. Lord George Hamilton, the First Lord of the Admiralty commented in the House of Commons that the new Webley was 'the most efficient weapon of its kind'. The endorsement meant this weapon was likely

113

Advertisement for Hudson's Acme Stentnor Megaphone. (Hudson's Whistles)

to be taken up by the merchant navy as well. The first five Marks were a continual series of minor improvements on Webley's original model of 1882, with birdshead grips and 4in barrels.

In 1896 Webley merged with W. and C. Scott of the Premier Gun Works, Lancaster Street, Birmingham, to form Webley and Scott. A year later the firm became a limited company – Webley and Scott Revolver and Arms Company

Limited – absorbing Richard Ellis and Sons in the process. Two years later, the Webley revolver proved itself in combat with British General Horatio Kitchener's troops at the Battle of Omdurman in the Sudan in September 1898. The Mark IV served as the standard British sidearm during the Boer War of 1899–1902. Webley manufactured some 36,700 Mark IVs between 1899 and 1914. The White Star Line and other shipping companies used the Mark IV, as it was a reliable weapon and packed quite a punch. Although there was no formal firearms training, it was common for merchant navy officers to own their own weapons, and shooting for sport was common in Britain prior to the First World War. The White Star Line ordered the firearms and ammunition directly from Webley and Scott, as they had to be registered to the company. Neither White Star nor Webley and Scott imagined that the guns would ever be used.

7

MIDLANDS CREW

The White Star Line prided itself on the quality of its officers and crew. The crew of *Titanic* were, like crews of all ships, from all parts of the country. It may surprise many to realise that the Midlands provided many men and women to the merchant fleets. In the case of *Titanic*, the senior officer was a midlander, Captain Edward John Smith from Hanley, Stoke-on-Trent.

Edward John Smith (or 'E.J.' as he would become known in later life) was born in 1850 at Well Street, Hanley, to Edward Smith, a shopkeeper, and his wife Catherine. Catherine had been married previously and her son Joseph (Hancock) from that marriage had left Hanley to join the merchant navy in Liverpool. Edward attended the Etruria British School until about the age of 14, after which he was employed at the Etruria Forge, one of Lord Granville's iron foundries. In the meantime, his half brother Joseph had carved out a career in the merchant navy, although not without incident. In 1856, while serving as second mate on board the 400-ton barque *Hymen*, Joseph, along with the whole crew of the ship, was taken captive by pirates off the Barbary Coast. After suffering for some weeks he was rescued by a Royal Naval force sent from Gibraltar. No doubt Edward heard the stories of his half brother's adventures at sea and it may have influenced him to consider such a career. In 1867, Edward and a group of friends went to Liverpool to meet up with Joseph and join the merchant navy. Joseph had risen to the rank of captain and was in command of the 1,297-ton sailing vessel *Senator Weber* of Andrew Gibson and Company. He arranged for Edward to sign on his ship as a 'boy' on the six months' voyage to Hong Kong. Thus was the beginning of Edward John Smith's naval career.

Edward's career followed the standard path, learning the ways of the shipping trade and more importantly the ways of the sea. It was a hard life of book learning and physical work, much of which was potentially dangerous. With ships visiting far away ports, the risk of disease or infection was great; only the fittest – both physically and mentally – would survive. The purpose, of course, of working one's way up through the ranks was to gain a full working knowledge of a ship, something that could not be done in a classroom. *Senator Weber's* next voyage was across the Pacific to San Francisco where, quite surprisingly, Edward was promoted to third mate. From San Francisco, *Senator Weber* sailed to the Peruvian port of Callao and then on to the Chincha Islands before heading south, rounding the notorious Cape Horn and across the Atlantic to Antwerp in Belgium, arriving on 28 October 1868. Edward's first experience of sea life had lasted eighteen months, and it seems he had found what he wanted to do for the rest of his life. In the New Year, Edward returned to *Senator Weber* for its voyage to Japan. From thence his life was to be ruled by the movement of ships and the sea. In 1871 he passed his second mate's certificate and signed on to the 1,039-ton *Record* bound from Liverpool to New Orleans.

Nearly two years later, following voyages on board the *Windsor* and *N Mosher*, Edward passed his first mate's examination. In May 1875 he passed his master's certificate, thus gaining the rank of captain. Captain Edward John Smith's first command was the 1,040-ton *Lizzie Fennell*, which left Antwerp on 13 May 1879 bound for Callao. At just over 174ft long and nearly 36ft wide it was a far cry from his final command. Following a short period of command of the *Lizzie Fennel*, Edward went aboard RMS *Britannic* to take a look around the White Star Line's record-breaking steamer, which was one of the ships that pointed towards the future of transatlantic travel.

It was soon after his tour in 1880 that he resigned from Andrew Gibson and Company and joined the White Star Line. Although a captain at Andrew Gibson and Company, he had to work his way up the ladder at White Star, one of the most prestigious shipping companies. He served as fourth and then third officer on board RMS *Celtic* under Captain Benjamin Gleadell on the Liverpool to New York run. From March 1882 to 1884, Edward served as second officer on RMS *Coptic*, sailing in the Pacific. The following year found him on *Republic* serving as first officer. His career was moving well and his ability to remain calm yet authoritative meant his temperament was ideally suited for White Star.

With his prospects on the rise he married a woman ten years his junior – Sarah Eleanor Pennington, the daughter of a farmer. They married on 13 January 1887 at St Oswald's Parish Church of Winwick near Warrington.

In April he tasted his first role as commander for White Star when he took temporary command of *Republic* before being transferred to *Britannic* as first officer. In February 1888, he passed his Extra Master's Certificate at the second attempt. A month later he was given command of *Baltic* and then of *Britannic* – the very ship that had convinced him to join White Star eight years previously. His career was certainly on the rise; the management perceived Edward as part of a tier of captains that would eventually lead the company in its rivalry against Cunard. White Star prided itself in the quality of its officers, and the fact that their commanders and officers were often members of the Royal Naval Reserve (RNR) enabled a passenger ship to fly the blue ensign rather than the red ensign. Edward applied to join the RNR in August 1888 and spent some time training on HMS *Eagle*.

In December 1888 White Star's new ship SS *Cufic*, a livestock carrier of 4,660 tons, completed its maiden voyage from Liverpool to New York with Edward in command. It was a big moment for Edward and the company who had entrusted a new ship to him. Following that command, he commanded *Republic* (to New York where she ran aground off Sandy Hook), *Celtic* (Atlantic), *Coptic* (to Australia and New Zealand), *Adriatic* (Atlantic) and then *Runic* (livestock carrier). In 1891 Edward once again took command of *Britannic* on the Liverpool to New York run, a command that would last for nearly four years.

In this period Edward went to the aid of the fishing smack *L'Active*, rescuing her crew, an event that made headlines much to the pleasure of White Star. That was not the only drama that involved *Britannic*, which also found itself battered by ferocious storms, hit by a monster wave and losing a crewman overboard. These hazards were par for the course in the career of any ship, and Edward's time with *Britannic* secured his reputation among passengers as the most congenial of captains. He was the ideal dinner guest and made himself available to passengers and crew. He was sought-out by first-class passengers, many of whom preferred to travel on the *Britannic* simply because he was in command. The management of White Star was quick to pick up on his popularity and Edward was being marked for progression.

In 1895 Edward took some leave while waiting to take command of SS *Germanic*, an opportunity perhaps to spend some time with his wife. His mother had died two years previously and now, quite unexpectantly, his half-brother Joseph, who was enjoying retirement after forty years at sea, collapsed in a Liverpool street and died. It may well have been Joseph's influence that had led Edward to go to sea, and now he was gone. Following two more voyages on *Germanic*, Edward was transferred to command *Majestic*, one of White Star's most popular ships. The 582ft-long, 9,965-ton ship had at one time held the Blue Riband (albeit for a fortnight) and remained one of the most popular ships afloat. Edward would command her for nine years, and take her to war when the ship was taken up as a troop transport during the Boer War, making two trips from South Africa with wounded soldiers. For his service, Edward was awarded the Transport Medal with South African clasp. Following the brief war service Edward and *Majestic* returned to transatlantic passenger service.

With the birth of his daughter, Helen, in 1898, Edward's family expanded and his career continued to progress. In 1902 the White Star Line became part of IMM, with consequent changes, and the rivalry with Cunard became more intense. White Star knew that Edward was one of their best assets and, along with captains Herbert Haddock and Bertram Hayes, he was now one of the principal commanders in the company and destined to be in command of one of the new 'big four' ships built in an attempt to dominate the North Atlantic route. Edward was given command of *Baltic*, which was twice the weight of *Majestic* and could carry nearly 3,000 passengers and crew. Edward commanded the ship from her maiden voyage in 1904 until 1907 when he took command of the last of the big four – *Adriatic*. At 24,541 tons, and measuring 729ft long by 73ft wide, *Adriatic* was the largest ship built for the White Star at the time. Her maiden voyage started from Liverpool on 8 May 1907, arriving in New York eight days later in heavy weather. It was while in New York that Edward responded to a question put to him from a local journalist about safety at sea – an answer that emphasised the overconfidence that had developed in British shipbuilding over the years: 'I will say that I cannot imagine any condition which could cause a ship to founder. I cannot conceive of any vital disaster happening to this vessel. Modern shipbuilding has gone beyond that.'

On her return journey via Plymouth and Cherbourg (France) she landed at Southampton instead of at Liverpool (the White Star Line had moved its principal port for liners bound for New York from Liverpool to Southampton). *Adriatic* was the first White Star vessel to operate from the new port, arriving to a very warm welcome on 30 May 1907 and leaving again on 5 June. Edward now commanded one of the finest vessels crossing the Atlantic and it became a popular ship, partly for its comforts and partly because of its friendly and affable captain. Yet, even as *Adriatic* started her successful career, Cunard had started work on *Mauretania* and *Lusitania*, leading Bruce Ismay of White Star to respond by ordering the construction of three even larger vessels. To make way for these ships, weighing over 45,000 tons, to operate out of Southampton, a new dock was constructed and *Adriatic* was transferred back to Liverpool. Edward was allocated the first of the new ships, *Olympic*, which was the class ship of a new fleet, containing within her steel walls the last word in luxury transatlantic travel.

Edward more than likely visited *Olympic* during her construction in Belfast, formally joining the ship in May 1911 in order to take her on her sea trials and taking official control on 31 May 1911 – the same day her sister ship, *Titanic*, was launched. Following sea trials *Olympic* made a brief stop in Liverpool before going on to Southampton to prepare for the maiden voyage, setting sail for New York via Cherbourg and Queenstown on 14 June, arriving at the Big Apple on 21 June.

The new big ships not only brought new standards of quality, but also new challenges in handling such large moving towns. On *Olympic*'s fifth voyage Edward encountered the Royal Naval cruiser HMS *Hawk* in the Solent. Both ships were running parallel to each other when *Olympic* put on speed and began to manoeuvre. *Hawk* soon fell back and was unable to manoeuvre away from the liner and collided with *Olympic*'s stern tearing two holes, one above and one below the waterline, and damaging a propeller shaft. *Hawk* was severely damaged, taking months to be repaired. It was a dramatic incident that led to legal action and prolonged debate on the effects of large vessels on smaller ones when in close proximity. George Bowyer, the pilot of *Olympic*, would be blamed for the incident by the official inquiry, although White Star management always contended that the blame was with William Blunt, the captain of HMS *Hawk*. In fact, it was caused by the effect of hydrodynamic suction between the ships – an effect that had been pointed out to the official inquiry by George Baker of the National Physical Laboratory.

Edward John Smith from Hanley, Stoke-on-Trent, was now the leading commander of one of the world's great shipping companies – in charge of the world's largest passenger liner and respected by management, passengers, and merchant seamen the world over. His experience on *Olympic* meant that he was destined to take out on her maiden voyage the next ship in the fleet, *Titanic*, still under construction in Belfast.

His last voyage in command of *Olympic* ended on 12 March 1912 when the liner docked into Southampton. Edward joined *Titanic* in Belfast on 1 April, relieving Captain Haddock who, in turn, went to Southampton to take command of *Olympic*. Edward now took charge during the brief series of sea trials to check the general working of the ship. The ship's designer, Thomas Andrews, and the Harland and Wolff Guarantee Group would remain on the ship for the voyage to New York, which was regular practice with new ships; just a year before, Thomas had been with Edward on *Olympic*'s maiden voyage. Although similar in design, *Titanic* was slightly heavier at 46,328 tons and 3in longer. There were interior and exterior differences between the two sisters, the most obvious being the partially enclosed A Deck, which had been open on *Olympic*.

In the early hours of 4 April, *Titanic* sailed quietly into Southampton's Berth 44 and made ready to be loaded with coal. A national coal strike had restricted sailings but *Titanic* had to sail on time. Being a member of IMM, owners of a number of shipping companies, it had the advantage of being able to transfer coal from their other ships to the new liner. Final preparations for the ship were being made, with final deliveries of material such as china and glass, food stores and, of course, the bulk of the crew signing on 6 April. Crews would hand over their discharge books hoping to be selected for the voyage. Old hands of White Star and those who had served on *Olympic* were likely to get a job, although with the coal strike many crews had gone away and there was a shortage of men.

Edward was not the only member of the crew to hail from Stoke. Leonard Hodgkinson was born in North Street, Stoke-on-Trent, in 1866. His father John was a presser in a pottery works. After Leonard served his apprenticeship as an engine fitter with Hartley, Arnoux and Fanning at the California Works, Stoke, he moved to Liverpool to work at Cammell Laird as a mechanical engineer and to train as a marine engineer with the aim of working on ships. He married Sarah Clarke, a local woman, in 1891 and had three children. After a successful time at Laird's he joined the Beaver Line in spring 1895. He remained with them for five years before joining the British and Foreign Steamship Company (Rankin, Gilmour and Company), reaching the rank of chief engineer and holding that position on the maiden voyage of the 3,000-ton cargo ship SS *Saint Jerome* in 1905, after which he joined White Star Line. His career with White Star began with voyages on *Celtic* serving as assistant engineer, fourth engineer and third engineer respectively. He then served on *Olympic* as assistant engineer before being promoted to fourth. He was on board *Olympic* during the collision with HMS *Hawk* and assisted in the immediate work assessing the damage to the propeller shaft. He joined *Titanic* in Belfast on 2 April for the delivery voyage and signed again on 6 April in Southampton as senior fourth engineer.

Longton was another Staffordshire town that was the original home to one other crew member who signed on *Titanic* on 6 April. Charles Christopher Mills was a butcher who had previously served on the American Line ship *St Paul* that sailed between Southampton and New York. Christopher (as he was known) was born in 1860, one of eight children to Richard Mills, a wheelwright and carpenter, and Elizabeth Lloyd. He married Selina Ellen Kemp of Fenton in Staffordshire in 1892 and had two children. Sadly, however, the marriage was shortlived, as he wife died in 1903.

James Richard Dinenage was a saloon steward who had just returned to Britain on the Royal Mail Steam Packet Company ship *Oruba* and, although based in his hometown of Southampton where he lived with his wife and child, he visited Walsall in Staffordshire to call upon his parents and sister. The coal strike had left ships stuck in port, and with little opportunity of finding work he took the opportunity to visit family. James had been born in Southampton, his father William Henry was from Bristol and his mother Jane was from Liverpool, and in their retirement they were living with their daughter Amiable (known as Amy) at 205 Bloxwich Road, Walsall. Amy dedicated her life taking care of her parents and took in boarders to raise money. Her father had been a coal agent making sixpence a hundredweight of coal and had to bring up a family of eleven children on 5*s* a week. Amy had been concerned that her parents might end up in the Old Spike, the local name for the Central Union Workhouse (later to become the Manor Hospital), so she decided to look after them. The couple had been married when they were only 18 and 17 respectively, celebrating their diamond wedding anniversary in 1910 and receiving a telegram from the king. William had served in the army, following his father Samuel who had fought at Waterloo. They moved to Walsall in 1880, as there was more work in the Midlands. James had gone to Liverpool to go to sea and served on various ships, eventually moving back to his hometown of Southampton. He married Alice Hallis Gouldon in around 1887 and had one son, Richard John, in 1891. It was while in Walsall that he received a message advising him that the White Star Line was looking for stewards for *Titanic*. James immediately left Walsall and headed to Southampton, leaving behind his sea chest and clothing, telling Amy that he would collect it when he returned from America.

Most crew members remained in Southampton ready to sign on the next suitable ship. Henry 'Harry' Brewer lived at 26 Palmerston Road, Southampton, but according to his declaration at signing he originally came from Birmingham and had previously served on *St Paul*. There is no trace of Harry in the records beyond the signing-on sheet. He appears to have been associated with Edith Wordon who worked in Southampton as a domestic servant. There is no record of them marrying prior to his joining *Titanic* as a trimmer, although Edith was around six months pregnant.

Henry Wood was another trimmer from Birmingham; born in 1881, he was the fourth child to Henry Wood, a glassblower from Dudley, and Lancashire-born Emily Lloyd. The family lived at various addresses in Aston, but while waiting for ships Henry resided in Southampton. At the time of his sign-on to *Titanic* he was at St Michael's House, having previously been aboard *Corinthian* of the Allan Line. Yet another Birmingham man joining the ship was 24-year-old George Gumery, who had originally signed on the IMM vessel *St Louis* as a mess steward; however, the coal strike had laid her up and so he transferred to *Titanic*. George came from Balsall Heath and had attended Tindall Street School, being the first secretary to the school's Old Boys' Association. He was well known to the members of the Moseley Road Congregational Church where he played an active role and had been a student at the Sunday school, he was also known for his amateur dramatic activities. His mother Harriet had passed away in 1889 and her sister Elizabeth Sherry had moved in to look after him and help out his father (also George). His father had worked in the confectionery trade, but the young George wanted to go to sea and not follow in his father's footsteps. His father passed away in 1909 and George helped out his aunt who took in work as a seamstress at her house in Sparkhill and he often stayed with her when on a break from stewarding.

Edward Ward, a 34-year-old bedroom steward from Birmingham joined *Titanic* in Belfast for the delivery trip and signed on again on 4 April. He had previously served on White Star's *Oceanic*.

Another Ward (but no relation) was William Ward who signed on to *Titanic* on 6 April as a first-class saloon steward. He was born in Handsworth in 1874, then a village in Staffordshire (now part of Birmingham). He was brought up in Handsworth and then Edgbaston by his parents John, an auctioneer and surveyor from Lanarkshire in Scotland, and Mary Emma. William's father was self-employed specialising in property auctions and, in particular, public houses. In 1891 he was working in Enfield in Middlesex.

William, along with his brother, John Henry, worked with their father as clerks in the business. William was one of fifteen children, and it may be that the rather crowded family led him to seek a life away working on ships. By 1902 he was in Australia working as a bar steward where he met and married Amelia Gleeson, having a son John. The family returned to England and settled in Southampton, the base from which he signed-on to various vessels. His previous ship to *Titanic* had been *New York*, which was laid up in Southampton due to the coal strike.

The fine city of Birmingham not only supplied trimmers and stewards but also a butcher. Frank John Roberts was a 36-year-old butcher who signed-on for the delivery trip from Belfast to Southampton, and then re-signed in Southampton as third butcher on a salary of £4 10s a month. His previous ship had been *Olympic*. He had wasted little time in getting on board the new ship, but this was the nature of a man who had left Birmingham to see more of the world. His father, Thomas, had come from Wednesfield in Staffordshire; working as a wheelwright he moved to Birmingham where he brought up a family of eight. Frank initially worked with his father as a blacksmith, but chose to train as a butcher. He married Comfort Maskell in 1896 and a year later had a daughter, Flora Louisa. In 1901 he volunteered for the British Army to fight in the Boer War. It was in the army that he gained two tattoos: a Victoria Cross with red, white and blue ribbon on his right arm and a dagger on his left arm. His military experience had a profound effect upon him and his family. He had another child, Doris Irene, in 1906, and following a move to Salisbury in Wiltshire he began to sign on ships. The family moved again, this time to Farnborough in Hampshire where his wife worked as a nurse at the Soldiers' and Sailors' Families Association. The one other Birmingham-born crew member was William Smith, who signed on as a seaman on 6 April after previously serving on *Minnewaska* of the Atlantic Transport Line. There is little known of the 26-year-old staying at 42 Bridge Street, Southampton, in 1912.

Titanic may well have employed the latest technology utilising electric lights, but the regulations still required some traditional methods of lighting. Oil lamps were still a requirement and the lifeboats were equipped with oil lamps. A lamp trimmer was therefore employed to take care of these lights in the person of Samuel Ernest Hemming from Bromsgrove in Worcestershire. His father was a coachman, and on leaving school Samuel became an errand boy. In 1884, at the age of 15, Samuel joined the Royal Navy as a landsman joining the training ship HMS *Impregnable* (originally named *Howe*). At the age of 18, Samuel signed on as a seaman, spending the next ten years serving on a number of training ships including HMS *Victory* when it was being used as a school for radio telegraphy. He was serving on the cruiser *Powerful* when, along with the cruisers *Doris* and *Terrible*, the battleship *Monarch*, the gunboat *Thrush* and a number of torpedo boats, it was deployed to the South African coast during the Boer War. He was a member of the Naval Brigade formed to take naval guns converted for field use to assist at the siege of Ladysmith, with Samuel taking charge of the 'big gun' at Wagon Hill that held off the Boers until relieved. He also served for just over two years on the battleship HMS *Revenge* when it was operating as flagship of the new Home Squadron. After leaving the navy on a pension, he began working on passenger ships. He married Elizabeth Mary Browning in 1903 and they had three children. He started working for White Star in 1907 serving on RMS *Teutonic*, followed by *Adriatic* and *Olympic*. He signed on to *Titanic* on 6 April 1912.

Worcestershire's neighbouring county of Herefordshire may have provided another crew member: M.W. Golder. He lists himself as being born in Hereford and signed on the 6 April as a fireman after previously serving on *Oceanic*. However, no further information has thus far been discovered of this man, except that he was staying at 15 Landsdown Road, Southampton.

Gloucestershire provided two stewards, a stewardess, and a fireman to the crew. Saloon Steward Arthur Henry Derrett was born in Wotton-under-Edge and was one of four children of Henry Thomas and Louisa Gazard. Arthur was educated at the local Blue Coat School and on leaving became a servant with the Huntley family at Boxwell Court near Leighterton, Gloucestershire. The experience he gained with the Huntleys set him in good stead for joining the merchant marine as a steward. He started his career with the Pacific and Orient Line before joining White Star as a first-class steward. He was serving on board *Olympic* when she collided with HMS *Hawk*, and was still serving prior to his joining *Titanic* for the delivery voyage. Arthur was engaged and planned to marry following the return trip on *Titanic*.

Another first-class steward was William Ford Kingscote who was born in Slimbridge, Dursley, the youngest of three children and only son of James Kingscote and Sarah Ford. James worked first as a waterman and then as a master mariner on the Sharpness canal, working coal trasnporters from Gloucester Docks to the River Severn. James' family were coal merchants, a trade he would continue later in life. William's mother died in March 1866 before he was 2 years old. His father remarried on 11 December 1866 to his late wife's sister Harriet, a shopkeeper. By 1890 William was working as a steward for the Inman Line serving on *City of Boston* and then *City of New York*. In 1892 he married Mary Willis and together they had five children. When the Inman Line became part of the American Line in 1893, as part of the conglomerate run by J. Pierpoint Morgan, Kingscote moved to Southampton. In 1911 he was living at 24 Elgin Road, Freemantle. His daughter Elsie had become a dressmaker and they had also taken in a boarder to help with the finances. His long career with *City of New York* came to an end when he signed on to *Titanic* on 4 April.

Kate Elizabeth Smith signed on *Titanic* as a stewardess on 6 April. She was born in 1867 in Bredon – a village near the Worcestershire–Gloucestershire border – and was the middle child of Charles William Smith, a solicitor's clerk, and his wife Harriett Evans, both from Gloucestershire. Kate's career at sea began with the Dominion Line in 1893 when she sailed on the 5,000-ton SS *Vancouver* from Liverpool, arriving in Quebec, Canada, on 21 May. She was placed in charge of immigrant children from Washwell House in Painswick, near Stroud destined for Marchmont Home in Bellville Ontario, a transit home from where the children would be fostered out to new parents. These immigrant children were just one group of many that were sent to Canada in the hope of finding a better life rather than struggling in the industrial towns and cities of Britain.

Between 1870 and 1914, 80,000 children were sent to Canada under schemes organised by various institutions and church organisations. In Birmingham, John T. Middlemore founded the Child's Emigration Homes, and sent around 5,000 children to Ontario, Canada in 1873, and later, from 1893, to Nova Scotia. Washwell House in Stroud was run by Harriett and Alice Wemyss who opened their first home for feeble-minded women in 1890, although they had been involved in sending orphaned children to Canada since 1873. Groups of children were always escorted and Alice had escorted previous groups.

On this trip, Kate Smith looked after them until they reached Quebec when they were handed over to the Reverend Wallace of the Marchmont Home. Her experience on *Vancouver* had given her the taste of sea life, and thus she signed on for voyages with Cunard, the American Steamship Company and the White Star Line, serving on over twenty ships, including *Servia*, *Umbria*, *Lucania*, *St Louis*, *St Paul* and *Olympic*. It was while serving on *St Paul* that she had the first of her two shipping incidents. On 25 April 1908 SS *St Paul* had left Southampton en route to New York, encountering a heavy snowstorm with strong tides and gale-force winds. Visibility was down to 800yd when the lookouts spotted the Royal Navy cruiser HMS *Gladiator* off Hurst Point, Isle of Wight. Although both ships manoeuvered it was too late and they collided. The glancing blow ripped open the sides of both ships. *Gladiator* foundered at once, while *St Paul* was able to remain afloat and launch lifeboats. A total of twenty-seven sailors were lost. Kate had another lucky escape when she was on board *Olympic*, leaving a room only a few moments before it was damaged by the collision with HMS *Hawk*. Unperturbed by these incidents she returned to serve on *Olympic* before signing on to *Titanic*.

Gloucestershire-born Joseph Wakefield Thomas signed on to *Titanic* as a fireman on 6 April. His father had worked as a labourer in a Gloucester shipyard and died at the early age of 41 when Joseph was only 6 years old. Joseph's mother, Elizabeth, remarried three years later to James Selwyn, a carpenter. Joseph appears to have begun working on ships soon after leaving school and moving down to Southampton. In 1909 he married Rosina Alma Barrow whose brother, Charles Henry, worked on ships as a butcher. Joseph and Rosina had a boy, Arthur, in 1910 and in 1912 Rosina was expecting again.

During Easter at 72 Maidstone Road, Perry Barr, Birmingham, John Thomas Hinckley, an engineer's fitter, was telling his children, Herbert aged 10 and Frederick aged 9, about the largest passenger ship in the world and how their uncle, George Herbert Hinckley, was going to be on board as a second-class steward. Born in Mickleover, Derbyshire, in 1872 George was the son of Herbert John Hinckley, a veterinary surgeon, and Mary Ann (Holmes), and was one of six children. Sadly, both of his parents died within a few months of each other in 1884 and along with his siblings he was taken care of by his maternal grandparents, John Brooks Holmes and his wife Elizabeth, in Burton-on-Trent. On leaving school George started work in service, employed as a hall boy for Colonel Edmund Arthur Le Gendre Starkie and his family at Huntroyde Hall, Padiham, Simonstone, Lancashire. By 1901 he was working as a footman for the shipping agent Frederick James Harrison at Maer Hall, Maer, Staffordshire. It may have been through his employer that he came to work for White Star Line from around 1906, eventually serving on *Olympic*. He had signed on to *Titanic* for the delivery voyage and then signed on again on 4 April. In a letter to his sister, dated Saturday 6 April, he wrote that he passed through Derby as he and about 100 others of the *Olympic* crew went to fetch *Titanic* from Belfast Lough to

Southampton. Speaking of the trip, he said they had a fine run down from Belfast, hardly knowing they were on board, and that *Titanic* seemed a great deal better than *Olympic*, which he called an unlucky ship.

Many of those working on *Titanic* were formally engaged by the White Star Line, signing the ship's articles; there were also others who were engaged through agents or other companies, such as the Marconi Company, which supplied radio operators. The ship's orchestra was supplied through the Liverpool-based agents of CW&FN Black. The musical agency was run by two brothers, Charles William and Frederick Nixon Black, who had been musicians themselves, and since 1909 supplied artists to hotels and shipping companies. In March 1912 they had agreed terms with White Star to be the sole suppliers of musicians to their ships, an agreement that had angered the Amalgamated Musicians' Union (AMU) who believed the deal would be detrimental to their members. J. Bruce Ismay of White Star had been keen to reduce costs and transferring musicians from crew to an agency saved him money and, it seems, the hassle of dealing with their demands for better pay and conditions. The deal resulted in musicians being registered as second-class passengers employed by CW&FN Black. Black's had similar deals with other British registered companies such as Cunard, Royal Mail and Booth Line, and thus no musician in the country could get a booking on a ship without working for the Black brothers.

Titanic had eight musicians divided into a trio (violin, cello and piano) that performed in the à la carte restaurant and the Café Parisien, and a quintet that played at teatime, after-dinner concerts, Sunday services and other occasions. As with everything related to *Titanic*, White Star expected the very best and the Black brothers needed to supply the very best musicians. The man chosen as bandleader was 33-year-old Wallace Hartley, transferred from Cunard's Blue Riband-holder *Mauretania*. The trio consisted of Roger Bricoux, a 20-year-old cellist who had been performing on Cunard's *Carpathia* with William (Theodore) Brailey, who would also join the trio on *Titanic* following a voyage with Hartley on *Mauretania*. The third member of the trio was Georges Alexandre Krins, a violinist who had been performing at the Ritz hotel in London. The quintet would be led by Hartley and comprised cellist Percy Cornelius Taylor from London; bass player John Frederick Preston Clarke, who had been performing in the orchestra at the Argyle Theatre of Varieties at Birkenhead and with the Vasco Akeroyd Symphony Orchestra at the Philharmonic Hall; John Law Hume (known as 'Jock'), a violinist from Dumfries in Scotland who had returned to Liverpool on *Carmania*; and John Wesley Woodward, a West Bromwich man who had become an accomplished musician specialising in the cello, but could also play the piano and violin.

Wesley (as he preferred to be known) was the youngest son of Joseph and Martha, née Barnett, of Hill Top, West Bromwich. As his Christian names imply he was, along with his six brothers and two sisters, brought up as a Methodist attending the Hill Top Wesleyan Sunday school at the Hill Top Chapel, of which his father was a trustee. By profession his father was manager of, and had an interest in, the Hilltop Foundry on Hawkes Lane, having followed in the footsteps of his father (also Joseph). The foundry produced hollowware and was established in 1799 during a period of growth of foundries in the area. Wesley's mother was from Tipton and her family, including two brothers and two sisters, was also involved in the manufacturing industry. Her father, William Barnett, was a manager at an ironworks and later owned Coppyhall Colliery at Stubbers Green, Aldridge. Joseph and Martha married in 1862 and, as was the manner of Methodists, their children were given a good education with the hope of improving their lot. Wesley's father died at the young age of 49 of stomach cancer when Wesley was only 5 years old. The executors to his Will, and fellow Hill Top Methodists, were his brother-in-law John Peters, a local iron merchant, and Isaac Johnson, a builder, who ensured Joseph's wishes were carried out. His gross estate was worth £703 5s, leaving Martha and her children well provided for.

As was tradition in the Black Country, sons followed their fathers in the same industry and often in the same place of work. Wesley's brothers also worked at Hill Top when they left school and began apprenticeships. By 1891 Thomas and Herbert were moulders, Roland was a patternmaker and Frederick was a draughtsman – both of them going through the standard training for a career in a foundry. Martha's father died in 1891 and he left her a total of £100 in his will, which helped secure the family. Thomas was musically inclined and had a local reputation as a chorister and was able to receive music tuition. He left in 1893 to become a chorister at Gloucester Cathedral, and a year later he successfully auditioned to become a tenor lay-clerk in the chapel choir of Magdalene College, Oxford. Soon thereafter Martha, with Wesley and Herbert, moved to Oxford. Samuel stayed in West Bromwich, pursuing a career in engineering, eventually moving in with his Aunt Elizabeth in Walsall Wood. Wesley, like his brother Thomas, was inclined to a musical career and Oxford was a suitable place to study music. After passing the Royal College of Music exams in 1900, Wesley was awarded a licentiate as a performer of the cello and was available for hire as a musician.

In the nineteenth and early-twentieth centuries, musicians and singers took bookings to perform at concerts held in hotels, schools, after teas or dinners and church services. Wesley gave performances with the cello as a solo artist and in string quartets formed for the particular concert. He became acquainted with various touring performers such as the Misses Price – the Price sisters (Edith and Mary) were the daughters of the Reverend Edward H. Price and usually sang at religious or fundraising events. Although there were many very talented amateurs on the circuit, there were many professional performers such as Henry Martin Dowson, Flora Von Leer and the singer C. Hayden-Coffin, with whom Wesley performed. Wesley developed a reputation as an excellent soloist, performing pieces such as 'Tzig Tzig' and 'Priere' by William Henry Squire, 'Serenata' by Gaentano Braga and 'Etude Caprice' by Georg Goltermann, although he was seen by some as principally an orchestral player. The venues were as varied as the performers finding himself at the school rooms in Sandford-on-Thames, the Kurlsaal in Bexhill-on-Sea, the Abingdon Corn Exchange, St George's Hall, Oxford, and the Oxford University Music Club.

As with all performers it is an advantage to have a good personality; Wesley was described as amiable, good natured and modest, which endeared him to the audience. To supplement his income as a musician he also taught cello. His personal interests did not just lie with music; he had an active interest in photography, which had developed in West Bromwich and brought him into contact with locals with a similar interest, including W. A. Benton, who in 1894 would be a founder member of the Handsworth Photographic Society. Wesley's interest was not merely in taking photographs; he also took pleasure in developing and printing in a small darkroom converted from a coal house in the garden at Hill Top. Wesley was also interested in engineering, and having a workshop in his garden he would spend hours constructing motors and other machines.

In 1907 he joined the newly formed Duke of Devonshire's band based in Eastbourne. Wesley joined at a wage of £2 15s per week for performing up to twelve times per week, more often than not at the Winter Garden. The music selection was a mixture of concert classical pieces and popular classical and was received with mixed reviews, although Wesley was singled out for praise in one review. A few months after the duke's death, in 1910, his orchestra was disbanded; Wesley then performed at the Grand Hotel. Following this engagement, on 10 December 1910 he set sail on the 5,455-ton RMS *Port Royal* from Bristol to Kingston in Jamaica to take up an engagement at the Constant Spring Hotel. It was most likely this trip that led Wesley to look at being an orchestra player on passenger ships.

Along with John Law Hume he signed on to the maiden voyage of RMS *Olympic*, leaving Southampton on 14 June 1911, and his own reputation grew among crew and passengers on White Star's newest vessel. He was on board *Olympic* in September 1911 when she collided with HMS *Hawk*, being in a room only a few feet away from where the ships made contact. The band was on its break from performing and the members were playing chequers when the collision took place. Wesley, with other band members felt the impact but continued their game. Like so many before him (and many afterwards) he enjoyed sea life – the change and variety appealed to him and he found it was good for his health. His next booking was on the 19,500-ton Cunard ship *Caronia* leaving Liverpool on 4 November for New York. He

Captain Edward J. Smith. (Avery Historical Museum)

reboarded the ship for three cruises to the Mediterranean before returning home where he would take up a booking on *Titanic*, being reunited with John Hume. For this trip Wesley brought with him his best cello, and just prior to leaving for Southampton accepted a booking to perform at the May dinner at Magdelen College, Oxford, on his return from New York.

For both men the summer sailing season was to have been their last. Wesley was planning to join the Devonshire Park Orchestra in Eastbourne for a new direction and a new future course.

Frederick Roberts, butcher. (PRO)

Samuel Hemming, lamp trimmer.
(Avery Historical Museum)

Leonard Hodgkinson,
engineer. (PRO)

John Wesley Woodward.
(Author's collection)

All crew members were up early on the morning of 10 April, *Titanic's* sailing day, as they had to be at the ship for 6 a.m, leaving their wives, girlfriends or parents behind with comments of, 'I'll let you know what the new tub is like.' For most it was just another trip. For the firemen it was time to get the boilers heated and ready to power the great engines, the trimmers to ensure the stability of the ship. The butchers examined the meat they would cut for the lavish and the not so lavish meals, and the stewards had to ensure everything was ready for the passengers who would start coming aboard in just a few hours' time. For Edward, it was the latest command during an illustrious career. The ship was soon busy, as what amounted to a small town came to life. Soon, the first of the trains from London would pull into the dock and passengers who were coming from all parts of the country would stream onto the ship, including passengers from the Midlands.

8

MIDLANDS PASSENGERS

At Berth 44 in Southampton the largest ocean liner in the world, designed to transport passengers across the Atlantic, awaited its passengers. They would come from far and wide, mostly by train. Some had come down a day or two early and had stayed in boarding houses or hotels until the day of departure. Many would, however, travel on the 10th, connecting with the London to Southampton trains laid on especially to meet *Titanic*. First-, second- and third-class passengers represented a cross-section of British society, and those coming south from the Midlands were as good a representation as from any other part of the country.

First Class

On Tuesday 9 April Tyrell William Cavendish and his wife Julia Florence, along with Julia's maid Ellen Mary Barber (known as Nellie), left their home at Little Onn Hall in Church Eaton, Staffordshire, with the ceremony that was accustomed and expected of an English aristocrat. Most of the servants were lined up in the driveway as Tyrell and Julia exited through the stone archway to the motor car that awaited. Julia's maid, Nellie, followed, carrying a small wicker basket. The servants acknowledged politely; Tyrell's butler, William Hill, wished his master a pleasant voyage and saw him to the car. It drove off, taking them to Stafford Station and arriving in time for them to catch the 3.45 p.m. LNWR express to London Euston.

Tyrell was born in Scarborough, Yorkshire, in 1875, the only son of Charles Tyrell Cavendish, a Justice of the Peace and deputy lieutenant for Staffordshire, and Elizabeth Anne (Dickinson). He was brought up at Crakemarsh Hall in

Uttoxeter, Staffordshire, and educated at Harrow. His parents were known in royal circles and his mother presented her sister-in-law, Mrs Edward Cousins, to Queen Victoria at Buckingham Palace on 5 May 1886. His father, Charles Cavendish, was committed to Cheadle Lunatic Asylum and died there in 1903; Tyrell had assumed the role as head of the family when his father had been committed, and it was important for him to keep the Cavendish line going and to secure the status of the family. In 1906 Tyrell married Chicago-born Julia Florence Siegel in Manhattan, New York, the daughter of Henry Siegel, a wealthy businessman who was the majority shareholder of the Siegel-Cooper department store located on Lower 6th Avenue, New York. With business interests in New York and Chicago, Henry Siegel became one of the wealthiest men in the United States. He brought up his daughter Julia in traditional style in Orienta Point in upstate New York, attending a convent school before being sent to a finishing school at Dresden in Germany. Julia, raised in an old European manner, did the rounds within the high echelons of British society, mixing with aristocracy during the season of lavish balls where young ladies could meet eligible bachelors. It was at one of these balls that she met Tyrell Cavendish; five days later they were engaged, marrying on Boxing Day in Buckinghamshire.

The union produced two boys: Henry Siegel born 1908 and Geoffrey Manners born 1910. The couple lived in Battlies House on the Rougham Estate in Suffolk before Tyrell moved them into Little Onn Hall in Staffordshire. Julia visited her family annually, usually with just her maid; however, in 1912 she was travelling with her husband to her father's country home at Orienta Point in Mamaroneck, New York. Ostensibly a family visit, it was also an opportunity for Tyrell's children to meet their grandparents. However, young Geoffrey fell ill and it was decided that the children should stay at home. Tyrell had another motive to visit his father-in-law. He had ambitions of entering politics representing Bury St Edmunds and hoped Henry Siegel would financially support his candidature. As part of Tyrell's strategy to become an MP, he had begun renovation of Thurston House in Suffolk, a large eighteenth-century house, as his new home. Travelling with the couple was Florence's maid, 26-year-old Nellie Barber from Penshurst, Tonbridge, in Kent. Her father, William Hopkins Barber, was a carpenter and the family lived in a property owned by her employer. Nellie had been employed as Julia's maid for a little over a year. This was to be her second trip to New York, and like all servants her passage was included on the Cavendish's ticket.

Tyrell and Julia spent a night in London before catching the *Titanic* express from Waterloo to Southampton on Wednesday morning. Leaving the station at Southampton Docks, they were led by a railway porter and then by a White Star Line steward onto the ship and escorted to their cabin C46. It would have been interesting if, as they were being escorted to their cabin, they came across William Edward Hipkins heading to cabin C39; he had also just got off the *Titanic* express after spending a couple of nights in London. Tyrell Cavendish was an example of old money – the aristocracy; William Hipkins was an example of new money. As managing director of the world's largest weighing equipment manufacturer, W&T Avery Limited based in Smethwick, he was heading to Milwaukee via New York to close a deal with the US Navy.

William Hipkins was 55 years old, and, along with his sister Bertha, was born and raised in Birmingham. His father, George Frederick Hipkins, had been a brassfounder, running his own business in Ashted, Birmingham, specialising in cabinet furniture and corkscrews. William's mother, Rebecca, was from Norton in Worcestershire and although dyslexic was very well educated. She was a good pianist and taught both her children piano, with William being a particular lover of Chopin. William's father died when he was only 6 and his uncle (also William Edward) came from London to run the family business. Tragically, just weeks later he died too. William's mother relied on the foreman to run the business while she concentrated all her energy into educating William to prepare him to one day take control of the business. To this end she brought in private tutors including the Reverend James Oliver Bevan of St James the Less Church in Ashted, who would become a family friend and almost a second father to William. William attended Kings Edward's School in New Street, Birmingham, before embarking on a tour of Europe and the United States with the Reverend Thomas Guest. On these tours he learned much about history, art, industry and commerce. On his return he became an apprentice in the family business, working his way up through various departments. At the age of 21, he formally took over the family firm, with it being restyled George Hipkins and Son. He developed this small brassfounders, applying all he had seen and learned on his travels, particularly what he had learned in the United States, and turning it into a highly successful venture. Such was his success that he was sought after to advise others firms such as Sansome, Teale and Company, a bicycle component firm located in Digbeth.

In 1890 came a remarkable opportunity for William. He was invited by a syndicate to take over as managing director of the rope-making firm of John and Edwin Wright Limited, Dartmouth Street, at the north-eastern end of Birmingham. The firm had been bought out by a consortium of businessmen and formed into a public limited company. William, known in business circles as simply 'Hipkins', stamped his own mark on Wrights. He sold his family business in 1892 to Vaughan Brothers, and just as he was becoming established at Wrights yet another opportunity fell into his lap. The weighing machine company of W&T Avery was thrown into turmoil when one of the owners, Henry Avery, died suddenly at the age of 34. His brother, William Beilby Avery, did not want to run the business so he approached Walter Chamberlain who, along with Wilfred Williams, started the process of transforming Averys into a public limited company.

The man they invited to be the new managing director was William Edward Hipkins. His reorganisation of the firm included the purchase of the famous Soho Foundry in Smethwick. Matthew Boulton and James Watt originally built the foundry in 1796 to manufacture steam engines. The steam engine firm of James Watt and Company had gone bankrupt in 1894 and the whole site and company was put up for sale, which William bought, thus becoming the last manager of James Watt and Company. Averys' other production facilities in the region were transferred to Soho, and by 1898 he had created the largest weighing machine manufacturing facility on earth. William extended Averys' reach by buying up weighing machine companies across the country and turning them into Avery branches. He began expanding into Europe, Asia, Australasia, South America and China.

In 1906 he opened a subsidiary company in the United States – the Avery Scale Company Incorporated located at Hopkins Street, North Milwaukee, Wisconsin. The American company had been a gamble, as the US was pressing hard on Britain's exports, imposing aggressive tariffs on British goods – tariffs that had been causing a number of problems for manufacturing firms in the Midlands. William made an annual visit to the American company to check on progress; however, progress had been slow. In January 1912 William received confirmation that the US Navy was placing an order for automatic weighing machines with the Avery Scale Company – a staggering achievement. His business gamble appeared to have paid off and he wanted to visit the United States to ensure the contract was progressing well. He booked his passage on *Titanic*, paying £50. He was of the opinion that, as he was a leading businessman, only the largest liner would suffice for the crossing, especially as he was doing business with the Americans because they would be impressed with his choice of ship. William would be travelling alone, as his wife Lavinia had died in 1910 after only four years of marriage. His sister Bertha lived with him at 16 Augustus Road, Edgbaston, and he had invited her to go with him, but she declined as she was recovering from a cold and felt a sea voyage would not be wise.

On Monday 8 April, the 8.20 a.m. City to City express train from New Street Station departed on time beginning its two-hour high-speed race to London Broad Street, calling only at Coventry on the way. Like all of William's activities he used his time efficiently, spending two days in London meeting with the managers at the London branch. Since the death of his wife he had been sharper with his managers and they did not relish his arrival. As always prior to a trip abroad, William wanted to ensure that everything was in order and everyone knew what was expected of them. On the night of 9 April, he double-checked everything and telephoned his sister to ask if she was feeling better. Next morning he took a motor cab to Waterloo Station. The *Titanic* express was waiting on platform 12; it was 9.15 a.m. The freshly cleaned green livery of the T-9 locomotive stood gently steaming with a rake of chocolate-brown and cream coaches coupled behind, their doors open, inviting passengers to board. William boarded and sat down in the soft, blue seats of the first-class compartment and opened his newspaper; just another business trip had begun. Promptly at 9.45 a.m. the train pulled out of Waterloo Station to race the 79 miles to Southampton Docks. On arrival, William left the train and walked up the gently sloping gangway to the first-class passengers' entrance on B Deck, where he was greeted by Chief Steward Latimer and his staff. William handed over his ticket and boarding card which was checked by the purser's clerk, Ernest King, against his list. William's ticket, No. 680, which had been allotted to cabin C39, was duly ticked off the list. William picked up his carry-on bag and went through the doors leading to the B Deck entrance hall and staircase. He went downstairs to C Deck; William would have been no doubt impressed by the fan-shaped spread of the oak staircase with wrought-iron scrollwork. He turned left at the bottom of the stairs and walked past the purser's office. A small passageway separated the purser's office from cabin C39. William was accustomed to quality accommodation on board ships as he had experienced on *Baltic* and *Oceanic,* and his cabin on *Titanic* didn't disappoint. The cabin could accommodate three persons, although on this trip he had it to himself. The decoration was not as ostentatious as the B Deck suites, but it was bright and comfortable with a WC and bath that was shared with cabins 35 (unoccupied) and 37 (occupied by Roberta 'Cissy' Maioni, maid to the Countess of Rothes). He settled in for a pleasant voyage.

Not all of those arriving were travelling for holiday or work, some were returning home. Constance Willard had been visiting her aunt, Florence Mackey, in Leamington Spa having spent some time with the Mackey family, attending the Warwickshire Hunt Ball in January. Constance's uncle, Frank Jay Mackey, was an American merchant who became involved in developing the Leamington Hotel in Minneapolis, Minnesota. He spread his life between the USA and Britain, having arrived in England in 1894. A regular traveller across the Atlantic he had sailed on such illustrious ships as *Lusitania*, *Mauretania* and *City of New York*. After three years he settled in Leamington Spa, purchasing Beauchamp Hall. He became actively involved in local life and was well known with local hunts and was a renowned polo player. His wife, Florence, also became involved in local life and they were well liked in the community. Twenty-two-year-old Constance was on her

Tyrell Cavendish.
(Author's collection)

Julia Cavendish.
(Author's collection)

William Edward Hipkins in 1912. (Author's collection)

way home to Duluth, Minnesota, after an enjoyable trip. The Mackey's had other friends joining *Titanic*; they were acquainted with William Carter, a fellow polo player who was travelling back to the States with his wife Lucille, two children, chauffeur and maid.

Avery Scale Company, Milwaukee. (Author's collection)

Second Class

Another American on his way home was 38-year-old Stanley Harrington Fox. He worked as a demonstrator for the Gleason Works Machine Tool Company of Rochester, New York, and had been on a six-week trip to Europe on behalf of the company, drumming up trade for the company's gear-making machines. The last leg of his trip found him in Birmingham staying at the Queen's Hotel, Stephenson Place, visiting a number of companies. On 4 April 1912 he wrote from the hotel to his general manager, James E. Gleason, stating that he would be sailing home on the 10th on the steamship *Titanic*. He booked his ticket through the Grand Trunk Company, paying £13. He arrived in Southampton on the morning of the 10th by the second- and third-class LSWR train from Waterloo Station and, along with other second-class passengers, entered the ship on C Deck.

The county town of Warwick is small and picturesque and dominated by the famous Warwick Castle. In the shadow of the castle is 14 Mill Street – in 1912, the home of George and Sarah Hughes with their son Charles and daughter Harriett Emily. George and his wife had brought up nine children in Warwickshire with one dying in infancy, six leaving home and the remaining two staying with their parents. Of those that left, Florence Agnes had immigrated with her husband, William Angle, to the United States in 1906. William came from a family that worked in the Staffordshire pottery industry in Newcastle-under-Lyme, Shepton and Hanley. His father George worked as a presser in hollowware and earthenware; his sister Mary Ann was a paintress of earthenware, his other sister Ellen was a potter's ground layer, his brother Thomas was a potter's presser and his other brother George was a machinist driller and married a paintress. William worked for Minton for a while specialising in their high-quality encaustic tiles, branching out as a specialist fixer of the tiles in various buildings. Encaustic tiles were very much in vogue in the latter quarter of the nineteenth century and into the first decade of the twentieth. These glazed ceramic tiles of two or more colours were extensively used in public buildings and baths – especially in the new Turkish baths. The correct installation of tiles on a floor or wall was a great skill, and the United States was a nation seeking skilled workers of all kinds. For this reason, in 1904 William, with six friends, decided to go to the States in the hope, like so many others, of finding a more prosperous life. William and his friends sailed to New York from Liverpool as second-class passengers on RMS *Baltic*, under the command of none other than Captain Edward John Smith. Once William had settled in New York and established himself he returned to England to marry his girlfriend Florence Agnes Hughes. Florence was born in Radford Semele near Leamington Spa in Warwickshire in 1876. Her father was a cowman working on various farms in the region, her two brothers also worked in agriculture and her younger sister Henrietta was a midwife, having followed Florence in a medical profession. Florence was an asylum nurse working in 1901 at the Warwick County Asylum in Hatton; by 1906 she was living in Woodlands, Devon. In November 1906 William brought over his new wife on RMS *Campania* and together they set up home at 460 West 24th Street, New York. He and his wife returned to Warwick in 1911 to visit family staying at Mill Street. They booked their second-class return ticket (226875) on *Titanic*, costing £26. On the morning of 9 April they caught the London Paddington train from Warwick at 8 a.m., spending the night in London before taking the second- and third-class express from Waterloo to Southampton. The 6ft-tall William with bright-blue eyes linked his arm with his wife Florence as they walked across the bridge to board *Titanic*.

A couple from Bromsgrove were also on the second- and third-class *Titanic* express. Leopold Weisz and his wife Mathilde Françoise were heading to Canada via New York. Leopold was born in Veszprem in Hungary in around 1875 to Jewish parents. His family moved to Vienna, the capital of the Austro-Hungarian Empire, while he was young and it is there he grew up and studied art, specialising in sculpture. At the age of 19 he left Vienna to work in Birmingham before taking up an appointment at the Bromsgrove Guild of Art in Worcestershire as a sculptor. Founded in 1898 by Walter Henry Gilbert, a cousin of the famous sculptor Alfred Gilbert, the guild produced work in a wide range of materials in the arts and crafts style. Designers from the guild were sought after for their ironwork, stained glass, plasterwork and garden statuary. Many of Britain's greatest works of wrought iron – the gates of Buckingham Palace, the Great Gates of Canada, the Liver Birds of The Royal Liver Assurance Building in Liverpool and the iron and bronze gates for The Mall – came from the guild. It was while he was working at the guild that he met and married in 1910 Mathilde Françoise Pëde, born in Ghent, Belgium. She had been running a successful dress-making business in Birmingham. In September 1911 Leopold crossed the Atlantic on *Lusitania*, travelling to Canada via New York. *Lusitania* was of particular interest to the guild as artisans from the guild had produced plasterwork and stained glass in the first-class lounge, as well as the bronze and glass enclosure for the passenger lifts. A large number of the guild's 150 workers were engaged on work for *Lusitania*, as well as for *Mauretania*.

Leopold began work in Montreal carving the frieze for the Montreal Museum of Fine Arts under the auspices of the guild's Canadian Agent, Edward Wren. Following completion of this work, the guild won a contract to carve stone shields representing Canada's nine provinces, which decorate the Dominion Express Building. Leopold and Wren got on well and the two planned to work together in what would have been a Canadian branch of the guild. The guild agreed to allow Leopold's wife to join him in Canada while he worked with Wren, so he returned to Bromsgrove to collect his wife and bring her over to a new life. They were scheduled to sail on *Lusitania*, but due to the coal strike were transferred to *Titanic*. They booked their berths in March 1912 with Houlder Brothers and Son and boarded *Titanic* at Southampton on ticket number 228414, which cost £26. Prior to sailing, Mathilde sewed their life savings of around £3,750 in money and gold in the lining of her husband's heavy coat for safekeeping.

Another couple who boarded *Titanic* may have looked a little nervous as the steward inspected their tickets. They informed him that they were newly married and then headed for their second-class cabin. However, Mr Henry S. and Mrs Kate Marshall were not all they appeared, as they were travelling under an assumed surname. Mr Marshall was actually 38-year-old Henry Samuel Morley, the senior partner of a chain of confectionery shops in Birmingham, Worcester and Malvern. His 'wife' was Kate Phillips, the 19-year-old assistant at his shop in Foregate Street, Worcester. They were eloping to San Francisco in the United States, with Henry leaving his real wife and young daughter behind in Malvern. As they boarded the ship they were heading for a new life, free from any scandal that might have arisen from their relationship.

Henry was born in Maidstone in 1874; his father William was a tailor's cutter from Bishop's Stortford who had followed in his father's footsteps, who had been a master tailor. Henry's mother Emily (Mace) was from North Walsham in Norfolk, and with William she had nine children, with six surviving beyond infancy. Henry was very close to his brothers Louis, Reginald and Ernest and in particular his elder brother Arthur, being 'thick as thieves' according to Arthur's wife. This closeness was strengthened by the untimely death of their father in 1889 at the age of 39. Henry's mother became a tailoress, with Henry starting in the business as a cutter; Arthur took work in a boot shop run by Freeman, Hardy and Willis. Henry married Worcester-born Louisa Price in 1899 at the Baptist chapel in Worcester. Louisa was one of six children, having four brothers (Thomas, Frank, George and Walter) and a sister (Emma). Her parents were associated with two industries for which Worcester was renowned. Her father, Thomas, had been a china potter and like Henry's father he died young; her mother Louisa (Long) was a gloveress, a trade in which her own mother before her had been employed, and her income was used to supplement Louisa's father's work as a china potter. Her brothers Thomas and Frank followed their father into the pottery trade, which proved to be important because in 1870 Louisa's father died of tuberculosis at the age of 43, just a few months after the birth of his sixth child. Life would have been very difficult, possibly quite a struggle. Louisa's mother remarried in 1877 to Richard Sanders, a widower who worked as a commissioning agent in Worcester.

Louisa didn't follow her mother into the glove trade, but entered the shoe trade instead, and it was through that trade that she met Henry Morley. Henry's brother, Arthur, who was working with Henry Massingham at a boot and shoe warehouse in Bristol, became acquainted with Louisa. Henry moved to the Bedwardine district of Worcester working as a grocer's manager and he met Louisa through his brother. A relationship developed between Henry and Louisa resulting in their marriage. At the time of the marriage Louisa was living at 27 Waterworks Road just a few doors away from an 8-year-old Kate Phillips; indeed, the Phillips family were known to Louisa. By 1901 Henry and Louisa were living at Vernon Park, Worcester, with Henry's younger brother Louis staying with them. His elder brother Arthur had already been married for five years and was a partner in M & M Boot Stores in Bristol. It was Arthur's move to Bristol that had prompted the other brothers to move to the Midlands. The Morleys were prospering, becoming successful with new families; later, in 1903, Henry and Louisa had a daughter – Doris Louisa. Henry's brother Arthur had three children – Laura, Arthur Vincent and Grace – and life seemed to be going well for him. In 1907 he moved to Birmingham, becoming manager of the Bull Street branch of Freeman, Hardy and Willis, one of their main stores. In the same year he entered into a business venture, with Henry opening two confectioner's shops in Worcester. Both brothers, along with Reginald, put capital into the business, with Henry managing the business and running the shop at 22 Foregate Street while his wife Louisa looked after the day-to-day running of the shop at 8 Broad Street. The title over the shops – 'L. Morley Brothers' – is interesting, the 'L' referring to their brother Louis, although he appears not to have taken an active role in the business. It appears the brothers were sticking together in business as they had at home. A year later, two of Arthur's children at ages 4 and 7 were christened at St Martin's Church in Birmingham. Whether this event signifies a change in the relationship he had with his wife Edith is not known, but soon thereafter he started an affair with Hattie Cole. The affair led to Arthur separating from his wife in what must have been a very traumatic time for all concerned. Arthur left the family home and moved to Cheltenham with Hattie, taking his son, Arthur Vincent, with him; his two daughters stayed with their mother. Arthur was given emotional and financial help from Henry, with money being taken from the L. Morley Brothers' account to fund Arthur to go to the United States. On 19 May 1909, Arthur, Hattie and Arthur's son left Southampton on board the White Star Liner *Majestic* bound for New York; they had booked their tickets as husband and wife in third class. The couple arrived in New York on 27 May and after clearing immigration they eventually settled in Dallas, Texas, where Arthur sold dry goods – successfully, it seems, because by 1910 he had two servants.

Henry continued to manage the confectionery shops, adding a new one in late 1909 at 36 The Shambles, Worcester. L. Morley Brothers Confectioners gained a reputation for high-quality confectionery in the form of chocolates, sweets and small cakes, which were not just bought in but were also manufactured at the back of 22 Foregate Street. Henry had another property at 336 High Street, Cheltenham, which may have been the house where his brother and Hattie had stayed. The business was very much a family affair, with the Morley brothers putting in the finance and other family members working in the shops. Henry and Louisa lived at the Foregate Street premises. Henry planned expansion, and to assist in the running of the shops he employed young female assistants. Between 1909 and 1911 there was a high turnover of staff, caused mainly by the fact that many of the girls did not get on with Henry's wife Louisa, who was seen as a tyrant with a jealous streak. From advertisements he posted in local newspapers, Henry tended to take on women of around 17 years of age; one such woman was Kate Phillips, who applied for a job in 1910 as an assistant at the Foregate Street shop.

Kate Florence Phillips was born in Balsall Heath, Worcestershire, in 1893 – the fourth child to Thomas Charles Phillips, an engine fitter, and Mary (Smith). Thomas' father had been a lock-keeper at the camp locks in Worcester and Mary was from Hallow in Worcestershire. Kate's upbringing appears unremarkable – she had a happy family life living at 34 Waterworks Road, close to where her father worked. The Phillips family knew Louisa from her time in the same street and the contact in a close-knit community led Kate, in 1910, to apply for and get the job – it seems Louisa felt she was giving the young Kate a start in life. Kate's duties varied from preparing confectionery for display to serving customers, essentially learning the ins and outs of the business.

In 1910, Henry took on a number of women to assist in other shops, as he was planning further expansion. The following year would prove to be a momentous one for the company and for the Morley families. A further two shops were added in Birmingham: a new one at Belle Vue Terrace, Great Malvern, and one that had relocated from Broad Street in Worcester to bigger premises at 27 The Cross. This brought the total number of shops in the chain to six.

Although the business was running well, the same could not be said for the Morleys home life. Henry and Louisa were no longer the happy couple they had once been; in fact, it seems that soon after the birth of Doris the marriage had cooled. For Henry and Kate, employer and employee working closely together day after day, a mutual attraction formed which became an affair. Such an event was not uncommon, but for conservative Worcester in 1910, and especially with an age difference of some nineteen years, it had the potential to become a scandal.

Henry had worked his way into a predicament, one with which his elder brother Arthur would understand, given the fact he had entered into a similar relationship – he had gone to the United States for a new life and while there Hattie bore him a daughter, Emily (named after Arthur's mother). Henry knew he could not live a double life without sooner or later being discovered. He had to get away with Kate, but what would happen to the business? Henry knew that his future, and that of his brothers', was tied up in the shops. He wrote to Arthur in the United States and Arthur duly returned to Britain, moving into 73 New Street, Birmingham, living above the shop with Hattie. Arthur's son moved in with Henry and his wife at 22 Foregate Street. It was a crowded establishment with Henry's daughter, mother and Aunt Alice living together. Arthur's affair had obviously caused much upset and Henry's wife refused to have anything to do with him. It seems the Birmingham shops were a way of keeping the families apart. It appears Louisa had no idea why Arthur had suddenly returned; perhaps she thought it was for helping out with the expanding business.

Henry and Louisa were growing further apart, and when the Malvern shop was up and running Louisa moved into the rooms above with her daughter. Louisa would run that branch, Henry's aunt managed the shop at The Cross, Henry continued to manage the Foregate Street premises along with its staff, and Arthur managed the Birmingham branches. Henry and Kate were free from the prying eyes of Louisa and perhaps from any scandal, although by late 1911 whispers were being heard among the young girls at Morleys. Another assistant, Emma Sheward, knew exactly what was going on and was taken into Henry and Kate's confidence.

With the business secure, Henry began making plans for a new life for him and Kate. The plan was that they would immigrate to the United States using an assumed name and claim to be married, and to avoid issues of parental consent Kate's age was given as 24. The aim was to settle in San Francisco and to open a confectionery shop. Henry's wife and daughter would be financially secure with the Malvern shop; his brothers would be secure with the others. The decision to go in 1912 was to forestall Louisa finding out about the affair until after they had gone. Arthur gave advice on how to navigate through US immigration as well as on how to set up in the States. On 28 February 1912 Henry drew up a new will with his solicitor, Charles Parkhouse, naming his brother Arthur as sole executor. He then began withdrawing money from the company accounts including a single draw of £400 to fund his trip and to provide for his and Kate's future life. In all, around £700 was withdrawn from the account in Worcester leaving little fluidity in the account – although the account only covered the Worcester shops, as the Birmingham shops had an account in Birmingham and Louisa looked after the account for the Malvern shop locally. She would have had no idea of what was happening in Worcester, which enabled Henry to bankroll his elopement in secret. Henry was hoping to have left Worcester by the time his wife found out.

On 3 March Henry left Worcester with Kate, first heading to Birmingham to stay with Arthur at 73 New Street, from where he purchased the ticket for *Titanic*, paying £26 for a second-class berth. Arthur had advised a different route, however, suggesting that he take the North German Lloyd steamer *Hanover*, departing Bremen to Galveston, Texas, sailing on 4 April 1912. But on hearing of the maiden voyage of *Titanic*, Henry decided to book on the new ship. Henry now moved around the Midlands with Kate, posing as husband and wife so that Louisa couldn't find them, and took on the name 'Marshall'. The name chosen was that of a friend of Henry and Arthur's – Arthur Marshall, a boot dealer; his sister Nellie worked in Morleys' shop at The Cross, Worcester.

Louisa had suspected something was wrong, and when a cheque could not be cashed to pay a supplier in Worcester due to insufficient funds in the Worcester account, Louisa enquired at the United Counties Bank where she was informed that Henry had been withdrawing money. Confectionery assistant Emma Sheward recalled Louisa arriving at the Foregate Street shop in a rage looking for Henry, but he had gone.

With Arthur's help the Marshalls, as they were now called, travelled to London to stay with Henry's relatives for a few days. Arthur, along with

Kate's parents, joined them and travelled with them to Southampton where they stayed overnight at the South Western Hotel. Henry had purchased new clothes for Kate and himself, and together they stayed in a variety of hotels before the move to London and finally to Southampton, spending around £60 with cheques prior to *Titanic*'s departure. On 10 April, Henry and Kate, accompanied by Arthur and Kate's parents, left the hotel and walked to Berth 44. Arthur said his goodbyes and wished his brother and Kate well and looked forward to hearing from them when they were settled. Kate said goodbye to her parents. What they made of it all one can only imagine.

When they entered their cabin they must have felt the beckoning of a new life; they had escaped Worcester and Henry had escaped Louisa, but he was leaving his daughter behind. What is more, unknown to both of them, Kate was pregnant with Henry's child.

Stanley Harrington Fox. (from *Birmingham Gazette*)

Henry Samuel Morley.
(Author's collection)

Kate Phillips with daughter Ellen.
(Author's collection)

Third Class

The arrival of third-class passengers to Berth 44 spurred the White Star port officials and crew into action. All third-class passengers had to undergo a brief medical inspection before boarding the ship – brought about by tighter controls by the US immigration authorities.

In 1892 an immigration station had opened on Ellis Island off the coast of New York in order to process people entering the country. In 1900, due to a fire destroying the original building, a larger facility had been constructed, and two years later an immigrant hospital had been built. The authorities were particularly concerned about the spread of disease through immigrant travel; a major cholera epidemic in New York in 1866 had been largely blamed on emigrants from Europe and the need to screen newcomers was seen as essential. The screening was also seen as a way to decide if immigrants were fit to enter the country, so people with certain infirmities would not be permitted to remain. The emphasis of the US government was to welcome working immigrants, bringing their skills to a country that was largely unskilled. On arrival in New York, third-class immigrants would be transferred to Ellis Island to be processed, undergoing a medical inspection. If deemed to be ill they would have to stay in the hospital for up to twenty-four hours; if they remained ill and saw no sign of recovery they would be sent back to their departure point at the cost of the shipping company that brought them.

Bruce Ismay of White Star was not keen to have non-paying passengers on his ships and thus insisted that all third-class passengers be inspected at Southampton or Liverpool prior to departure. The passengers would line up and wait their turn to be inspected as a medical orderly examined each passenger for any signs of illness, checking through hair and beards, looking at the back of the throat and teeth and checking eyes and general appearance. Even the slightest problem might result in rejection. Third-class passengers often wore their Sunday best in order to look nice and clean and children's faces would be rubbed with a pumice stone to make them look rosy and healthy. Mothers would turn to their children and say, 'For God's sake, don't cough!' First- and second-class passengers also had to undergo an immigration check, but this was carried out on board the ship in New York.

Such was the lot of the third class, but they expected no better and the rules were there so it was best to rub along. In the line stood William Henry Allen who had travelled from London after spending a few days with his parents. He had given up his job as a fitter at the Birmingham Metal and Munitions Company Limited at Adderley Park in the hope of starting a new life, joining an uncle in New York. As a fitter his skills were needed in the United States and the US Consulate in Birmingham had been more than helpful to process his application. William was from Lenton in Nottinghamshire, born to a family of three boys and three girls. His father, Alfred, was from Birmingham and had progressed upward in the world of engineering, starting out working with his father in an ironfoundry before progressing to become a mechanic at a wagon works in Lancaster, and then as a lace-machine fitter in Nottingham where his son, William, joined him to learn the trade. Alfred eventually became foreman at the lace machine factory before moving to London to become a stationary engineer. He was prepared to move around the country to improve himself, and this ambition influenced his son who was prepared to do the same.

After working with his father in Nottingham, William took his skills to the Midlands, initially working in Coventry before taking a job at the Birmingham Metal and Munitions Company in 1911, moving in with his aunt and uncle (Frederick and Harriett Hunt) at 78 Queen's Road, Erdington. He had ambitions to travel to the United States and would have done so earlier, but he wanted to go with money in his pocket, hence he took work in Coventry and Birmingham. It was at the Birmingham firm that he met John Thomas Hinckley, an engineer's fitter whose brother, George Herbert, was a steward with the White Star Line. His choice of sailing on *Titanic* was influenced by the fact that George Hinckley would be serving on board. Harriett suggested to William that he travel in second class, but William insisted he would save money by travelling in third. He entered the offices of Josiah Frances Brame shipping agent at 7 City Arcade, Birmingham, and paid the £8 for his ticket. Incidentally, Harriett's son, Claude Frederick, sailed on board RMS *Cymric* the same day as *Titanic*; he left from Liverpool to Portland Maine on route to Canada. Brame's also took another booking for *Titanic*, that of a Mr Franks; however, he transferred his booking to another ship sailing from Liverpool a couple of days later. After leaving his parents' home in London, William took the second- and third-class *Titanic* express to Southampton, and once he cleared the medical inspection he boarded the ship.

Standing patiently in line for the medical inspection was Henry John Spinner, a glove cutter originally from Worcester who had had an interesting life and was seeking a better future for his family. Henry (known as Harry) was born in Worcester in 1880 the son of George Spinner, a glove cutter, and Ellen (Taylor). He attended Angle Street Congregational Church where he was a member of Mr Hunt's Bible class and was an active member of the local YMCA, playing in their football team. He followed his father's trade, being employed as an apprentice glover, starting as a glove cutter at Fownes Brothers and Company, a manufacturer of high-quality gloves. He made a name for himself as a local hero when at 16 years old he dived fully clothed into the Worcester canal to rescue a small boy who had fallen in.

Henry left Fownes in 1900 after completing his apprenticeship and joined the Royal Marine Artillery where he served for five years serving on board HMS *Ocean* in the South China Sea during the Russo-Japanese War. Upon leaving the Marines, he returned to Fownes in Worcester. He was married in 1907 to a local woman, Harriett Alice Walker, a gloveress machinist he met at Fownes. A year later the couple had a daughter, Alice Maud Winifred. The family moved to Yeovil in Somerset where Henry worked as a glove cutter at a subsidiary of Fownes. He wanted a better future, and Fownes offered it to him when, in 1907, the Worcester firm opened a manufacturing facility at Gloversville, New York. Gloversville became the hub of American glove-making and Henry wanted to be part of it. His wife and daughter moved back to Worcester, staying with Harriett's sister in Lowell Street. Henry travelled to London Paddington from Worcester Shrub Hill Station, spending a night in London before catching the train from Waterloo to Southampton on 10 April, enabling him to board with ticket number 369943.

George Green, a farrier from Dorking, had travelled to Southampton from Coventry. His wife Theresa Jane and his three children were staying with her parents at Spon Lane, Coventry, while he went on to the United States to establish himself in the mining district of Lead City, Dakota. They were due to follow him in about a month's time.

The lure of finding a new life and possibly making one's fortune in the United States was attractive to many who worked in the industrial Midlands. For five brothers of the Davies family in Harwood Street, West Bromwich, the lure was irresistible. Their grandfather, Thomas, had been an iron puddler – a process of converting pig iron into wrought iron. His son Richard had followed him into the trade and three of Richard's sons followed thereafter in the traditional family occupation. Richard was born in Ettingshall in 1859, a region famous for its metalworkers, and it was no surprise that when he turned 15 he joined his father, learning the art of a puddler. He married Mary

Ann Cox in 1885 and together they had nine children (six boys and three girls). The eldest, William Thomas, became a bricklayer; his brothers Alfred, John and Joseph became ironfounders, with Alfred being a cupola worker at Izons and Company hollowware manufactures. John and Joseph worked with their father at Edward Page and Sons iron manufacturers at Roway Iron Works, Albion; of the two remaining brothers, Richard became a baker and Arthur, the youngest, born in 1906, was still at school.

The girls, Alice May, Matilda Doris and Mary Gladys, stayed at home. The eldest daughter, Alice, suffered from what was then called cretinism, a condition of severely stunted physical and mental growth due to untreated congenital deficiency of thyroid hormones, now referred to as congenital hypothyroidism. There was no treatment in the early twentieth century, thus Alice would have been kept at home. In 1906 William Thomas had travelled to the United States to answer the call for people with building skills to work in San Francisco to help rebuild the city following the disastrous earthquake earlier in the year. William did well in the USA, finding good opportunities and becoming a building contractor. Having moved to Michigan, Illinois, in 1908, he married Isabella Mundie, a Scottish émigré who had moved to the United States via Canada with her parents in 1905. Eventually they settled in Pontiac, and with the breakdown of his parents-in-law's marriage, his mother-in-law Isabella moved in with him and his wife. In 1911 William had a son whom he named Richard, after his father. In West Bromwich the family followed William's exploits with great interest and began to think that they would all be better off in the United States.

In December 1911 William returned to West Bromwich to visit the family and introduce his wife and son to his parents and siblings. William told of his successful life and that the opportunities in America were endless for those who had skills and worked hard. It was not only the Davieses that were interested in emigrating; William's aunt, Alice Cox, had in 1900 married James Lester, a galvaniser who worked at George Adams and Sons Limited, Mars Iron Works, Wolverhampton, and they had a son, James Dennis. James senior came from a family of metal workers, with his father, Joseph, and brothers, Samuel, Joseph and John, all involved in various aspects of the trade. James was convinced that the best future for his family lay across the Atlantic. In early 1912 the Davieses and James Lester visited the US Consulate at Newton Chambers, Cannon Street, Birmingham, where they were given advice by E. Harker, the deputy consul. Following his advice the Davies family decided that they would all immigrate to the United States, although Alice May would not be able to go. Due to her condition she would not be permitted to enter the country and would, therefore, have to be left behind with members of her mother's family. It may seem a harsh decision, but Alice May was not expected to have a long life, as her health would continue to deteriorate over time.

The Davies' set out their plan. William would return to Pontiac with his family, taking with him his 20-year-old brother Richard. Alfred, Joseph and John would work out their notices at their employers, and, along with their uncle, James Lester, would follow in a few weeks. Once all were settled and working they would send for their parents, their sisters (except for Alice May), their Aunt Alice and Cousin James. Alice and James Jnr moved in with her sister in order to save money. On 1 February 1912, William, with his family and brother Richard, set sail on RMS *Baltic* from Liverpool bound for New York.

The remaining Davies brothers started to make plans for their new life, with Alfred having special plans to make. He had been going out with Ann Maria Cartwright, who was working as a domestic servant in Moseley, Birmingham, for Samuel George Wareham, a commercial dealer in bedsteads. Alfred worked with Ann's father John at Izons, and it was from their friendship that he met Ann, whom he wanted to marry and take with him to America.

Initially, it was thought that Joseph, being only 17, would have to wait until his parents were going to America to make the trip, which made him somewhat downhearted that his other brothers would leave without him. However, it was decided that he could travel after all with his brothers, and he accompanied them and his uncle to Houlder Brothers and Company shipping agents at Ocean House, Navigation Street, Birmingham, to book passage on RMS *Baltic*, scheduled to leave Liverpool for New York on 28 March. But the shipping clerk informed them that all third-class berths for the voyage were booked and recommended they sail on RMS *Lusitania* instead. However, they were foiled again – the 6 April sailing was also fully booked, possibly due to the national coal strike, which had rendered many ships stuck in ports for want of coal. The clerk suggested the maiden voyage of *Titanic*, as maiden voyages were rarely fully booked. Thus, the Davies brothers and James Lester found themselves booked as third-class passengers on *Titanic*, paying £8 1s each for their tickets, totaling £32 4s. Joseph wrote to his brother in Pontiac to tell him the news:

Dear Sister and brother,

I was the happiest chap in West Bromwich when I knew that I was able to come there and join you. Alfred and Jack told me they were crossing on the *Baltic* but that boat being all reserved we have decided to come on the *Titanic*, the largest boat afloat. The boat starts out on Easter Day [*sic*] I will conclude by sending love to you all.

From your loving brother Joe.

The National Coal Strike had affected Black Country industry with factories closing due to lack of coal. The Davies brothers' father, Richard, found himself laid off when Page's ironworks had to shut down. John Davies wrote to his brother William for the last time before he set off:

Dear Sister and Brother,

I write a few lines to let you know some news from our family. The strike has not yet been settled but I think it will be this week, Father will then go to work again. I could hardly believe Mother when she told me Joe was going over with me. He was very downhearted when he thought he had to stay here. I think this is the last news you will hear from England, so I will conclude by sending best love to you all.

Mother sends kisses,
From your brother.

The excitement of heading to a new life across the Atlantic was heightened by the emotion of a wedding. On 8 April, just two days before *Titanic* set sail, 24-year-old Alfred James Davies married 21-year-old Ann Maria Cartwright at Oldbury Parish Church. The following day the brothers and their uncle began their voyage to the New World. The goodbyes were long as the brothers left their parents and sisters. Alfred left his new wife with her mother and James Lester kissed his wife and young son goodbye, and then they were off to Snow Hill Station to catch the train to London Paddington. Where fate had contrived to put them on *Titanic*, it now seemed to be trying to prevent them from reaching the ship.

Due to a mix-up in the train times, thinking their train left at 7 a.m. when in fact it left at 5 a.m., the travellers found themselves running late. They raced to Birmingham via tram. When they made it into Snow Hill Station they ran past the parked limousines and carriages, past the famous station clock and onto the platform where their train was pulling out. Cries went up as they hurtled down the platform with their suitcases. Suddenly, doors of carriages were opened and railway employees shouted at them to hurry and throw their bags on board. The same workers then leaned out and helped the men on board to the amazement of others on the platform and in carriages. After they arrived in London they headed to Waterloo where they booked into a boarding house for the night, sharing a room between them.

On the 10 April they caught the second- and third-class *Titanic* express and steamed down to Southampton, arriving straight into Berth 44 passing over Canute Road. They lined up for their health inspection and looked up at the huge liner docked ahead of them. They passed the inspection without any trouble and headed up the gangway to be greeted by Sixth Officer Moody, who sent them in the direction of their bunks. After dropping off their cases in the cabin they immediately went to the poop deck, which was the third-class recreation deck. They wanted to see the ship pull away from the dock, so they worked their way to the railing where they could look down at the quayside. The time was 11.55 a.m.; *Titanic* was due to set sail in five minutes.

Henry Spinner.
(*Berrow's Journal*)

Alfred Davies. (Courtesy of Cheryl Lynn Lewandowski)

John Davies. (Courtesy of Cheryl Lynn Lewandowski)

Joseph Davies. (Courtesy of Cheryl Lynn Lewandowski)

Alfred and Ann Maria Davies. (Courtesy of Cheryl Lynn Lewandowski)

Arthur Davies. (Courtesy of Cheryl Lynn Lewandowski)

Richard Davies. (Courtesy of
Cheryl Lynn Lewandowski)

Alice Lester. (Courtesy of
Cheryl Lynn Lewandowski)

US Consulate, Birmingham, in 1912. (Author's collection)

9

MAIDEN VOYAGE

As the passengers waited for the throbbing of *Titanic*'s engines and her propellers to turn, most were not aware of the large amount of work that had gone into preparing the ship for her maiden voyage; in the very early hours of 4 April, *Titanic* had slipped into Southampton and docked at Berth 44, where the work began preparing the ship for the voyage. The first task was to load the ship with coal, a rare commodity due to the coal strike, but White Star's parent company, IMM, had arranged for the transfer of coal from some of their other ships in Southampton, notably *Majestic*, *City of New York* and *St Paul*. Trimmers such as Henry Brewer and Henry Wood now had their work cut out helping to load and store the nearly 4,500 tons of coal coming aboard, adding to the 1,800 tons of coal already on board. The stowing of coal on a ship presented a number of problems: balancing the ship, reducing dust and the risk of fire. While in Belfast, a small fire had broken out in the coalbunker at the forward end of Boiler Room 5, where it continued to burn. Coal fires were not uncommon on ships and the technique to extinguish them was well known to the firemen and stokers; using a hose to quench the bunker with water was the most common method, coupled with the use of the heated coal for the boilers first, thus removing the fuel for the fire. A greater risk existed when a coalbunker was empty and coal dust blew about, creating a fire hazard. Empty bunkers were damped down with water to reduce such a risk. This was routine to the crew below decks, and although a small fire did simmer away for some time, there was no immediate threat to the ship. Through a mixture of quenching and the removal of coal, the fire was extinguished by 13 April.

On the upper decks, crew were also busy taking deliveries of crockery, glass, utensils and stores, all of which had to be checked and stored. Stoniers' warehouse in Southampton had been filled with material for *Titanic*, and almost as soon as the ship arrived this material began to be loaded. As well as a large quantity of china, glass from Stuart and Sons was loaded on board, including the 200 champagne glasses that had been produced by Webbs. An interesting delivery on Saturday 6 April was a number of metal bedsteads from Hoskins and Sewell. These were delivered unassembled. Two men from the Southampton agent for Hoskins and Sewell went on board to set up the beds. William Cole of Henry Pooley and Sons boarded the ship on Saturday morning to calibrate the weighing machine in the Turkish bath and to deliver several boxes of tickets on to which passengers could record their weight. As was his usual practice, he put a couple of tickets bearing the name of the ship in his pocket as a souvenir.

The weekend was a frenetic time on *Titanic* as a number of workmen came on board to add finishing touches. Three gilders from Elkingtons in Birmingham were touching up any carving and ironworks that had bump marks – they were escorted by Joey Thompson, a member of the Harland and Wolff Guarantee Group responsible for painting and decorating.

A parcel was delivered to the ship's barber, Augustus Henry Weikman, containing a quantity of pin badges depicting a ship's wheel with the name 'RMS *Titanic*' inscribed around the edge. These, along with a quantity of other designs, had been produced by P. Vaughton and Sons of Birmingham. Augustus would sell these as souvenirs in his barbershop. From Huntley and Palmers at 49 Newhall Street, Birmingham, came 100 special tins of quality biscuits, and the famous Birmingham firm Cadbury, located in Bournville, supplied 150 boxes of luxury chocolates. Both the biscuit and chocolate tins had lids depicting an Olympic-class ship. Cadbury also issued a small card with their cocoa showing the largest liners in the world.

With all of the excitement in Southampton, the rest of the country would only hear about the maiden voyage through their local and national newspapers. In an age before radio and television, the printed media was the main source of information on local, national and international events. The Midlands had a number of newspapers that were published daily and weekly, with each of the major towns having their own publications. These newspapers played a vital role in not just informing the public, but also, at times, guiding public opinion. During the week leading up to the maiden voyage of *Titanic*, the news media covered the main stories of the day, notably the national coal strike, the home rule for Ireland debate and the Turkish–Italian war. The Birmingham press covered some interesting stories that at the time were just curiosities but would later become major talking points, and a number of local stories that over 100 years later would seem all too familiar. On 6 April the *Birmingham Weekly Mercury* carried a prophetic story about icebergs entitled 'The Truth About Icebergs', in which a Mr H.J. Shepstone discussed the size and nature of icebergs, informing the reader that some can have pinnacles that tower 1,000ft above the water and are so wide that they resemble islands. The article pointed out that icebergs can be of various colours and that the amount of the berg submerged can vary. There was another item about Captain Scott with the headline, 'News of Captain Scott – has he Succeeded?' alluding to Captain Scott's attempt to reach the South Pole – the latest news suggested he was 150 miles from his goal. There was also a piece about the development of trams in Birmingham – a similar article appeared in the *Birmingham Post* 104 years later!

On the morning of Wednesday 10 April 1912, the people of Birmingham and the Black Country prepared for work. It was just another day. The main news items in Wednesday morning's press were the speech by Andrew Bonar Law on home rule for Ireland, of which he was fervently opposed, and the latest news on the national coal strike and how local industry was trying to get back to normal. Local gas supplies had been cut since Easter due to the lack of coal, but were about to be reinstated as the first deliveries of coal for some weeks were now arriving. In Sparkbrook there had been a large fire at the shop of Profitt and Westwood corn and seed merchants on the Stratford Road; Arthur Edward Vickers of Riddings Lane, Tysley, appeared in court charged with bigamy; and there was a report that shots had been fired at an aeroplane that had been mistaken for an eagle. In news about shipping there was a report that all steamers for Canada were fully booked for two months, as many skilled workers from Britain were emigrating. In the *Evening Dispatch* there was a small piece reporting that the largest liner afloat, the White Star Liner *Titanic*, was given an enthusiastic send-off on her maiden voyage.

In Southampton, the last passengers boarded *Titanic*. Revelling in the excitement of the new ship was White Star's chairman J. Bruce Ismay enjoying the luxurious suite of rooms on B Deck, rooms that contained a great deal of Midlands' material. The ship's principal designer Thomas Andrews was also making the trip, along with nine members of Harland and Wolff whose job it was to see how well the ship performed in service.

William Hipkins had settled himself into his first-class cabin. He looked at the gold watch that had belonged to his father, it was 11.57 a.m.; it would soon be time to depart. William ensured that the connecting door to the bathroom was locked and then left for the deck. He walked up the stairs, eventually reaching A Deck with its marvellously decorated entrance with carved oak panelling. From the bottom of the stairs he looked up to the top-most landing where a great, carved wooden clock 'Honour and Glory Crowning Time' was fixed into the panelled wall. To top the whole staircase was a magnificent wrought-iron and glass dome. He walked up the stairs and looked closely at the exquisite carving of the clock before moving on to the boat deck. Many people were rushing about, others were standing looking over the side or admiring the ship. Some young boys were excitedly running about exploring. It was a cacophony of noise – people talking and shouting, motor engines, various whistles, horns – all signifying a busy dock. Due to the coal strike, however, *Titanic* would be leaving in style while a number of other ships stayed moored up like forgotten pets outside a shop.

On the bridge Captain Smith stood with the pilot George Bowyer and made his final checks before ordering Fourth Officer Boxhall to signal the engine room to begin.

At midday on 10 April, ships' horns sounded a traditional send-off for a vessel on her maiden voyage. *Titanic's* propellers turned and the great ship began to slowly pull away from the dock. The deck of *Titanic* was full of passengers waving goodbye to Southampton and crowds of people had gathered to see the event. The Davies brothers stood on the poop deck in third class excited that the voyage had started and looking forward to arriving in New York. On the second-class promenade, Henry Morley and Kate Phillips took their last look at Southampton, perhaps wondering what lay ahead – a new life? – and perhaps also reflecting on what they were leaving behind. On the first-class deck, Tyrell and Julia Cavendish watched the crowds who wanted to be there when the largest ship in the world started its maiden voyage. Tyrell may have felt a little uneasy; the ink was only just dry on his will.

A special correspondent for the *Birmingham Gazette and Express* was at the quayside to watch the departure of the great ship; he described in detail the events of 10 April:

Having looked down on the world from the *Titanic's* boat deck, I went down onto the quay and looked up at the projecting heads of the passengers. It was like standing by the wall of St Paul's Cathedral and craning your neck to get a glimpse of the Apostles on the roof. It was just noon when the vast steel wall in front of us began to move. For the first yard a caterpillar might have raced the *Titanic*. It was difficult to imagine such a tremendous object moving, so slowly. I walked along to the end of the deep water dock and saw her come by at a slow pace within a stone's throw of the quay. Her propellers churned the green sea up to liquid grey mud. She had to go round a bend to the left; it was while trying to round this bit of a bend that the *Titanic* pulled the 10,798-ton *New York* liner from her berth.

The Leyland liner *New York* was moored at the dock, tethered to the land and unable to sail as her coal had been transferred to the great ship now edging past her. Stewards Kingscote and Ward were too busy to notice *New York*, a ship with which they were all too familiar. As *Titanic* began to pass *New York*, the smaller ship's stern began to move towards the larger vessel. Suddenly cables snapped and it seemed that there was to be a collision between the two ships. The pilot and bridge crew on *Titanic* were quick to react, stopping her engines, and the tug *Vulcan* threw cables to the stern of *New York* – a collision had been avoided, but it had been a close call, with both ships coming within 12ft of each other. The *Birmingham Gazette and Express* reporter on the scene reflected on what he had seen:

> What was said to have happened seemed a fantastic absurdity until I saw the frayed end of a steel wire hawser about as thick as a man's wrist, lying on the key. 'It snapped like the crack of a gun,' a man told me who saw it break. Broken hemp cables hung down the *New York*'s side. The crowd was breathless with excitement; people climbed into railway trucks to see what was going to happen.

The incident added to the excitement of the occasion, although to some it seemed an inauspicious start. *New York* was shepherded back into place and *Titanic*'s maiden voyage began one hour later than scheduled. Had William Hipkins seen the incident he would have known the breaking strength of the cables involved, having written a technical book on the use of steel cable.

With the excitement of the departure now settling down, William, along with Tyrell and Florence Cavendish, responded to the bugle call to luncheon and went down to D Deck, walking through the reception room and into the immense dining saloon, which could seat over 500 diners per sitting with tables arranged in a typical restaurant fashion and some small tables set into recessed bays for private parties or family groups. William sat at his table and looked at the menu for the first meal of the maiden voyage; it was a choice worthy of the White Star Line:

LUNCHEON

Consomme Jardiniere   Hodge Podge
Fillets of Plaice
Beef Steak & Kidney Pie
Roast Surrey Capon

FROM THE GRILL

Grilled Mutton Chops
Mashed, Fried & Baked Potatoes
Rice Pudding
Applesattan   Pastry

BUFFET

Fresh Lobsters   Potted Shrimps
Soused Herrings   Sardines
Roast beef
Round of Spiced Beef
Virginia & Cumberland Ham
Bologna   Sausage Brawn
Gelantine of Chicken
Corned Ox Tongue
Lettuce   Tomatoes

CHEESE

Cheshire, Stilton, Gorgonzola, Edam
Camembert, Roquefort, St Ivel.

The luncheon was accompanied by music played by the ship's band. For John Wesley Woodward it had been a busy morning; the band had to play in the first-class reception to welcome the wealthiest clientele before reassembling in two groups at the dining room and à la carte restaurant.

The routine of a ship at sea had begun: brief moments of activity followed by food. In the first few hours of the voyage passengers of all classes acquainted themselves with the facilities, finding their way around the corridors, up and down stairs and strolling along the promenades. In second class the Marshalls enjoyed the lounge, library and deck space. Being only 19, Kate may have been slightly overawed, but her lover Henry was worldy and guided her through the social niceties. In third class, the Davies brothers and James Lester were no doubt enjoying the spacious public areas allocated to them, as well as ample space on the poop deck for taking in the air and watching their homeland slip further away.

At 6.30 p.m. that evening, *Titanic* arrived at Cherbourg in France. The bugle call for dinner had already sounded, and while the passengers went to dine, *Titanic* received more passengers via the tenders *Nomandic* and *Traffic*. Boarding the ship at the French port were those who had been on the European tour: John Jacob Astor and his young wife Madeleine – like the Marshalls, a couple with a large age gap – who had been in Europe avoiding the press following the divorce from his first wife; Margaret Brown, the vaudeville star whose husband had hit it rich in silver mining in Colorado, made her entrance as only she could; and Benjamin Guggenheim, another multi-millionaire on his way home with his French mistress Leontine Pauline Aubart for company. Second- and third-class passengers also joined at Cherbourg, with the third-class emigrants coming from all parts of Europe and the Middle East.

Next morning *Titanic* arrived at Queenstown in Ireland (now reverted to its original name of Cobh); it was while here that a lifeboat launch had to be demonstrated to meet local regulations. A number of passengers left the ship, namely those who had joined in Southampton in order to say they had been on the largest ship in the world on her maiden voyage. These passengers included Father Francis Browne, a Catholic priest who had taken a number of photographs of the vessel, which would become of immense historic value. Irish emigrants lined up at the quay waiting to board the tender *Ireland*. Many of these emigrants had sold almost every possession in order to fund a new life in the United States.

It was around this time that back in the Midlands people were reading the reports of *Titanic*'s departure from Southampton in their morning newspapers, the only available information to friends and families of their loved ones on board until a postcard or letter arrived from Southampton, Cherbourg or Queenstown. At Queenstown, passengers had a last chance to send a message home before arriving in New York. Third-class passengers had a complimentary postcard to send home; the Davies brothers took advantage of this, writing that they were 'having a most pleasant voyage'. William Allen also took advantage of the last post before New York, sending a letter to his Aunt Harriett in Erdington stating that the voyage to Queenstown was 'a smooth passage, nothing worse than being on a train'. He ended the letter stating he would write again as soon as he was on land.

At 1.30 p.m. *Titanic* raised her Noah Hingley-made anchors and cable chain and began her voyage across the Atlantic. In total, there were a little over 2,200 passengers and crew, somewhat short of capacity, but all were looking forward to a pleasant voyage.

As was usual with a maiden voyage the trip would be a steady one. Not all of the boilers were lit and, with clear weather expected, a smooth, uneventful crossing was what Captain Smith envisioned.

Tyrell and Julia Cavendish fitted well into high society. Tyrell by birth and Florence by training – the European finishing school had prepared her for the dinners and social events of first class. William Hipkins, by experience and training, fitted in well too; he was the new generation of businessmen that created wealth through industrial commerce. He was acquainted with several of the first-class passengers through business including Charles Melville Hays, president of the Grand Trunk Railroad, with whom he had corresponded over the possibility of Averys supplying weighbridges to his company. As a reserved man, William would not have been enthusiastic to join any parties; instead, he would read, work through his papers and use the voyage for a rare chance of relaxation in his busy life. No doubt William, being a keen Francophile, sampled the delights of the Café Parisien, although it is likely he did not appreciate the ragtime music that was performed there. More to his taste were the popular classical pieces played during luncheon and dinner. West Bromwich-born John Wesley Woodward played the cello and was enjoying his booking. At times the band also played in second class, much to the appreciation of the passengers. Wesley made a good impression with one second-class passenger – Kate Buss.

Cadbury chocolate tin.
(Author's collection)

Cadbury cocoa card.
(Author's collection)

Kate was from Sittingbourne in Kent and was on her way to be with her fiancé in San Diego, California. She referred to Wesley in a letter to her brother Percy as 'Cello Man' and he was clearly a favourite of hers, writing: 'Every time he finishes a piece he looks at me and we smile.' Kate, considering him to be a superior musician, was keen to hear him play a solo and, accompanied by Dr Ernest Moraweck and Leopold and Mathilde Weisz, went to hear the band play. Mathilde agreed to sing and after the recital the group sat with Wesley to talk. He spoke of his time on *Olympic* and of the collision with HMS *Hawk*. He clearly made a great impression with Kate and she wrote in her journal that he was 'quite gentlemanly'.

The Marshalls, also in second class, behaved as if on honeymoon. The young Kate must have been carried along in the moment. Just a few weeks ago she was an assistant in a confectionery shop, now she was on board the largest liner in the world enjoying fine food and service.

In third class there was no ship's band; instead, the musical entertainments were provided by the Irish passengers who enlivened the public rooms with jigs and reels. The Davieses may well have danced along with the other nationalities on board – the Swedes, Finns, Germans, French, Belgians and even Lebanese.

Regardless of the surroundings and entertainment, passengers in first, second and third class all congratulated themselves on being on the largest, most luxurious liner in the world, and no one thought that anything could go wrong.

10

SUNDAY 14 APRIL 1912

Sunday 14 April 1912 began as any other day on the voyage. The only break to the routine was the Sunday services held in the restaurants. The ship's orchestra would play in first class as Captain Smith led the service. The stewards were momentarily relieved of their duties servicing the passengers to carry out those little jobs that they simply didn't have time for, especially as the department was short-staffed. Due to the coal strike many stewards had gone home to their families, just as James Dinenage had done when he went back to Walsall. He saw it as good fortune that he was able to get to Southampton in time to sign on to *Titanic*. The stewards had had a busy time of it, not simply because the passengers were demanding, that was part of the job, but it was a new ship and although similar to *Olympic* it was not identical and the stewards had to learn their way around.

Arthur Derrett, having been with the ship since Belfast and previously been on *Olympic*, knew his way around well and knew how to look after passengers. All good stewards made a careful note of passengers' particular likes and dislikes and remembered regular travellers. For example, William Edward Hipkins in C39 always liked to have drinking chocolate before he went to bed, and his steward ensured he had it every night. Stewardess Kate Smith had her hands full assisting with the first-class children as well as her general duties.

One task scheduled for the stewards on the Sunday was lifeboat drill, but it had been cancelled due to strong winds making the swinging out of a lifeboat too hazardous. The stewards were probably relieved as they had enough to do.

Two men who had been extremely busy were the radio operators, John Phillips and Harold Bride. They worked for the Marconi Company, which had the contract to operate a radiotelegraph, primarily for the passengers to send and receive messages, but also to receive and send messages for the ship, such as weather reports and notice of any hazards. Along with *Olympic*, *Titanic* had the most powerful radio set at sea, and with two operators it was able to have a twenty-four-hour service. Most ships sailing across the ocean did not have radio, and those that did usually had only one operator who shut down at 11 p.m. With the excitement of the maiden voyage passengers were all too keen to send messages.

From 12 April there was a steady stream of messages from other ships reporting icebergs and ice fields. The temperature began to drop and walking the deck became a somewhat chilly experience. On Sunday 14th, ice reports came in from *Caronia*, *Amerika*, *Baltic* and *Noordam*. Captain Smith left orders for the officers that *Titanic* was to change course, turning towards New York, known as 'turning the corner', at 5.50 p.m. – somewhat later than expected. This would take *Titanic* a little further south, thus avoiding any ice that may lie in her path. He also ordered that the cold boilers be warmed up so that by evening they would be travelling faster; this was not a common move on a maiden voyage, but the extra speed would enable the ship to make up time for the later turn and arrive in New York on Tuesday evening rather than Wednesday morning. Contrary to many reports *Titanic* was not going for a record – she didn't have the engine capacity and could never attain the Blue Ribband. It was also common practice in this period that if a ship was facing some risk such as bad weather, the ship was to put on speed to get out of the area as quickly as possible and put the danger behind them; a practice that was acceptable so long as conditions were clear – and conditions were perfectly clear.

When evening came and passengers began to take their seats for dinner, *Titanic* was sailing in a perfectly flat, calm ocean with a crystal-clear sky and stars shining brightly. The sea was so calm that it acted like a mirror reflecting the night sky; from a distance it would have looked as if *Titanic* was flying through space. At 7 p.m. on the bridge, First Officer William Murdoch had relieved Second Officer Charles Lightoller so that he could have dinner. A quarter of an hour later Samuel Hemming reported to Murdoch that the lights had been set for the evening. Murdoch ordered him to close the forward scuttle hatch to prevent a glow of light that might affect the lookouts' ability to see ice. Lightoller returned from dinner at 7.30 p.m. and continued his watch.

The passengers were enjoying their dinners too. In first class the orchestra played while passengers selected from a lavish menu on which the White Star Line prided itself.

William Hipkins took his seat, more than likely in a quieter part of the restaurant. Since the death of his wife Lavinia two years previously, he had lost any desire for large social gatherings – not that he was ever confident in the company of lots of people. Tyrell and Julia Cavendish were different, not only enjoying such gatherings but seeing them as a necessity. Tyrell, the budding MP, had to be adept at meeting all kinds of people and his wife had been schooled in such matters in Dresden. They fitted in well to the social graces and intrigues of first-class passenger travel.

In second class, Kate and Henry 'Marshall' dined without a care in the world – for them the voyage was the interval between an old life and a new one. Still a teenage girl, Kate was beginning to get a taste for the better things in life, a far cry from Waterworks Road in Worcester. Second-class dining on *Titanic* was as good as in many first-class restaurants on other ships. The first course was consommé tapioca, with a choice for second course of baked haddock in sharp sauce, curried chicken and rice, spring lamb with mint sauce, or roast turkey with cranberry sauce – all came with a choice of vegetables. The third course was a mouth-watering choice of plum pudding, wine jelly, coconut sandwich, American ice cream, assorted nuts, or fresh fruit, followed by cheese, biscuits and coffee.

Mathilde Weisz had had a very enjoyable voyage joining in with impromptu musical activities, and as she sat down with her husband for dinner she may have wondered what more excitement was to come before they reached New York. By contrast, Florence Angle had rested throughout the voyage; with her health problems she welcomed the opportunity for a week's rest – as the weather had got colder she had avoided walking the deck in the evenings. Stanley Fox was also using the trip for a break after a hectic period travelling through Europe and the comfort of the restaurant on a cold night, knowing he had no business meeting on Monday, enabled him to relax.

Down in third class the mood was also upbeat. The meals served were of a high standard, with three courses available, although the choice more limited: first course was rice soup with fresh bread and cabin biscuits; second course consisted of roast beef, brown gravy, sweet corn, boiled potatoes; third course was plum pudding with sweet sauce and fruit. In addition, a tea was served of cold meat, cheese, pickles, fresh bread and butter, stewed fig and rice. To

R.M.S. "TITANIC"

APRIL 14. 1912.

DINNER

HORS D'ŒUVRE VARIES
OYSTERS

CONSOMME OLGA
CREAM OF BARLEY

SALMON, MOUSSELINE, CUCUMBER

FILET MIGNONS LILI
SAUTE' OF CHICKEN, LYONNAISE
VEGETABLE MARROW FARCIE

LAMB, MINT SAUCE
ROAST DUCKLING, APPLE SAUCE
SIRLOIN OF BEEF, CHATEAU POTATOES

GREEN PEAS - - CREAMED CARROTS
BOILED RICE
PARMENTIER & BOILED NEW POTATOES

PUNCH ROMAINE

ROAST SQUAB & CRESS
COLD ASPARAGUS VINAIGRETTE
PATE DE FOIE GRAS
CELERY

WALDORF PUDDING.
PEACHES IN CHARTREUBE JELLY
CHOCOLATE & VANILLA ECLAIRS
FRENCH ICE CREAM

Iced draught Munich Lager Beer 3d. & 6d. a Tankard.

First-class menu, 14 April 1912. (Author's collection)

add to the quality of third class, a supper of gruel, cabin biscuits and cheese was available. The quality of food for emigrant passengers was important, so as to meet international regulations, and the Davies brothers would not be complaining. Alfred, John and Joseph with their uncle, James Lester, must have enjoyed the music of the Irish players and the dancing in the public rooms. No doubt they took their turn on the poop deck, maybe even taking a look at the starry night sky on that Sunday night. Perhaps they had met William Allen and chatted, both parties having come from the Midlands. Alas, we will never know.

Captain Smith had been enjoying dinner with the Widener family: George Eleanor and Harry had thrown a small party in his honour. After an enjoyable evening, Smith left the dining room and went to the bridge, arriving just before 9 p.m. He discussed with Lightoller the conditions, making a note that the sea was calm, it was very cold, there was a clear sky and that they expected to be able to see any ice at a reasonable distance. Smith told Lightoller that if there was any haze they would have to slow down, but if there was any doubt the officer of the watch should contact him. After briefly stopping in the chart room Smith went to his cabin. Lightoller ordered the lookouts in the crow's nest to be instructed that they were to make a special watch for small ice and growlers. It would be a routine night: cold, dark, quiet.

At 10 p.m. there was a change of watch. First Officer Murdoch went onto the bridge to relieve Lightoller and Robert Hitchens took over in the wheelhouse. The lookouts changed watch too, with Frederick Fleet and Reginald Lee taking their places in the crow's nest, receiving instructions about ice in the process. Lightoller and Murdoch exchanged information and once Murdoch's eyes adjusted to the darkness Lightoller left the bridge.

In first class the diners had more or less left the restaurant. The men had retired to the smoking room and were spending a pleasant time enjoying cigars and brandy. William Hipkins had returned to his room; as was usual in an evening, he would read for a while, perhaps even write a poem – a pastime that helped him to relax. His order of hot chocolate arrived, the steward politely knocking at his door. In second class, Mathilde Weisz had joined in with an impromptu musical session with fellow passengers Dr Alfred Pain playing the flute and Douglas Norman on the piano. She performed the 'Last Rose of Summer' to great success. The last verse trailed off around 11.05 p.m.:

So soon may I follow,
When friendships decay,
And from Love's shining circle
The gems drop away.
When true hearts lie withered,
And fond ones are flown,
Oh! who would inhabit
This bleak world alone?

She was then joined by her husband and they walked the deck. They shivered slightly in the cold air and looked at the countless stars above their heads, shining so brightly that one might imagine reaching out and touching one. A beautiful night on a beautiful ship, yet Mathilde told her husband that she felt uneasy for no apparent reason and she went to the library. Leopold walked the deck for a while and when they met up again he was shivering and said to Mathilde, 'I guess we're in the ice.' They headed to their cabin.

In the crow's nest, Lee and Fleet were cold too. It was 11.39 p.m. but they still had a couple of hours of their watch left. They stared ahead and suddenly they saw it, a black mass that seemed darker than the surrounding darkness – it was an iceberg. Fleet rang the bell three times and picked up the telephone linking the crow's nest to the bridge. Sixth Officer Moody answered the phone, 'What did you see?' he asked calmly.

'Iceberg right ahead!' shouted Fleet down the phone.

'Thank you,' came the reply. Moody then turned to Murdoch who was already starting to react, having heard the bell.

'Hard-a-starboard!' he shouted and then dived onto the ship's telegraph to order the engine room to stop engines and then reverse both. Murdoch was attempting to steer the ship around the iceberg, but was he too close?

Leopold and Mathilde had just gone to bed when they felt a tremor. They looked at each other; Mathilde wanted to get up to find out what had happened but Leopold told her not to go, telling her she was mad to think about going upstairs. In cabin C39 William Hipkins was reading when he felt a vibration. He looked up at the small cabinet on top of which was a silver-framed picture of his late wife; if he was able to look out of his porthole he may well have seen a white mass pass by. As nothing else happened, William went back to his book. Leopold and Mathilde remained in bed but Mathilde was getting nervous; whatever the tremor was it didn't seem to be important, but it aroused the curiosity of many passengers.

Captain Smith had heard the bell and felt the vibration and his experience told him they had hit something, he ran on to the bridge to ask Murdoch what they had struck.

'An iceberg, sir. I put her hard-a-starboard and run the engines full astern, but it was too close,' replied his first officer.

Smith checked that the watertight doors had been closed and that the warning bell had been rung, which they had. The firemen and trimmers were all too aware of this as the watertight doors began to close and some men heard the jarring of the hull plates as the iceberg had grazed by. Boiler rooms 5 and 6 were flooding, much to the consternation of the men there. Coal in the bunkers had spilled over with the force of the collision and the trimmers were surveying the mess. With the night crew adjusting to the situation, crewmen who were asleep in their beds were woken either by the collision or by the noisy commotion of people moving about.

Samuel Hemming had been in bed; the collision disturbed him and he got up, got dressed and went to find out what was happening. He looked out of a porthole but saw nothing. He then heard a loud hissing sound and went to investigate. Coming across storekeeper Frank Prentice they both went to find the source of the noise. Having found no flooding in a storeroom they continued their search at the forecastle head just forward of the anchor crane. It was here they found air hissing with great force out of a vent pipe, which meant that the peak tank – the compartment farthest forward – was flooding rapidly. Chief Officer Henry Wilde, accompanied by Boatswain's Mate Albert Haines, carried out their own investigation. Wilde asked Hemming what the hissing was and Hemming told him that the forepeak was flooding. Wilde left them, at which point both Hemming and Prentice with nothing to do went back to their bunks. Technically speaking, as they were off duty, anything that was happening was none of their business until they were called.

John Hutchinson burst into Hemming's room and said, 'If I were you, I would turn out you fellows, she is making water, one two three, and the racquet court is getting filled up.'

No sooner had the carpenter left the room than the boatswain turned up, 'Turn out you fellows, you haven't half an hour to live. That is from Mr Andrews. Keep it to yourselves and let no one know.'

Hemming jumped up and got dressed and headed for the boat deck. His boat station was number 16, but he went to the foremost boat on the port side where Second Officer Lightoller was preparing boats to be launched.

The off-duty firemen were up and about. Being located at the bow they had felt the collision and soon found that water was entering the ship. Many gathered their belongings and left their cabins, with trimmers Brewer and Wood and firemen Golder and Thomas among them.

The contrast between the lower decks of the bow and the rest of the ship was startling. Throughout the ship passengers were wondering what had happened. Those on duty on the upper decks knew little of what was happening below. Stewards found themselves bombarded by questions from passengers and without any firm information they simply told passengers to go back to bed and not to worry. Handsworth-born steward William Ward lay on his bunk awaiting any orders. He had felt the collision and assumed that one of *Titanic*'s propellers had been lost. He heard the running about of people but only knew that an iceberg had been involved when two or three people called upon him excitedly telling him about the iceberg – one even showed him pieces of ice gathered from the deck. He heard the commotion of third-class passengers racing down the corridor from the bow, carrying life jackets and suitcases with them. He took a look at them and noticed some were wet, yet he returned to his bunk.

Meanwhile on the bridge Captain Smith had ordered 'all stop' and asked the ship's carpenter to sound the ship. Other officers, such as Chief Officer Wilde and Fourth Officer Joseph Boxhall, had already discovered that the ship was taking water and went to report to him. Boxhall pointed out that the mail room was flooding and Smith could see the ship's commutator indicating that the ship was listing; he left the bridge to carry out his own inspection. As he went through the ship he could see people running about. In the boiler rooms firemen were drawing the fires to reduce pressure and prevent an explosion, as the pressure had been building up since the 'all stop' command.

The release valves sent towering jets of steam out of pipes attached to the funnels and the accompanying noise was deafening. Meanwhile, officers and crew started to prepare the lifeboats for launching in case they were needed. Smith came across the ship's designer, Thomas Andrews, who was also inspecting the ship; the two of them discussed the situation for a while and then separated. As Smith headed back to the bridge he was seen by a number of first-class passengers and the expression on his face told them that whatever had happened was serious. On arrival at the bridge, Smith ordered the call to all hands and the mustering of the passengers; he still had no firm information on the amount of damage.

The off-duty stewards were now being called to duty. Many of them had lifeboat stations which they needed to get to, others started knocking on cabin doors to rouse the passengers. Many passengers were already roused – the noise of the steam escaping and the chasing around of officers and crew had stirred them. At first the stewards had ordered passengers back to bed, but now they were asking them to return to their cabins, put on warm clothes and a life jacket and return to the deck.

William Hipkins waited, perhaps a little irritated that so many passengers would trouble themselves to wander about the ship so late. Then came the polite knock on his door followed by a steward asking him to put on warm clothes and a life jacket. William knew then that something was wrong.

Tyrell Cavendish was already up and about; like so many first-class gentlemen he was curious as to what had been happening. He returned to his room to fetch his wife. In second-class the Marshalls received a similar call. For one reason or another they were delayed in getting ready; perhaps Henry didn't believe that the ship was in any real danger.

Florence Angle wrapped herself up well and along with her husband headed for the boat deck.

Mathilde Weisz had not settled even though her husband had said nothing was wrong. She heard people running about and became frightened, urging her husband to get up, but he stayed in bed. Mathilde couldn't hold herself back so she got out of bed, put her overcoat on over her nightdress and ran upstairs to see what was happening.

She asked a steward about all the commotion but he simply replied, 'I'll be very glad if they'll turn the hands of the clock round so I can go off duty. Nothing has happened.'

She ran downstairs again and back into her cabin. Leopold was still in bed. She begged him to get up but he wouldn't. Suddenly they heard a steward shout, 'All hands on deck!' Leopold finally got up and dressed, putting on his overcoat weighed down heavy with their life savings in the lining. He turned to Mathilde and said, 'Don't worry, they always do this at sea.' Once he was dressed they headed upstairs.

There was the most confusion in third class. Passengers located on the bow were already heading aft with their belongings, the Davies brothers amongst them. Third-class stewards were trying to get order, calling on passengers to put on life jackets and assemble in the public rooms. Some stewards thought they would be given an additional order to escort the third-class passengers to the boat deck, but not all of the stewards thought this as some third-class passengers were taken to the boat deck reasonably quickly.

Saloon Steward William Ward, who had stayed in his bunk, was now up and ready for duty. On reaching D Deck, he came across Steward George Dodd, who was gathering a group of stewards together to see if anyone was in the saloon area and, if so, he directed them to the boat deck to gather as many lifejeckets as possible and take them to the cloakroom. Ward headed to the boat deck helping passengers into their life jackets before reporting to lifeboat 7 on the starboard side. The other Midland stewards, Arthur Derrett, James Dinenage and William Kingscote, were all directing passengers to the lifeboats. Stewardess Kate Smith was assisting women with children, helping to put on their life jackets, much to their reluctance.

John Wesley Woodward and the rest of the orchestra found themselves in an interesting position: they were not crew, neither were they strictly passengers, and therefore they had no boat station. Their leader, Wallace Hartley, led them to the boat deck to cheer things up. Their playing was met with polite applause and the atmosphere became calmer. At about 12.25 a.m., Captain Smith discussed the situation with Thomas Andrews, who informed him that with the five forward, watertight compartments filling, *Titanic* would eventually sink. If only four had been open to the sea the ship could have stayed afloat, but with the bulkheads only going as high as E Deck the weight of water would pull the ship down by the head, and then spill along the corridor and pour down into the sixth compartment, then the seventh, and so on. One can only imagine what Captain Smith must have felt; he asked how long the ship had left and Andrews replied, 'An hour perhaps an hour and a half.' Smith ordered the loading of the lifeboats and headed to the radio room. He ordered Jack Phillips to send the regulation distress signal 'CQD MGY' – 'CQ' for attention all stations, 'D' for danger and 'MGY' was *Titanic*'s call sign.

First Officer Murdoch was sorting out boat 7 and calling for women and children. William Ward, now at his boat station, assisted in the loading but there were problems convincing passengers to get into the boat, most thinking the whole exercise a bit of a joke. The ship was well-lit, the heaters were on inside and to the casual eye the ship did not seem to be in any immediate danger. With the order to fill the boats there was added urgency as stewards and stewardesses more assertively roused passengers and grabbed additional life jackets and blankets. First- and second-class passengers, who had more or less ignored the original calls to go to the boat deck, now found stewards banging hard on their cabin doors to get them out. Tyrell Cavendish put his overcoat on his wife, she added a wrap and they headed to the lifeboats. The Marshalls now finally made their move. Kate put a coat on over her nightdress as Henry led her up to the stairs. Like so many others, Henry probably still thought that nothing was seriously wrong and that the evacuation was a matter of form, for even though he had a large sum of money in the cabin he didn't take any of it with him. On C Deck, William Hipkins saw the mayhem as ladies were queuing to get their jewellery from the purser's office. He would have been irritated to see such behaviour; he walked past the crowd and up the stairs.

Down in the boiler rooms, trimmers, firemen and a mix of others ran pumps to try and keep ahead of the flooding; they were just buying time. When the order came through to man boat stations the men began to leave. It was just in time, as the bulkhead between boiler rooms 5 and 6 gave way.

It was 12.40 a.m.; William Ward watched as boat 7 was lowered into the smooth sea. The first boat launched carried twenty-eight people; it could have held sixty-five. Technically, William should have been on board the lifeboat, but he moved down to assist with boat 9. The deck was full of people dressed in a variety of clothes from evening dress to nightdresses and overcoats, many still seeing the lifeboat activities as something of a night out. Captain Smith looked in on the radio operators and asked them what ships they had. Jack Phillips replied that they had *Carpathia* only 58 miles away, *Frankfort* 150 miles and *Olympic* 500 miles away. Smith checked what signal they were sending. Phillips replied, 'CQD.' His colleague Harold Bride then suggested sending the new signal 'SOS', adding that it might be the last chance they would have. Phillips laughed and changed the call.

Smith returned to the bridge and ordered Quartermaster George Rowe to fire distress rockets, one every five or six minutes. This was in response to Fourth Officer Boxhall's possible sighting of the mast light of a steamer through his binoculars. The flash and rapport of the rockets should have impressed upon the passengers the seriousness of the situation, but officers still had trouble getting people into lifeboats.

The band continued to play – John Wesley Woodward standing with his colleagues. William Hipkins was probably standing on deck watching the events. Stewards Dinenage, Derrett et al. were trying to coax women and children into lifeboats. Chief Officer Wilde joined Second Officer Lightoller on the port side and asked him if he knew where the firearms were kept.

Lightoller, having originally joined the ship as first officer, had stored the revolvers supplied by Webley in the first officer's cabin. The revolvers were distributed along with ammunition to those in charge of loading the lifeboats.

Boats 7, 5, 3 and 8 had been launched, next was boat 6 on the port side. Florence Cavendish was near this boat as her husband led her forward. She looked at him and he kissed her, followed by a long look into each other's eyes. Florence would have known at that moment that things were serious; another kiss and Tyrell disappeared into a crowd of men. Florence entered the boat. Lightoller ordered Samuel Hemming, who had been assisting in its preparation, into the boat. Along with him were Quartermaster Robert Hitchens, who had been at the wheel when *Titanic* had struck the iceberg, and Lookout Frederick Fleet, the first man to see the iceberg. Lightoller prepared to lower away; however, due to a shortage of men no one was on the aft davit. Realising this, Lightoller called out for a seaman on the after-fall. Hemming was aware that there was no one available so he called out, 'Aye aye, Sir,' and got out of the boat and manned the davit. The boat was lowered away at 1.10 a.m. Hemming was then ordered by Captain Smith to ensure that the lifeboats were fitted with lights, so Hemming left the boat deck and started to light lamps and distribute them to the boats.

Meanwhile, on the starboard side, William Ward continued to assist in the loading of boat 9, with a large number of women and children being helped in by stewards. The loading was quite slow and more men were needed to assist; these men included Managing Director Bruce Ismay. Ismay had had a strange evening; Fifth Officer Harold Lowe had admonished him for interfering with the launching of boat 5, so he was now assisting quietly. Ward and other stewards loaded boat 9 with great efficiency and in a variety of ways, with one passenger being swung in by her arms from the deck. The step down from the deck to the boat was quite large and Ward assisted Madeleine Aubert (Benjamin Guggenheim's mistress), who had fallen and hurt herself getting in. The boat was lowered away at 1.30 a.m., with Ward aboard as one of the crewmen.

Fifth Officer Lowe was having problems with boat 14, when a group of men rushed the boat. Lowe took out his Webley waved it in the air and shouted, 'If anyone else tries that, this is what he'll get!' He then fired it three times down the side of the ship.

Five minutes later it was Florence Angle's turn to leave the ship; her husband led her forward to boat 11, which was being loaded through the open windows on A Deck. It was thought by some that loading boats from this deck might be easier. Stewardess Kate Smith was also admitted to boat 11, which was overloaded, carrying at least seventy people with some standing. Florence witnessed the efforts to free the boat from the falls when the after-tackle jammed and the near swamping of the boat by water from a pump discharge outlet.

Leopold and Mathilde Weisz had been on deck watching as boats were being loaded. Some women refused to get into boats without their husbands, but, although Leopold had thought there was no danger, he noticed the slant of the deck as the bow of the ship began to get lower. Lightoller was loading boat 10 on the port side and calling for women. Mathilde had hung back staying with her husband. The band was still playing cheerful ragtime tunes, but now people were beginning to realise that something was seriously wrong as crewmen became more vigorous in getting women into the boats. Mathilde was frightened and slightly tearful, but Leopold turned to her and said, 'Don't upset yourself, there is no danger.' Lightoller saw them and took her arm, leading her to the boat; she broke away and returned to her beloved husband and kissed him. Leopold kissed her tenderly and told her to be brave and stay calm, adding that he would be all right. Mathilde then turned and got into the boat. It was lowered away at 1.50 a.m.

Kate Phillips and Henry Morley had waited with all the other passengers and no doubt witnessed some incredible scenes, although nothing is known for certain of their whereabouts or which boat Kate entered. All that can be said is that Henry watched as his young lover was taken by a crewman and placed into a boat. He saw the boat being lowered and then stepped into a group of men and was gone. Kate was in the boat with nothing but a nightdress, shoes and topcoat. In third class some passengers and stewards were awaiting orders that would not come; many passengers would discriminate against themselves, believing that they had to wait until their betters went first. Whether the Davies brothers and their uncle ever made an attempt to get to the upper decks we will never know.

On the bridge, Captain Smith had been watching the evacuation, monitoring the ever-increasing list to the bow. He called in on the Marconi operators and informed them that they would not have power much longer: *Titanic* had not much time left. Harold Bride sent a message to *Baltic*, transmitting that the engine room was flooded. By now the forward well deck was awash and efforts were being made to prepare collapsible boat C for loading. First Officer Murdoch called for more women for the boat and ordered crewmen to board including butcher Christopher Mills. Captain

Smith released Quartermaster George Rowe and he also got into the boat. As the boat was ready to go, Bruce Ismay and a male passenger jumped in and were lowered to safety.

It was 2 a.m. when Captain Smith returned to the Marconi room and released the operators, telling them, 'You have done your best and you can do no more, you had better take care of yourselves.' Smith then returned to the bridge.

On top of the bridge, either side of the forward funnel, were the two remaining collapsible lifeboats, A and B, and Lightoller called out for some hands to help get them off the roof. The call was answered by a number of men including two Marconi operators, Harold Bride and Samuel Hemming. Lightoller was surprised to see Hemming as he thought he had gone off in boat 6 and asked why he hadn't gone. Hemming replied, 'Oh, plenty of time yet sir.' Hemming had been helping Lightoller all night. The spirit and enterprise of Hemming had helped launch at least four lifeboats and he had sorted the lamps for even more, but now he was involved in probably the hardest task – getting the two collapsible boats off the roof.

On the ever-sloping deck, passengers and crew were milling about, not sure where to go; many were heading to the stern, keeping away from the water engulfing the bow. John Wesley Woodward and the orchestra stood on the boat deck – they had been playing all night and now there was time for just one more piece. Legend says it was 'Nearer My God To Thee', although in reality no one is exactly sure what was played at the end. All that is certain is that they *did* play, and to the very end. Tyrell Cavendish had been busy since he placed his wife into a lifeboat, assisting with other boats and helping women and children into them. Now he stood on the deck with a few men. One known to him reportedly said, 'Well chum, don't you think it is time for us to get busy?'

'Well, there are no more boats to fill, so we will shake hands and hope that we will meet again soon,' replied Tyrell. At which point he and the nameless man leapt into the sea.

From the lifeboats that had been launched people watched *Titanic* with fascination and horror. The strains of the orchestra could be heard across the water along with screams and shouts. The stern was slowly rising, yet all the lights blazed away, as the electrical engineers had stayed at their posts. Leonard Hodgkinson, like the rest of the engineers, remained, overseeing the firemen and trimmers, ensuring that the pumps remained working and that the lights stayed on.

Lightoller and the crew managed to free one of the collapsible lifeboats from the top of the bridge, but it fell on the deck upturned so they concentrated on the other one. Samuel Hemming struggled with the others to get it free; the bow of the ship began to dip lower. Captain Smith entered the bridge for the last time. Some say that he picked up a megaphone and called, 'Abandon ship!' before entering the bridge, but nothing is certain except that soon after he entered the bridge it was engulfed and *Titanic* began her death throes. As the bridge went under, the men trying to free the remaining collapsible boat found the ship disappear from beneath them. Lightoller found himself pressed against a ventilator before a rush of air from deep inside the ship threw him clear. Hemming dropped down a set of falls and swam towards boat 4, grabbing hold of one of the boat's lifelines. He pulled himself up above the gunwale and saw his friend Jack Foley standing in the boat. He called to him to give him a hand and Hemming was taken on board.

Titanic's lights flickered out and the hull began to split with the stern section falling back slightly before rising once more to be almost perfectly vertical. After hanging there for what seemed an age the stern began to sink, with many people still hanging on at the poop deck. Then she was gone. The largest, most luxurious ocean liner in the world had sunk; it was 2.20 a.m. For those in the lifeboats it was not yet over. Surrounded by the majesty of the heavens and a pitch darkness that was so tangible one could touch it, taste it, they were faced with the cries from the water as people struggled to survive in the freezing-cold temperatures. Mathilde Weisz called out for her husband in the hope that he was nearby. Arguments broke out in the lifeboats about whether or not they should go back and rescue people. Many felt the boats would be swamped if they went back, leading to the loss of everyone. As it turned out, only one boat went back into the mass of bodies after *Titanic* had foundered. Fifth Officer Lowe searched for survivors, but only found four still alive after about an hour. The cold had taken its toll.

A cold, eerie silence fell among the lifeboats as the survivors shivered under the stars. A little after 4 a.m., the Cunard ship *Carpathia* was nearing the scene after racing beyond its normal top speed in answer to *Titanic's* distress calls. Captain Arthur Rostron would spend the next six hours picking up each and every lifeboat, taking on board 705 survivors – a figure which indicated that over 1,500 had perished. Mathilde searched *Carpathia* looking for her husband and when she couldn't find him she broke down, calling hysterically for Leopold. She was taken to the ship's hospital, and to calm her down she was told that Leopold could have been picked up by another ship; after two hours she recovered her composure.

Kate Phillips just remained quiet, probably not fully realising what had happened. Like Florence Angle and Julia Cavendish she had lost her man, and like Mathilde Weisz they all hoped their men had been rescued by another vessel.

Carpathia headed for New York and a world that was not prepared for the news.

11

MIDLANDS' REACTION

While *Titanic* was at sea, life continued its normal routine in the Midlands. Family and friends of the Midlands passengers and crew knew they would have to wait at least two weeks before hearing how their loved ones had enjoyed the maiden voyage and how they were enjoying the United States. The local newspapers had reported the exciting start of the voyage, but since then there had been nothing, nor was anything expected. On 13 April, the *Birmingham Weekly Mercury* ran the headline that the national coal strike had come to an end; there was a report on the continuing saga of Birmingham's trams and the *Birmingham Gazette* reported the death of John Ernest Berry, the secretary of the Birmingham Trades Council, in a motor accident.

The coming week was expected to be of particular excitement, as on the 17th there would be an eclipse of the sun, part of which would be visible in the Midlands. Astronomers at the University of Birmingham were advising on how to prepare smoked glass to observe the phenomenon, and many companies, institutions and schools were preparing for the event. For those not interested in the eclipse, Birmingham theatres were providing plenty of entertainment. At the Prince of Wales Theatre, the famous comedian Weedon Grossmith was starring with Stanford Hilliard, Spencer Geach, Amy Willard and others in the farce *Baby Mine*. The Theatre Royal was hosting *The Dollar Princess* starry Deborah Volar, while the Hippodrome was host to Betty Barclay. The *Weekly Mercury* advised Midlanders to book early at the Grand Theatre (Birmingham) to see *The Eternal Waltz* starring Christine Roy, the most successful operetta ever produced. All in all, it was just another working week.

The first news that something had happened to *Titanic* flashed across the American press on 15 April and, due to the five hours' time difference between New York and London, the British press picked up the story for morning editions on the 16th. The Associated Press sent out a notice that at 10.25 a.m., New York time, *Titanic* had called CQD after striking an iceberg. Initial reports suggested that women and children were taking to the boats and the great ship was down by the head, but there was no statement that *Titanic* had sunk. The *Denver Post* reported:

2,000 LIVES ARE SAVED OFF WRECKED *TITANIC*, BY WIRELESS: VESSEL IS REPORTED SINKING.

The *Evening Sun* in New York reported:

ALL SAVED FROM *TITANIC* AFTER COLLISION.

London newspapers started to get the same reports, and due to the time difference the morning editions of Tuesday 16 April reported that *Titanic* had collided with an iceberg, but all were safe. The *Daily Mirror* reported 'Everyone Safe' and that *Titanic* was being towed to Halifax (Nova Scotia). Yet in New York, something was not quite right; the White Star Line's New York offices were being inundated with enquiries from relatives of passengers. White Star vice president, Philip Franklin, issued the fateful statement of, 'We believe that the boat is unsinkable.' Yet the general silence from White Star as to details of the accident was causing concern. The managing editor of the *New York Times*, Carr Van Anda, joined the dots of the various statements and decided that *Titanic* had in fact sunk, probably with a great loss of life.

In Birmingham family and friends of passengers were concerned when they read the *Daily Mirror* on Tuesday morning. In the Black Country, the *Express and Star* also used the initial reports, stating that the passengers were safe, which gave some relief to the Davies family in West Bromwich. The *Birmingham Daily Mail* was essentially a copy of the London news with a few local stories added, and thus followed the line taken by the London Press. The *Birmingham Gazette and Express* was, however, telling a different tale by stating that *Titanic* had in fact sunk, contradicting all other newspapers:

APPALLING DISASTER AT SEA
TITANIC SUNK AFTER COLLISION WITH ICEBERG
VAST LOST OF LIFE

The *Gazette* had an advantage over the other newspapers; they received information of telegraph messages from a radio ham in the Black Country. This unknown amateur radio enthusiast had constantly supplied information to the *Gazette* for some months and had been receiving the station-to-station messages from the various ships that had received *Titanic*'s CQD. The *Gazette* also went to press a little later than the London editions, as the proprietors insisted on waiting for the 2 a.m. telegrams from the Associated Press and Reuters before printing an edition. This meant that the *Gazette* was several hours ahead of news, and with the time difference with New York, it enabled the *Gazette* to have the scoop of the century. The *Gazette*, along with the *New York Times*, was the first to tell the world that *Titanic* had sunk with great loss of life.

Immediately, families and friends started to call in at the *Gazette*, visit the shipping agents and send telegrams to New York in a desperate attempt to get some firm information. Houlder Brothers in Navigation Street, Birmingham, found themselves swamped by enquiries and competing journalists trying to get a look at their copy receipts naming local passengers. Once again the *Gazette* had been the quickest off the mark, and while reporters from the *Express and Star* and the *Birmingham Daily Mail* tried to convince the shipping clerk to provide them with the list of names, a *Gazette* reporter had already copied the list:

MIDLAND PASSENGERS
FOUR MEMBERS OF WEST BROMWICH FAMILLY MISSING

The following telegram has been received at the Birmingham office of Houlder Bros. and Co. Ltd:-

Mathilde Weisz on board *Carpathia*. Many more names still to come in, but not expected until late to-day. Ismay.

Messrs. Houlder Bros. and Co. Ltd. issued two bookings in March to Mr. and Mrs. Weisz of Bromsgrove and the above telegram shows that Mrs. Weisz is safe. Nothing however, has been heard of Mr. Weisz.

Other passengers hailing from the Midlands and of whom no news has been received are:

Mr. W.E. Hipkins managing director of Averys Ltd, Birmingham.

Mr. William Allen a fitter who lived with uncle and aunt at Queen's Road Erdington.

Mr. Fox an American who had been on a visit to Birmingham.

Alfred Davies (24) of Harwood Street West Bromwich.

John Davies (23) of the same address.

Joseph Davies (17) of the same address.

James Lester (39) of the same address.

The three Davies' were brothers and all lived at home with their parents.

The Board of Directors at W&T Avery wanted clarification of what had happened to William Hipkins, with Walter Chamberlain and Arthur Gibson both trying to ascertain the truth; initially, they had received assurances from White Star that the ship and its passengers were safe. Charles Beakbane, president of the Avery Scale Company in Milwaukee, made enquiries of his own. William's sister, Bertha, was aware of the story and on hearing the reports that everyone was safe simply thought how William would have enjoyed the drama. Within a few hours after the first reports, however, the optimistic remarks from White Star officials had turned to expressions of regret. In an age when communication over long distances was by Morse telegraph, accurate information was often difficult to come by. A special board meeting was convened at Averys with Walter Chamberlain, Arthur Gibson and Alfred Lloyd. The meeting was short and no official mention of William and the disaster appears in the minutes, but it is clear why it had been called. In the event that William had died, the company would have to move fast to ensure all ran smoothly.

When William's life long friend, James Bevan, heard the news he physically shook. Apart from William, his friend Henry Forbes Julian was also a first-class passenger who lost his life. James knew he would have to go to Birmingham to be with Bertha. Bertha herself was notified by Arthur Gibson, who called upon her. Bertha collapsed on hearing the news, and although Gibson did say that William could be one of the survivors, there was a sense that he was not.

Thousands of miles away in the North Atlantic, the Cunard liner *Carpathia* was steaming to New York with the 705 survivors from *Titanic*. William was not among them but the world had to wait for the news, and until such a time there was speculation. The *Milwaukee Sentinel* of 16 April carried reports of Milwaukeeans on board the ship and mentioned William:

Grave apprehension is feared for the safety of W.A. [*sic*] Hipkins of Birmingham, England, and a member of the Board of Directors of the Avery Scale Company of Milwaukee, of which C.F. Beakbane, 594 Farewell Avenue is president. Mr. Beakbane received word from Mr. Hipkins stating that he was about to sail on the *Titanic*. Mr. Beakbane fears that he may have perished with the hundreds who went down with the boat.

Charles Beakbane in the United States and Walter Chamberlain in the UK awaited news from White Star. The news, when it came, was bad, although hope was offered in that the officials had yet to receive a complete list of survivors. The *Birmingham Daily Mail* published a list of survivors. Chamberlain and Gibson scanned it; there was no listing for William. The report added that Benjamin Guggenheim, John Jacob Astor, Major Butt and Isador Strauss had also survived, but this information was incorrect. There were also reports that other survivors may have been picked up by other ships, which serve to highlight the level of misinformation around soon after the disaster. Beakbane remained in constant communication with White Star Line offices in New York and Philip Franklin cabled Beakbane to give him the news he had been dreading, but half expecting:

> Regret to inform you that the SS *Titanic* foundered on April 15th at 2.20am. From the list we have received from the SS *Carpathia*, Mr. W.E. Hipkins' name is not among the survivors.

Beakbane sent a cable to Chamberlain and the news was official. Arthur Gibson took the bad news to Bertha at her home in Augustus Road, Edgbaston, where she was being consoled by James Bevan and her servants.

The loss of *Titanic* was the subject on everybody's lips. The shock that hit the UK had never been previously experienced and there was a sense of disbelief. The shock was bad enough for members of Averys' workforce, but it reached a new level on Wednesday 17 April when the various departments at Soho Foundry were called together for a special announcement. At the same time across the country at the various branches, workers were called to hear a special announcement from the Avery Board of Directors. At Digbeth in Birmingham and in Belfast, Cardiff, Leeds, Liverpool, Glasgow, Sheffield, Newcastle, Nottingham, London and Manchester, workers and staff gathered together to hear the branch managers read the four-line announcement. At Digbeth, Francis MacKenzie looked as white as his freshly starched shirt collar – William had been good to him and he was visibly shaken by the news. In the engineering department at Soho Foundry it was the general manager,

Richard Gibbs, who delivered the message; even the tough Gibbs found it hard to articulate. In the offices the company secretary, Alfred Lloyd, gave the news. In the foundry, the foundry manager read the announcement to the gathering of men in leather gowns. All across the Avery empire at 10 p.m. the message was read:

> It is with great sadness that I have to announce the death of our Managing Director Mr. W.E. Hipkins, who lost his life in the tragic loss of the SS *Titanic* last Monday. On behalf of you all the firm will pass on our condolences to Mr. Hipkins' family. We will be taking a collection which will be presented to the Titanic Relief Fund for the families of those lost in this tragedy.
> Walter Chamberlain.

There was a stunned silence for a few seconds, as if nobody knew what to do. One of the foundrymen spat on to the ground and said, 'Right lads back to work.' Most of the staff and workers were shocked and saddened but there were some, many of the older hands who had resented the change in working practices that William had introduced at Averys, who not only shed no tears but openly commented, 'Good riddance.'

For Bertha, however, it was a tragic loss. She had lost her mother, sister-in-law and brother in just a few years. Arthur Gibson was not only an accountant, he was also a lead writer for the local media and he wrote up a biographical piece about William Hipkins that was printed in the *Gazette* on 19 April.

Julia Cavendish's father, Henry Siegel, in New York was anxious and sent a message to *Carpathia* on 16 April:

> Mrs. Tyrrel V. Cavendish Carpathia.
> Anxious to know if both safe
> your father
> Henry Siegel.

On *Carpathia* Captain Rostron limited the use of the radio for survivors to send messages to their families. Julia Cavendish took the opportunity on 17 April, sending a message to her father with the words, 'Tyrrel not here have you news.' The next day she sent the message, 'Saved not Tyrell yet Julia.' She then sent another message to her father, 'I am saved Julia.' Two hours later she sent yet another message, this time directly to her father's company asking for:

25 coats, 19 trousers medium weight for destitute deliver immediately to pier 54 to Officer C.H. Lightoller. Julia.

Julia Cavendish was thinking of the less fortunate on the ship, a rather incredible gesture given her grief. The press picked up that Tyrell Cavdendish of Little Onn Hall was not on *Carpathia* and reported his loss.

The White Star Line struggled to supply accurate information to the press, but with Morse code there were errors, transmission problems and simple mistakes, which led to a confusing situation. White Star was able to supply the names of crew members who had signed on giving a Midlands link. The Birmingham papers included the names of those from Derby, Oxford, Bristol and Gloucester as midlanders. With the biggest story in the world every link, even the tenuous, was exploited for circulation:

SECOND OFFICER [sic] A COUSIN OF A STOURBRIDGE MAN

Lieutenant William Murdock, R.N.R. the second officer [sic] of the Titanic was a cousin of the rev. Dr. Ewart of Stourbridge. Lieutenant Murdock was only 35 years of age and had a distinguished career. He was transferred to the Titanic from the Olympic along with Commander Smith who was a Staffordshire man.   (*Express and Star* (Wolverhampton) 17 April 1912)

In Stourbridge Walter Barringer was waiting for news of his brother Arthur William who was a storekeeper on *Titanic*. Walter told a reporter in Dudley that his brother had served under Captain Smith a number of times, but this was to be his last voyage as he was planning to retire from the sea to run a hotel in Bournemouth with his wife.

Captain Edward John Smith from Hanley attracted special attention, with details of his career being printed. There were, however, very few facts. *Carpathia* was keeping silent, apart from a few personal messages, and it would not be until the ship reached New York and the survivors disembarked that any details of the disaster would be heard. Thus, the press was eager to get hold of any snippet of information.

The shipping agents Houlder Brothers and Company were a main source in the Midlands, and the agents were constantly in contact with White Star in New York trying to ascertain if their clients had survived, and eager for news. Worcester newspapers published the latest information about the Weisz couple, stating that Mathilde was safe but there was still no news of her husband. On the same page there was a report that the family of Harry Spinner was still awaiting news.

With initial reports suggesting that other ships may have picked up survivors there was always hope for the families of the missing. Newspapers reported daily, offering a glimmer of hope. The press, like the rest of the world, was hungry for information and the only way to obtain it was from the survivors who were on *Carpathia*.

It was late on 18 April when *Carpathia* arrived in New York; the weather was appalling, with driving rain, thunder and lightning, yet this did not stop thousands turning out to see the ship arrive. When she docked and the survivors disembarked then, and only then, did the realisation of what had happened truly hit home. The press were eager to interview the survivors and learn the truth of the disaster, and in the Midlands people waited to see who had actually survived.

In West Bromwich the Davies family sat in their living room at 29 Harwood Street waiting for news. The telegram the Davies' dreaded arrived on 19 April, another 'Regret to inform you' telegram. Richard Davies, his wife Mary and sister-in-law Alice sat grief-stricken. Mary and Alice locked in each other's arms sobbing pitifully. Richard sat staring into the fire, sobbing and talking softly to a reporter from the *West Bromwich Chronicle*.

'It's too much for us to bear; it will about break our home up – all three sons gone! It's awful, it's terrible.' The reporter noted down every word Richard said. 'Better lads no-one could possibly have.' The heart-rending story of the Davies family stole the hearts of the Midlands. Alfred's young wife, a widow after only one week of marriage, seemed to symbolise the fragility of life.

The Worcestershire newspapers found themselves with a developing story that in the twenty-first century would have made the front page, but in a more restrained period it was a story that would require sensitive treatment. On hearing *Titanic* had gone down Arthur Morley knew a major crisis was at hand. He sent a cable to the White Star offices in New York; Henry Marshall was not on the survivors' list, but a Mrs Kate Marshall was. He knew that sooner or later the news of the elopement would emerge so he had to manage the information. At this early stage the press were taking information at face value. The details of Henry and Kate posing as a honeymoon couple were reported in the *Aberdeen Journal* as follows:

Mr. and Mrs. Marshall on a honeymoon trip to California. Mr. Marshall was a partner in a big boot business in Scotland.

This story now put Arthur's friend, Arthur Marshall, in a spot as some of his friends thought *he* was on *Titanic*. Kate Phillips' arrival in New York posed a number of problems for her: she was travelling under an assumed name, claiming to be married and claiming to be of age when she was actually only 19. Added to this she had no money and only the clothes she was wearing when she left the ship. Like all those who arrived in New York she went through the immigration process that was carried out on board *Carpathia*. Once processed she was passed to the New York Women's Relief Committee for the Survivors of the SS *Titanic*, an organisation that had been rapidly formed by fifteen women concerned for the welfare of the survivors en route to New York. The committee co-ordinated with other institutions such as hospitals, homes, department stores, the Red Cross and the American Seaman's Society, to mention but a few. By the time the *Carpathia* docked, the committee had arranged clothing, hospital beds, transport, accommodation and money to those in distress. Each passenger received a medical examination and his or her personal circumstances were assessed. Those that had friends or family in the United States would receive help to go to them, otherwise temporary accommodation would be sought. Kate was assessed; she didn't need medical treatment. She was given some new clothes and placed with a volunteer who would take her to their home until a more permanent solution could be found. Kate's assessment showed she had no money or valuables, so she was made a special case and awarded $200. Cunard and White Star, in co-operation with the Marconi Company allowed survivors to send a cablegram to family. Kate sent one to her father in Worcester stating she had survived.

Apart from Kate, Florence Angle was in a difficult position. Due to her poor health she was taken to hospital suffering from breathing problems; she was treated as a special case and allocated $100 for herself along with some new clothes. She sent a cable to her father in Warwick.

Mathilde Weisz arrived in a daze; she had been near to hysterical on *Carpathia* when she couldn't find her husband, and although now calmer she was still looking for Leopold. There was concern for her well-being and she was taken to St Vincent's Hospital. Mathilde had only the clothes she was wearing when she left the ship; the family savings had been stitched into the lining of her husband's coat and was lost with him. She wanted to continue her journey to Canada where she could meet up with her husband's business partner Edward Wren. The Relief Committee arranged for two payments of $150 and later $600 to cover the cost to transport and bury her husband's body in Canada. Julia Cavendish and her maid, Ellen Barber, were met by Julia's father who arrived by motorcar. Julia made sure that her request for clothes had been met; her father confirmed this and added that extra clothes had been made available and had been distributed to the Relief Committee.

In Worcester the newspapers found more local links:

LOST IN THE *TITANIC*

Mr. Henry J. Spinner, one of the two Worcester men lost on the *Titanic* was a son of George Spinner, of Wolverton road, a glover in the employ of Messrs. Dent. The unfortunate man followed the business of his father, but in the service of Messrs. Fownes Brothers and Co. until twelve years ago, when he joined the Royal Marines. The last that was heard from him was a postcard dispatched from Queenstown and Cherbourg. He left a wife and child in Worcester, with whom much sympathy is manifested. (*Berrow's Journal* 20 April 1912)

TITANIC'S WIRELESS OPERATOR
REDDITCH ASSOCIATIONS

The *Titanic*'s first wireless operator Mr. J. Phillips, the son of Mr. and Mrs. G.A. Phillips of Farncombe, Godalming, Surrey, is a cousin to Mr. F.G. Heaphy of Redditch. Upon enquiry Mr. Heaphy said the following telegram had been received from jack's father: 'Have not heard officially. No hope.' 'Jack' explained Mr. Heaphy is the only son. He has twin sisters, thirteen years his senior. (*Birmingham Evening Dispatch* 22 April 1912)

The news via telegram that Kate Phillips was safe was welcomed by her father and Arthur, but how to break the news of Henry's death to the wider community and to his estranged wife Louisa? The rumour mill had been working overtime. In Waterworks Road there had been gossip about Kate and Henry, and the assistants in the Morley shops had enjoyed the gossip. Although the elopement was common knowledge in a select group, the wider community was unaware, and the absence of Henry was explained by Arthur saying that he had gone to California for health reasons. When Arthur heard that Henry was definitely a casualty and that Kate had survived, the truth would have to come out.

For the press, the *Titanic* disaster was a once-in-a-generation story and competition was fierce between the various publications. The *Birmingham Gazette* had stolen the lead on the other papers with their 16 April edition, but now all papers wanted a local link to *Titanic* and their journalists were sent to find them, no matter how tenuous. In Worcester there were a number of newspapers run by three publishers: Berrow's produced the *Daily Times* and *Berrow's Journal*; Worcestershire Newspapers and General Printing produced the *Chronicle*, *Herald* and *Echo*; and George Williams produced the *Advertiser*. All wanted details of local passengers and crew and all relied on the Associated Press and Reuters for information, which their local journalists would follow up.

A 32-year-old veteran journalist, Harry Ginn, was doing the rounds of the shipping agents, pulling details for the *Worcester Daily Times*. In the same manner Silas A.T. Smith ('Sats' to his friends), the 29-year-old Swansea-born journalist, was doing the same for the *Berrow's Journal*, using a junior reporter, 18-year-old Norman Richard Pegg, for the footwork. Norman was from Newark, New Jersey, USA, and had come to his parents' country to take up journalism. He had got a taste for the profession from seeing the rivalry between New York newspapers, and his aim was to start small in a local newspaper learning the trade. Worcester seemed a suitably small city in which to start; little did he know that he would cut his teeth on the story of the century. Like other reporters he checked the contract ticket list supplied by White Star Line and then visited the shipping agents. Something caught his eye on ticket number 250655 allocated to Mr and Mrs Marshall. Their address had been given as 73 New Street, Birmingham, which he found was, in fact, Morley Brothers Confectionery Shop, and living above the shop was Arthur Morley.

Morley's was well known in Worcester with the shops at Foregate Street, The Cross and The Shambles. Who was Mr Marshall? The Mrs Marshall was a Kate Marshall who had supplied her father's address of 34 Waterworks Road, Worcester, to New York officials. Norman knew someone who lived in Waterworks Road: Arthur Booth, a typeset printer at *Berrow's*. Not only that, he lived next door to number 34; additionally, living at number 42 was Ernest Brook, a clerk in the newspaper office. Norman learned of the gossip on the street that Kate Phillips had run off with her boss Henry Morley, with Henry leaving his wife and young child behind. Silas Smith was presented with a real coup and immediately he and Norman went to Birmingham to speak to Arthur Morley. Arthur stuck to the story that Henry was going to California for his health, and admitted to seeing him off at Southampton. Next Silas and Norman spoke to the shop assistants at the Foregate Street and The Cross shops, including Emma Sheward. Kate's father wouldn't speak to the journalists and neither would Louisa Morley. In 1912 journalists in the UK did not put the same pressure on people as they do in the twenty-first century and respected the privacy of bereaved relatives. Nonetheless, the evidence was there, but how to report it without seeming insensitive? The result was a masterpiece of subtlety:

FORMER RESIDENTS OF WORCESTER DROWNED

It has been rumoured for several days past that Mr. H.S. Morley, who formerly carried on business in Worcester as a confectioner was on board the *Titanic*, and that his name was not among the list of those reported to have been saved. The latest telegrams to hand indicate that he went down with the ship. It is understood that he sailed in the name of Marshall, and that although persons of that name are among the survivors, Mr. Morley is not one of them. It is, however, known that a young Worcester woman, who had booked in the name of Kate Marshall, was saved. The widow, Mrs. Morley is the proprietress of a business in Malvern.

There is now no longer any hope that Mr. H.J. Spinner who was on his way to Gloversville has survived, and much sympathy is felt by his widow, who like Mrs. Morley, is left with one child. (*Berrow's Journal*, 20 April 1912)

The Worcester papers decided against giving the real surname of Kate, but the *Birmingham Evening Despatch* didn't, stating, 'A young woman named Phillips of Sandy's Road Worcester is among the rescued.' Sandy's Road was one of the addresses that Kate and Henry stayed at during the period of their elopement. Residents of Worcester (and Birmingham) were under no illusion as to what had happened. Arthur arranged for all the Morley Brothers' shops to close for one day as a mark of respect.

Louisa was not only embarrassed and humiliated but was also a widow with a young child. She did receive sympathy, unlike the Phillips' in Waterworks Road, who found themselves the target for scorn and condemnation. Their teenage daughter had run-off with a married father. It couldn't get much worse, but it would. Kate was out of the field of fire in New York, and perhaps if she could find work she could still make a life for herself, certainly she had little doubt that Henry, in the event of his death, would have made provision for her.

Provision for the dependants of the dead was on everybody's minds. The Mayor of London set up the Mansion House Fund to raise money for the victims' families. People from across the country donated with local newspapers such as the *Express and Star* (Wolverhampton), *Birmingham*

Gazette and Express, Walsall Observer and *Worcester Daily News* acting as local subscription collectors. Businesses, civic leaders, the scout movement, schools and individuals gave generously. The goods department of the LNWR in Wolverhampton (responsible for transporting *Titanic's* anchors) donated £2 19s.

Saturday 20 April was the last day of the football season; Aston Villa were at home to Newcastle United. The Football Association issued a notice to all clubs:

> The Council recommends that clubs belonging to the The Football Association make collections at their matches in aide of the Lord Mayor of London's Fund, and that the proceeds be sent to The Football Association. The Council consents to matches being played on or before May 4, 1912, the gross proceeds to be contributed to the Lord Mayor of London's Fund, and that the proceeds be sent to The Football Association.

There were remarkable scenes at Villa Park on the last day of the season with a crowd of over 30,000. Prior to kick-off, the Aston Prize Band took up position in the centre of the pitch and played the 'Dead March from Saul' by Handel. Immediately, everyone in the stands rose in their places and there was scarcely a man who did not uncover his head in honour of the *Titanic* dead. At half-time the band once again set up at the centre of the pitch and played 'God Be With You Till We Meet Again', the crowd again rising en masse, and a collection was taken raising £35. Incidentally, Villa won 2–0. West Bromwich Albion had reached the FA Cup Final; playing against Barnsley at the Crystal Palace they drew 0–0. Money was raised at the match for the fund and from the replay, which Albion lost 1–0. Special charity football matches were played, such as Bournville Athletic versus Bournbrook, which raised £4. On Sunday 5 May a Stafford Rangers Old Stars team played a game in pouring rain raising £6.

Bands, orchestras and theatres in the region organised special performances to raise money. On Sunday 21 April, the Birmingham branch of the Salvation Army staged a concert, parading through the centre of the city raising £9 5s. In the same afternoon a concert at the Citadel, Corporation Street, raised just over £2, while a sacred concert was held at the Opera House, Burton-on-Trent, where members of the George Edwardes' 'Merry Widow' Company raised just over £7. A parade was held by the Dudley Prize Band in the centre of the town, which raised £5 from passers-by.

Mr Murray, the manager of the Grand Theatre in Wolverhampton, arranged for a matinee performance on Thursday 25 April as a fundraiser. The George Alexander Dramatic Society performed *Billy's Little Love Affair*. On Saturday 27 April many thousands of people gathered at Victoria Square in Birmingham when the band of the 5th and 6th Battalions of the Royal Warwickshire Regiment, by kind permission of Lieutenant-Colonel J. Barnsley, V.D., Lieutenant-Colonel E. Martineau, V.D. and officers of the regiments gave a concert lasting an hour and a half, arranged and conducted by Heinrich Suck under the patronage of the Lord Mayor W.H. Bowater. This large event clashed with a matinee performance at the Grand Theatre in Birmingham, which boasted a host of stars including the Stella Girls, the Aerial Smiths, Arthur Slater, Violet King, Wood, Wells and Wilkins, and Willie Pantzer and his brothers performing feats of strength and balancing, as well as a full orchestra. The variety show was not as well attended as expected, which was disappointing, but those attending fully appreciated the show and their enthusiasm made up for the lack of numbers. The following night a *Titanic* fundraising concert was held at Birmingham Town Hall featuring Gladys Ashton (soprano), Bergitte Blackstad (contralto), Mr J. Alban Cohan (tenor), Charles Collier (harpist) and Wymark Stratton (accompanist). Selections of music were also played by the City of Birmingham Military Band conducted by Heinrich Suck. The entire audience at the town hall stood and sang hymns including 'Nearer My God To Thee'. On 5 May, Birmingham's Alexander Theatre staged a charity concert featuring a grand orchestra of sixty performers. The theatre was lent by Leon Salberg and all of the performers gave their time free of charge.

Collections were also made at church services across the region. Sunday 21 April was the first Sunday following the sinking and *Titanic* was the only subject of the sermons. The Bishop of Birmingham, Dr Russell Wakefield, spoke at a confirmation service at St Basil's Church where he commented on how much attention was given to every comfort of the passengers at the expense of safety. At Birmingham's Parish Church of St Martin's a special service was held followed by an organ recital by Dr W. John Reynolds, who played Mendelssohn's 'Funeral March in E minor', Beethoven's 'March in A flat' and Chopin's 'March in C minor'. At Moseley Congregational Church the service had a particular interest as the congregation remembered George Gumery, one of their flock who had gone down on the ship. In the morning service, the choir sang the Gaul's anthem 'No Shadows Yonder' and the hymn 'Nearer My God To Thee' was sung. The Reverend Thomas Towers preached from the text, 'And the sea shall give up their dead which were in it', and asked, 'Could their faith see anything beyond the scene of desolation, the engulfing wave which swallowed up more than 1,000 precious lives?'

The Reverend F. Oscar Lane at Moseley Parish Church said that their 'hearts went out to the survivors many of whom had lost one or more of those near and dear to them'. A similar event took place at Moseley Baptist Church, and at the Society of Friends meeting in Moseley Road Friends' Institute Barrow Cadbury gave out the hymn 'Nearer My God To Thee', which was sung with such feeling. At the Carr's Lane Chapel, the Reverend Thomas Nicholson of Paddington referred to the *Titanic* disaster. At St Phillip's Cathedral, Canon William Hartley Carnegie expressed the feelings of everyone, stating that they were stunned and overwhelmed by the appalling character of the catastrophe. At the Central Hall, the Reverend Luke J. Wiseman conducted a memorial service, which opened with the playing of 'O Rest in the Lord'. Churches in Handsworth all found themselves packed for their memorial services. At St James Church, the Reverend T.S. Cave spoke of the splendid behaviour of the Anglo-Saxon race, referring to the men who stayed on board as women and children were put into lifeboats. In Lozells, during a memorial service at St Paul's, the Reverend Canon F. Dale Roberts spoke passionately of repentance, while in Lozells Street Hall 1,200 people sang 'Nearer My God To Thee'. The Reverend John Wills, the new pastor of the Lozells Congregational Church, when speaking of the *Titanic* disaster, mentioned that the late William Stead had been a great friend and that he was also an intimate acquaintance of the Marconi operator, Harold Bride.

In Dudley, Mayor Sir George Bean, along with members of the corporation, attended a memorial service held at the Dudley Parish Church of St Thomas in the high street. The service was conducted by the Reverend A. Gray Maitland and the organist T.W. North, who played the 'Dead March (from Saul)'. The Mayor's chaplain, the Reverend B.J. Marriott, gave a short address to a packed congregation. Across Worcester, churches found themselves with more attendees than they had seen for some time. Canon Wilson at Worcester Cathedral announced that the evening's service had been adjusted in remembrance of those who had died and that the 'Dead March' would be played at the end of the evening. Services in churches in Worcester were more poignant because 'two of her sons are among the lost and she rejoices in the historic heroism of the great tragedy upon the trackless waters, for one of her daughters is saved'. So it was across the whole Midlands, in Coventry Cathedral, local chapels, churches and meeting houses in Warwick,

Stourbridge, West Bromwich and Leamington Spa, and in hundreds of other places the outpouring of grief was, and probably remains, unprecedented.

Grief was not limited to church services; people poured out their feeling in poetry. A number of these poems were published in newspapers. William Bargery was a 42-year-old insurance agent living at Osborne Road, Sparkbrook. He was so moved by the disaster that on 30 April he sent a poem to Her Majesty Queen Mary, which was subsequently published in the *Birmingham Weekly Mercury*:

THE LOSS OF THE TITANIC
by William Bargery

The nation's head is bow'd to-day,
Those whom we lov'd have pass'd away,
Claimed by the greedy sea.
O God, how awful was their fate
The great ship's signals were too late
We trust they are with Thee.
Lord of the earth and sea and sky,
Hear, O God hear the orphans' cry,
Dry up the widows' tears,
O, be there comforter and friend,
Be mindful of them to the end
And drive away their fears.
O may they place their hand in Thine,
Thou'lt safely lead them through time,
And land them safe in Heaven,
The widow then shall join her mate,
The orphan sing, and dance and prate,
With joy his heart is leaven'd.
Their lov'd ones have but gone before,
They have now reach'd a calmer shore,
No breakers are ahead.
Calm are the waters of Heaven's sea,
Lash'd by the winds they'll never be
No shipwrecks there they dread.
A nobler ship ne'er left a port,
A thing on beauty, no-one thought

That she could ever sink.
Man's ingenuities are vain
'Gainst fate, which follows in his train.
No matter how he thinks.
The nation's head is bow'd to-day,
In meekness we would humbly pray
May we a lesson learn.
With carefulness to plough the main,
That it may not occur again,
The lesson deep in burn.

As more details emerged, the fate of the Midlands passengers and crew became clear. Captain Smith had gone down with his ship and some reports had suggested he had committed suicide, others that he was last seen holding a child in the water, and another report had him calling through the Hudsons' made megaphone, 'Abandon ship, every man for himself!' The truth was no one was sure what had happened to Captain Smith, after he was seen entering the bridge shortly before the bow went under the water. The other midland crew members who perished were: Henry Brewer, Arthur Derrett, James Dinenege, M.W. Golder, George Gumery, George Hinkley, Leonard Hodgkinson, William Kingscote, Frank Roberts, W. Smith, Edward Ward and Henry Wood. Apart from Captain Smith, the highest-profile member of the ship's company was bandsman John Wesley Woodward from West Bromwich. The almost mythological image of the band playing 'Nearer My God To Thee' as the ship was sinking stirred the imagination and emotions of midlanders and the title 'hero' was instantly given to the cellist from the Black Country.

There was good news, too. Stewardess Kate Smith from Gloucester was saved, so too was Third Butcher Christopher Mills, Handsworth-born William Ward, and most amazingly of all Samuel Hemming the heroic lamp trimmer who, with the rest of the surviving crew, had been called to give evidence at the American inquiry. The local press was keen to get interviews, but the crew had been silenced by their appearances at the inquiry, and then again when the British inquiry was in session. Afterwards, those who wanted to work for White Star again thought it was best that they kept away from the press.

With the crew of *Carpathia* remaining silent, the Midlands' press tried alternatives. The *Express and Star* found a passenger from one of the potential rescue ships, SS *Virginian* of the Allan Line. Herbert William Fairall had returned to Wolverhampton after spending three years in Canada. He set sail on *Virginian* on 12 April, calling at St John's before heading for Liverpool the next day. In the late evening of the 14th, *Virginian* picked up the distress call from *Titanic* and altered course to go to her aid. Mr Fairall described how the crew of *Virginian* began to prepare the ship to receive *Titanic*'s passengers, making the spare cabins ready and preparing for casualties. Select members of the crew were chosen to man the lifeboats that had been uncovered and ready to be lowered. Then a message was received that *Carpathia* had recovered all of *Titanic*'s lifeboats. *Virginian* immediately stood down and altered course. As Fairall described the scene, *Virginian* must have got close:

> In our case it was necessary to change the course owing to ice, and even after responding to the appeal of the *Titanic* for help we had to round a floe about twenty miles in length. We saw in the distance some exceptionally big icebergs. There would be twenty in sight at once but we kept well clear of them.

Virginian had communicated with other ships and the New York press had incorrectly suggested she was carrying survivors. It was *Carpathia* though that brought the news of the lost.

Of all the Midlands passengers, the loss of Tyrell Cavendish and William Hipkins in first class demonstrated to some the heroism of the Anglo-Saxon race. In second class, Henry Morley's story was only hinted at; William Angle of Warwick, Leopold Weisz of Bromsgrove and the American Stanley Fox had all perished waiting on the deck as the women and children were lowered away in the few lifeboats. The third-class passengers from the Midlands probably stirred more emotions than the others; William Allen of Coventry and the tragedy of the Davies brothers, John, Joseph and Alfred, along with their uncle, James Lester, seemed to symbolise the inequalities in society.

Yet, even with the shock of the losses, there was more to come. SS *Mackay-Bennett*, a cable-laying ship under the command of Captain F.H. Lardner, was sent to the scene of *Titanic*'s sinking to try and find bodies. Loaded with over 100 coffins and carrying a team of embalmers the ship would find 306 bodies, 116 of which were buried at sea with the remainder taken to Halifax, Nova Scotia. Of those buried at sea one was George Hinckley, listed as:

> Body Number 66, Male. – Estimated Age: 50 – Hair- Dark. Clothing- blue serge suit, blue striped flannel shirt, black boots and socks. Personal effects: a silver watch and chain, match box, bunch of keys, letters to G. Hinckley, 2 Oxford St., Southampton.

The body of butcher Frederick Roberts was also recovered:

> Body Number 231 - Male. - Estimated Age, 32. – Hair- Dark; Moustache- Fair. Clothing - Blue serge pants; green overcoat; flannel belt; drawers marked 'F. Roberts.' Tattoo on right arm: Victoria Cross and red, white and blue ribbon; on left arm, dagger. Personal effects a set of Ship's keys.

Frederick was buried at Fairview Lawn Cemetery, Halifax, Nova Scotia, on 8 May 1912.

Tyrell Cavendish's body was recovered. Listed as number 172, he was wearing a black-striped flannel suit and had on his person a gold watch, a pair of gold cufflinks and £7 in cash. His body was returned to his wife Julia on 3 May, under the care of Simpson, Crawford and Company. He was cremated on 4 May at North Bergen, New Jersey, following a funeral service conducted by the Reverend Frank F. German at the Episcopal Church in Mamaroneck, New York.

Stanley Fox's body was also recovered and eventually returned to his wife, but not before there had been an attempt by a woman claiming to be his sister-in-law to claim the body and personal effects. The woman was forestalled in what appeared to be an attempt at insurance fraud.

Leopold Weisz's body was recovered, much to the relief of his wife Mathilde. He was found still wearing his black, fur-lined coat with Astrakhan collar. His personal effects were a key chain and keys, gunmetal watch, cigarette case, two pocketbooks, bank book, gold watch, silver wrist watch, two cuff buttons, one gold ring, one pin, one gold chain, £56 in gold, £30 in notes, $1 in coins and $26 in notes. When the body and personal effects were returned to Mathilde she found their life savings still inside the lining of the coat. Leopold was buried on 5 May 1912 in Montreal. She wrote to her friend Marie Weingartnen in Bromsgrove giving details of her experience. Leopold had worked with Louis Weingarten at the Bromsgrove Guild to where Louis and his wife had moved from Switzerland. The letter was published in the *Worcestershire Weekly Messenger*, and perhaps more than any other Midland report it demonstrates the tragedy of that night:

I cannot wait any longer without writing to you to tell you that my husband's body has been found. I need not tell you the terrible shock dear, I know that you would read the papers. I do hope that you have not upset yourself too much. I wish I had the luck to be with you to tell you everything. It is terrible. I cannot realise it; it seems like a dream. When the shock came to the boat, dear, I got up out of my bed, but Herr Weisz would not let me go upstairs. He said I was mad. I went to bed again, and heard people going about, and I began to be frightened, and ran out on to the top deck. When I came back Herr Weisz was still in bed. I prayed of him to get up, and he would not. Then they shouted 'All hands on deck,' dear, and he got up and dressed himself. I only had on my nightdress and my coat. You can imagine what a terrible thing it was. No one believed that there was any danger until the last minute. Herr Weisz said 'Don't upset yourself; there is no danger.' The officer took me away from him, and I went back to kiss him, and that was the last I saw of him. He kissed me tenderly, and told me to be brave and calm, and said he would be alright. You can imagine how I felt when I was put into a small boat, and when we went away I was calling Herr Weisz all the time, not knowing what to do. We were eight hours on the water in the bitter cold, but in good hopes of meeting our husbands at the other end. When we came to the *Carpathia*, and I found Herr Weisz was not there, I became very ill. My nerves gave way, and I was like a mad woman. I was taken to the hospital on the boat, and two hours after I became myself again, being in hope that Herr Weisz had been picked up by another boat. Some of the women went mad and died, and were buried at sea. I thought I would meet Herr Weisz in New York, and that gave me hope again, but to-day I had a wire to say that his body had been found, and so I shall have him buried in Montreal, where I can go and see his grave. As soon as I am strong enough I shall go and start work, as I have lost everything. I had some clothes given to me, but they tell me I shall get something. If I could be with you I could tell you a lot more. You cannot imagine how it was. It was terrible, terrible.

To make ends meet Mathilde set up a dress-making business, similar to the one she had ran and sold in Birmingham years before. Her new life in Canada had begun.

The British Consulate staff did what they could for the survivors and worked with the US authorities, who took a sympathetic approach. Even with the sympathy and support of the community, life for Kate Phillips was difficult – in a foreign country with no details of who Henry Morley's contacts were she was on her own. Her true identity had been established and the US authorities would have been understanding if it was just her, but when she discovered she was pregnant with Henry's child, it was clear she would have to return to England. The US authorities did not want her child being declared an American citizen. The White Star Line had made provision for those who wanted to return and it was reported that she left for England on RMS *Celtic* on 25 May. Her father collected her and brought her home to Worcester where she had to face the accusing looks and cruel remarks. She was assured in her own mind that her lover would have made some provision for her in his will.

Although the people of Worcester may not have been charitable to Kate and her family the same could not be said for the overall response to the victims of the disaster. The Royal Orphanage, Wolverhampton, offered ten places to orphans of the officers of *Titanic*. Supporters of the orphanage were so impressed by the offer that money was donated to the orphanage in order to support it. As it transpired the offer of ten places was not required and the governors of the orphanage wrote to their benefactors offering to refund their donations or use the money to take in extra children. There was a unanimous response agreeing to take in additional children, which amounted to four boys and two girls. Soon thereafter the orphanage received a letter from the Lord Mayor of London stating that a widow of one of the passengers wanted her 10-year-old son admitted to the orphanage. This application was from Alice Lester, the widow of James Lester. Her son was James Dennis Lester who was living with the Davies' at 29 Harwood Street. With the loss of James, times had become very hard for the family. James had been earning up to £100 per annum and when *Titanic* went down Alice suddenly found she had no income. Alice's application was for a temporary placement, as she was expecting an award from the Titanic Relief Fund. James Dennis Lester's application was approved by the governors on 21 October 1912 and he was duly admitted to the Royal Orphanage.

The money raised for the Titanic Relief Fund was generous and the *Titanic* disaster would set the precedent for all future appeals. The fund had been instigated by the Lord Mayor of London for the aid and relief of the widows, orphans and dependant relatives of the persons (whether crew or passengers) who lost their lives by reason of the foundering in the Atlantic Ocean of SS *Titanic*. Those who believed they qualified had to apply to one of the regional administrators. The process, although very well administered, did take time. The dependants of the third-class passengers and crew members were likely to be those in most need. Alice Lester had placed her son into the Wolverhampton orphanage while her application was processed. Once processed Alice received 15s per week, plus 2s 6d for her son, making an award of 17s 6d a week.

The Davies family, losing three sons who they were expecting to send for them to live in the United States, were in a sorry state. The Titanic Relief Fund paid for their tickets to travel to their remaining two sons in Pontiac. On 16 February 1913 Richard James Davies, with his wife Mary Ann, daughters Doris and Gladys and son Arthur, set sail from Liverpool on board RMS *Carmania* of the Cunard Line. They arrived in New York on 24 February, where they were met by their sons Thomas and Richard. A new life was about to begin.

Henry Spinner's body was never recovered or identified; his wife Harriet received £1 0s 6d per week for herself and daughter Alice. Florence Angle, although living in the USA, qualified as a British subject and received £1 per week due to the loss of her husband.

Second-class passenger Kate Phillips had moved in with her parents in Worcester and suffered the consequences of being a teenage girl, pregnant with a married man's child, albeit he was dead. If she expected to be financially secure through Henry's will she was in for a disappointment. Henry's wife, Louisa, expected that she and her daughter would inherit the confectionery business. She would be disappointed too. Henry's executor was his brother Arthur, with probate being granted on 28 September 1912. The will was a shock for Louisa, as her late husband's wishes stated:

> I give my business of a confectioner carried on by me at Number 18 Belle Vue Terrace, Malvern and the premises on which the same is carried on (but none of my other shops and businesses) unto my wife.

The will went on to state that the remainder of his shops and businesses were to be given equally to his brothers Ernest, Arthur and Louis to 'share and share alike'. Louisa was not even mentioned by name, which suggests that had he eventually divorced, or Louisa had died, whoever was his wife at the time would have inherited the business in Malvern. What incensed Louisa was that there was no mention of his daughter Doris at all. To add insult to injury he named Kate Florence Phillips as a beneficiary to receive £50 per annum to be paid quarterly from the fund of an insurance policy of £500, which would be invested and administered by Arthur Morley. The net value of Henry's estate came to £704 9s 10d, the bulk of which went to his brothers. Louisa applied to the Titanic Relief Fund and received a weekly allowance of £1 12s 6d for herself, 3s 6d for her daughter and 3s 6d was allotted to Henry's mother Emily.

Kate Phillips was not happy either; she felt she should have received more and she could not apply to the Titanic Relief Fund. When she gave birth to a daughter (Ellen Mary Phillips) on 11 January 1913 at the Waterworks Road home of her parents, she could not legally add Henry's name to the birth certificate. Her dream of a new, comfortable life in California was gone; instead she was an unmarried mother in a very conservative environment. She left Worcester and her parents brought up her daughter, with Kate visiting once in a while. After a while Kate's father could no longer tolerate the scandal and in 1915, along with his wife and young Ellen, moved to Chesterfield.

The families of the first-class passengers did not apply to the Titanic Relief Fund, but the families of the crew had to accept weekly allowances with no lump sums:

Henry Brewer's wife: she was pregnant at the time he set sail and gave birth to a son, Harry Marks Brewer, on 6 July 1912. She remarried and thus did not qualify for a grant, but Henry's son was allocated 2s 6d per week.

Arthur Derrett: father Henry received 3s per week.

James Dinenage: his widow Alice received £1, his child James 3s, and his parents 10s per week respectively.

M.W. Golder: his mother Marian received 2s 6d per week.

George Gumery: Aunt Elizabeth Sherry received a grant of £15.

Leonard Hodgkinson: his widow Sarah received £1 12s 6d, his children Caroline and Stanley 5s 6d, and his mother Caroline 6s 3d per week.

William Kingscote: his widow Mary received £1 and his children Lillian, Robert, Winifred and Ethel 8s per week.

Frank Roberts: his widow Comfort received 12s 6d and his children Flora and Doris 4s 6d per week.

Joseph Thomas: his widow Rosina received 12s 6d and his son Arthur 2s 6d per week.

John Wesley Woodward: his mother Martha received 17s 6d and his brother Herbert 2s per week.

The hardships of the dependants of victims could be aided by the Titanic Relief Fund. The survivors had their immediate needs catered for, but in many cases the *Titanic* disaster would have long-term effects. *Titanic*'s barber, Augustus Weikman, had helped fill lifeboats with women and children; he was thrown clear of the ship after the bow started to go under and he swam for a lifeboat. He was injured in his escape and was, for a time, in a wheelchair. Although hailed as one of the heroes in the American press, this did not stop his creditors chasing him, as the following letter from him to John More and Company (leather-harness manufacturers of Wolverhampton Street, Walsall) attests:

March 28th 1913

I have just returned to England from New York and found your statements [indecipherable] ordering my payment. I am extremely sorry I am unable to pay you at present. My terrible miserable time in the SS *Titanic* where I lost everything onboard savings (£1000) all my clothing and valuables I am without any insurance and was badly injured by the explosion and also severely frozen legs and fact have been so bad. I have been unable to do anything since owing to my injuries. I was saved more dead than alive. But I am very glad to say I have recovered sufficiently to work again after a whole year of stress and idle. I expect to get another ship and have applied for the *Olympic* and shall no doubt get her. I owe about £150 so I am unable to pay. All the firms I dealt with have offered to share my losses and gifted me all goods I want for a new start. If I get the old ship [indecipherable] I will be able to pay something from my old bills. So I hope I will be strong enough to hold out for the coming season but I think that when I once more get to work again I should recover better by getting my mind employed and keeping busy. I don't suppose you know what was the unfortunate [indecipherable] on the *Titanic* my two assistants who were lost …
[Two lines indecipherable]
… my legs in fact badly frozen but I am thankful of escaping the awful fate of the others on that terrible night. I was badly injured but alive. Now with your kind consideration and patience I will do the best I can towards your account.

Thanking you very much in anticipation and hoping to hear from you soon.

I am respectfully yours

A.H. Weikman

Late 1st Barber of SS *Titanic*

Weikman did return to work and managed to rebuild his life.

The people of the Midlands like the rest of the population had been shocked and fascinated by the sinking of *Titanic*. Over the weeks following the disaster they followed the details that were revealed at the US and British inquiries in the local newspapers. At the US inquiry, eighty-two witnesses were examined, including Samuel Hemming and William Ward. The Senate Committee made a number of recommendations, including the requirement of lifeboat space for all passengers and crew, lifeboat drills, increase in bulkheads and the addition of searchlights. The British inquiry was chaired by the wreck commissioner, Lord Mersey, and came to similar conclusions as the US committee. Lord Mersey found that insufficient lookout had been kept and that the course should have been adjusted and the speed reduced due to the reports of ice. The ultimate responsibility for the course, speed and lookout arrangements were those of Captain Smith and, therefore, he was in essence (according to the inquiries) to blame, although most people saw that it was complacency as much as anything else that was the real problem – an over confidence in design and ability. The outdated Board of Trade Regulations for lifesaving equipment were updated and design changes were made to new ships and existing ones were modified during their overhauls. The myths and legends grew, especially as the survivors and families of victims did not talk about *Titanic*. It was almost as if by speaking about the ship one was invoking an evil spirit. Officially, too, the ship was not spoken of. Bruce Ismay, although exonerated at both inquiries, was pilloried in the press and would leave White Star Line. The third sister ship was renamed *Britannic*, as the original name *Gigantic* seemed to echo the boast of *Titanic*. The same Midlands' firms that supplied *Britannic*'s sisters would also supply her.

The last official act to mention the name *Titanic* was the unveiling of a statue of Captain Edward J. Smith in Beacon Park, Lichfield, in 1914. An influential committee had been formed in 1913 chaired by the Right Reverend Bishop William Boyd Carpenter, with the aim of setting up a fitting memorial to Captain Smith in a form that might appeal to his many friends and acquaintances, as well as to others who might wish to have an opportunity of joining in a tribute to his strenuous career, his patriotism, his self-sacrifice and his heroic end. The aim was to raise a subscription to design, build and install a memorial. It was clear from the onset that Stoke-on-Trent was not interested; there were no subscribers from the town and no officials were interested, perhaps due to the notoriety of the *Titanic* disaster. However, his hometown of Hanley reacted differently.

A number of subscribers were found but the actual site for the memorial was to be in Lichfield. The Mayor of Lichfield, H.J.C. Winterton, took a personal interest in the project, expressing the opinion that the city of

Lichfield, being the centre of the diocese, would welcome a memorial to Captain Smith. Subscriptions came in from various quarters and from some notable individuals, including Waldorf Astor, Lord and Lady Pirrie, Sir George Hingley and Thomas R. Bayliss of Birmingham. At a meeting of the Memorial Committee on 19 November 1913 in Westminster it was arranged that Lady Kathleen Scott, the widow of Captain Robert Falcon Scott who had lost his life returning from the South Pole, would be commissioned to sculpt a statue of Captain Smith to be placed in Lichfield. In addition to the statue a stained-glass window was to be erected in the new cathedral at Liverpool. Any surplus money would go to the Seamen's Orphanage for Boys in Southampton. The bronze statue of Captain Smith shows him defiant, with his arms folded; standing nearly 8ft tall on a plinth of Cornish granite, it cost £750.

It was a sunny Wednesday afternoon on 29 July 1914 when Captain Smith's daughter Helen Melville Smith performed the unveiling ceremony by declaring, 'I hereby declare this statue, unveiled,' whereupon a group of buglers played 'The Last Post'. There was then a speech by Admiral Lord Charles Beresford who opened by saying, 'Mr Mayor, your Grace, my Lord Bishop, Ladies and Gentlemen. We are met here today to pay respect to the memory of a conspicuously brave man.' The attendees included the Mayor of Lichfield, Councillor R. Bridgeman; Millicent, Duchess of Sutherland; Lady Kathleen Scott; The Bishop of Willesden; Sarah Eleanor Smith (Captain Smith's widow) and numerous others, all of whom wanted to pay their respects.

The bronze tablet beneath the statue reads:

> Commander
> Edward John Smith, R.D., R.N.R.,
> Born January 27th, 1850
> Died April 15th, 1912,
> Bequeathing to his countrymen the
> Memory and Example of
> A Great heart,
> A Brave Life, and
> A Heroic Death

This was to be the last officially sanctioned act connected with *Titanic*. The great ship would, for a while, disappear from the forefront of people's thoughts, for just five days later the First World War began.

News stand in Worcester following the sinking. (*Worcester News*)

Commemorative postcard depicting Captain Smith. (Author's collection)

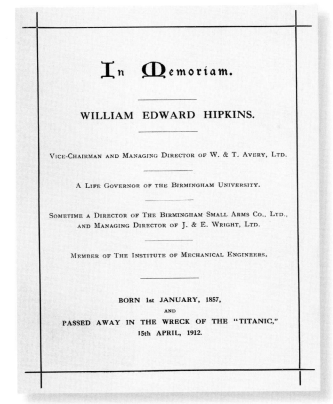

Memorial book for William Hipkins. (Author's collection)

Unveiling of Captain Smith's statue, 29 July 1914. (Author's collection)

EPILOGUE

For the survivors and families of the victims of *Titanic*, life would never be the same again. Financial, psychological and relationship problems would blight many of their lives, although for some who took a philosophical approach, they moved on. Many of the survivors did not speak of their ordeal, and those who did found themselves subject to public cross-examination, especially if that person was a man. The media had been outraged that so many third-class women and children had died when, in proportion, such a large number of men of first class had made it into lifeboats. All male survivors had to explain to a suspicious public why they had survived, and it was prudent therefore for surviving men to keep a low profile.

There were some men who didn't have to keep a low profile – those seen as heroes, the men who had helped women and children into the boats and had been thrust into the sea when the ship sank. Samuel Hemming was one of these men; he did not seek publicity and, being a man who coped well under stress, he simply continued with the rest of his life and went back to sea. He died on 12 April 1928 in Southampton. Saloon Steward William Ward had been ordered into a lifeboat and his actions that night also brought praise. He continued to work at sea, eventually going to Australia with his family. Following the death of his wife Amelia he remarried, to Mary Gertrude Aldous. They had a son named Kenneth who was born in Sydney on the *Titanic* anniversary – 15 April 1928. William Ward died in Sydney on 19 July 1941.

After *Titanic*, Christopher Mills joined RMS *Oceanic* in May 1912 and continued his career. On a visit to his son and daughter-in-law in 1930, he told them to prepare his grave, as he would need it soon; within an hour he collapsed and died.

Kate Smith returned to Britain with the other stewardesses, arriving at Plymouth. She continued her career at sea inconspicuously, not speaking about the events of that night in April. Her eventual fate is not known.

The loss of trimmer Harry Brewer was a bitter blow to his pregnant wife, Edith. She gave birth to a son, Harry Marks Brewer, on 6 July 1912. It was the convention in society at the time that widowed mothers should remarry sooner rather than later, and so was the case with Edith who remarried in 1913 to William Edward James Prewitt, a boilermaker. The couple had four children. In 1925 the family immigrated to Canada, sailing on the White Star liner RMS *Doric* on 23 October 1925. Living in Welland, Ontario, Edith and William had another son, Vernon, in early 1928. The family crossed into the United States on 30 November 1928, settling in New York. Edith's husband passed away in 1981 and she followed ten years later. Her son, Harry Brewer, died in Florida in 2001.

Saloon Steward James Dinenage's widow Alice moved to Baddesley, Hampshire. She never remarried and passed away on 23 December 1946. James' son Richard worked as a carpenter and died in Romsey, Hampshire, in 1974. James' great-nephew is Fred Dinenage, the well-known television presenter who was born in Birmingham in 1942. Fred is famous for his appearances in television series such as *How*, *Pass the Buck* and *Gambit*, as well as presenting the news and a variety of factual programmes.

Leonard Hodgkinson, along with the other *Titanic* engineers, was hailed as a hero for staying at his place during the disaster. He is remembered on a number of memorials, notably the Southampton Engineers' Memorial in East Park. He left an estate of £116 10s 10d to his wife Sarah, who died prematurely at the age of 47 on 25 January 1914. His son, Leonard Stanley, served with the White Star Line and later Cunard–White Star Line as a marine engineer, sailing on RMS *Majestic, Queen Mary* and *Queen Elizabeth*.

Saloon Steward William Kingscote left an estate of £84 9s 4d to his wife Mary. She never remarried and passed away in 1939.

John Wesley Woodward, one of the men who played to the end, was unmarried and left an estate of £1,195 3s 5d to his mother Martha. Martha Woodward, who was greatly affected by the loss of her son, passed away in 1926 aged 87. As one of the heroic band members, John Wesley Woodward found posthumous fame throughout the world, with his name appearing on a number of memorials. There are also some personal memorials at

Eastbourne, Sussex, opposite the Central Bandstand and Grand Parade, and another in All Saints' Church, Oxford, which reads:

TO THE GLORY OF GOD AND IN MEMORY OF
JOHN WESLEY WOODWARD
BANDSMAN ON THE SS TITANIC
WHO WITH HIS COMRADES
NOBLY PERFORMED HIS DUTY TO THE LAST
WHEN THE SHIP SANK
AFTER COLLISION WITH AN ICEBERG
ON APRIL 15 1912.
BORN SEPT: 11, 1879.
NEARER MY GOD TO THEE.

The Woodward family plot also bears his name, although his body was never found. The family gravestone is in Heath Lane Cemetery, West Bromwich, and was renovated as part of the *Titanic* centenary commemorations.

First-class passenger William Edward Hipkins' body was never recovered or identified. The premature departure of Averys' managing director threw the old firm into a managerial vacuum, albeit only briefly. Gilbert Christopher Vyle, an outsider, was appointed as a director on 18 June 1912 and a month later was given the post of managing director. At Averys, Vyle would oversee great changes made in order to meet the changing economic conditions resulting from the First World War. In 1914, Averys merged with their great rivals Henry Pooley and Sons. Vyle also made the decision that the US subsidiary, the Avery Scale Company Incorporated of Milwaukee, should be closed; this factory was the reason why William was on *Titanic*. It was closed in 1914 with all the records being crated up for returning to Soho Foundry in Smethwick. On 1 May 1915 the records of the Avery Scale Company left New York on board RMS *Lusitania*, which six days later was torpedoed and sunk off the coast of Ireland. A memorial plaque to William Hipkins was placed at the entrance to Soho Foundry, which sadly disappeared in the late 1980s. In 2013, a new memorial plaque was placed in the reception. The family plot at Warstone Lane Cemetery is the only publicly accessible memorial to William. William's sister Bertha, who was the principal beneficiary from his will, moved to Chantry Road, Moseley, in Birmingham, for some time before finally buying a house in Great Malvern (living not far from Louisa Morley). Bertha never married and rarely spoke of her brother in relation to *Titanic*. She passed away in 1940.

In 2005 William's cabin, C39, was photographed during an exploration of the ship by James Cameron.

Julia Cavendish, with her maid Ellen Barber, returned to her home in Staffordshire and continued her life raising her children. Julia never moved into their house in Thurston, but instead she sold the property and moved into her husband's family home of Crakemarsh Hall in Staffordshire. She did pay for the land and building of a community hall in Thurston, which was named after her husband. The hall is still in use today. Julia never remarried, but continued to travel, visiting her father in the United States. She died at Crakemarsh on 16 January 1963.

Mathilde Weisz remained in Canada and married her late husband's business partner, Edward Wren, in 1914. King Leopold III of Belgium awarded her the Médaille de la Reine Élisabeth for her contribution to the war effort. Mathilde had raised $57,000 for Belgian charities by singing. She was interviewed on the twentieth anniversary of the sinking, commenting:

> Time has passed so quickly. I do not often talk about it, although this week I have been thinking much about it as I have been very ill. But it is very true that saying, 'Laugh and the world laughs with you, cry and you weep alone.'

William Hipkins' family plot, Warstone Lane Cemetery. (Author's collection)

Janet Pickard unveils a memorial plaque to William Hipkins at Soho Foundry in 2013. (Author's collection)

Mathilde performed in theatres during the Second World War, raising more funds for charities. She passed away on 13 October 1953 in Montreal.

For Kate Phillips, life after *Titanic* was not a happy one. The scandal of her elopement with Henry Morley, and the birth of his child, had resulted in Kate leaving Worcester and moving to Ealing, London. Her parents had been looking after her daughter, Ellen, in Worcester, until the pressures of the scandal became too much and they left for Chesterfield. Kate only managed to visit her daughter once a year. This separation meant that Ellen thought her grandparents were her real parents and had no idea who the woman was who visited. Her grandparents treated Ellen as if she was their own, dressing her well and sending her to a good school. In 1918 Kate married Frederick Henry Watson, a driver in the Royal Horse Artillery. After leaving the army he took work as a window cleaner before moving to Ramsgate to start a café business. In 1919 Kate gave birth to a second daughter, Joan M. Watson. In 1921 Kate collected Ellen from her grandparents and took her to live with her and her new family.

Life for young Ellen was not as good as it had been in Chesterfield. Kate apparently told the 9-year-old Ellen, 'You're not a lady now so you won't have to wear clothes like that anymore.' Kate was receiving £12 10s per quarter from the money allotted to her from Henry's will, which according to Ellen stopped when she reached the age of 16. However, the payments were not made specifically for Ellen and would only stop when the investment of the allotted fund of £500 came to an end; it is possible that the payments came to an end around 1923, which would explain why Ellen was taken from Chesterfield by her mother, or perhaps the money was being used to fund the café business. Kate did not treat her daughter very well and used her to do housework, and if she did things wrong Kate would hit her and lock her in a cupboard. This poor treatment only stopped following court action and the intervention of Ellen's stepfather, who treated Ellen much better than her mother did. Kate's relationship with her daughter was never easy, and whether this was due to her being reminded of Henry Morley and the life she missed out on one can only speculate.

Kate never told her daughter much about her father, and Ellen only knew anything from one of her aunts, who showed her a photograph of Henry in around 1927 (later Ellen claimed she first saw a picture of her father in 1989). Over time, Kate's behaviour became more erratic, resulting in an attempted suicide by drinking acid and being committed to Leavesden Asylum near Watford. Frederick was unable to cope with or tolerate Kate's behaviour and left her. When old enough, Ellen also left and remained estranged from her mother, leaving her to deal with her demons. Details of Kate's life from then on are sketchy; she died in Hendon in 1964. Ellen in the meantime had met and married Lawrence William Farmer, a grocer's assistant, in 1935. Six months later, Ellen gave birth to a son, Robert William. Sadly, the marriage didn't last. Ellen remarried in 1944 to a bus driver, Frederick Walker. Ellen was not notified of her mother's death until after she had been buried, and although she always wondered about her father, she didn't think about tracing any details until after she retired from her job at the Passport Office in London.

In 1988, at the age of 75, Ellen moved to Pershore in Worcestershire, close to her ancestral city of Worcester, in an attempt to 'get back to my roots and find some relatives of Henry'. It was by chance that she saw an article about Worcester's *Titanic* connections in *Worcester's Memory Lane* by Michael Grundy. She contacted Michael Grundy at the *Worcester News* and Ellen's story was published, with Ellen believing that she was conceived on *Titanic*, thus making her the de facto youngest survivor. (It cannot be ascertained with certainty that she was conceived on *Titanic*, and on the balance of probabilities Kate was already pregnant was she boarded.)

Ellen also had three items that she believed connected her mother with the ship: a sapphire necklace purportedly given to Kate by Henry, either just before or during their voyage on *Titanic*; a purse; and a set of keys thought by Ellen to be Kate's cabin keys (although clearly they are not cabin keys).

Ellen hoped that some relatives would be found, and a distant relative of the Morleys did come forward. From then on she sought to have Henry Morley formally recognised as her father, seeking out those who might have been able to assist her. Her story was told in numerous newspaper articles, being told and retold with some variation, including the story of the necklace. The necklace was sold to a collector in Southampton prior to 1995 and then later to a collector in Scandinavia. Although, with no corroborating evidence and the fact that, according to contemporary sources in the United States, Kate Phillips was carrying no valuables when she landed in New York, the story of the necklace must remain a legend (a suggestion that it inspired the necklace in James Cameron's film *Titanic* is not true). Nonetheless, Ellen continued her quest to be recognised as a *Titanic* survivor and to have her father's name added to her birth certificate. Ellen's efforts for recognition were frustrated by the various *Titanic* enthusiast societies and she was not invited to survivor reunions. Ellen, suffering with dementia, spent her last days in a nursing home in Worcester. She passed away at the age of 92 in 2005. In 2012, 100 years after the sinking, Ellen's granddaughter, Beverley Farmer, met with Deborah Allen, the great-granddaughter of one of Henry Morley's sisters, and was able to wear the necklace.

While many 'Titanoraks' are swept up by the romance of the story, there is a very serious element that is often lost in the hype. There are two forgotten victims of the *Titanic* disaster: Louisa Morley and her daughter Doris. One can imagine the shock and humiliation when Louisa discovered that her husband had run off to the United States with one of his shop assistants, and with a girl whom she knew. As mentioned in the previous chapter, Henry did not mention his wife by name in his will, nor mention his daughter at all. Louisa had been left the confectioner's shop in Great Malvern and she continued to live and work there, bringing up her daughter. She had no

Ellen Walker. (Author's collection)

communication with her brothers-in-law, and especially none with Arthur. She did, however, form a close bond with Arthur's estranged wife Edith, both of them having similar experiences of Morley brothers running off to the United States with women.

Arthur, with his brother Reginald, continued to run L. Morley Brothers, expanding the business; by 1916 new shops were opened in Worcester and Birmingham. Arthur was doing well. With his lover Hattie Cole he had two more children, Hattie and Samuel. He was not, however, to enjoy his command of the Morley empire: he died of infective endocarditis at the shop run by his mother at 31 Horse Fair on Christmas Day 1916. In his will he left the bulk of his estate to his 'housekeeper' Hattie Cole and the children he had with Edith; the business was left to his brothers, leaving nothing to his legal wife. Three years later his wife Edith died of tuberculosis. Reginald Morley then ran the confectionery business and expanded it further. In November 1917 L. Morley Brothers Limited was formed with a nominal capital of £3,500, with the registered address being 73 New Street, Birmingham. The new company soon expanded, adding a new shop at 3 Hill Street, Birmingham.

The remaining Morley brothers were hoping that their fortunes were on the up but tragedy would strike them again. On the 18 September 1922, Reginald Morley was the passenger in a car being driven along Lordswood Road, Harborne, by a business acquaintance, William Hardcastle of Mackintosh and Sons Limited in Halifax. The two had been to Stratford-upon-Avon until about 5.10 p.m. From there they took tea at the White Swan, Henley-in-Arden, before spending some time at the Nag's Head in Hockley Heath, leaving there around 9.30 p.m. When they reached the top of Lordswood Road, William Hardcastle swerved to avoid some pedestrians and then, seeing a car heading for him, he swerved again. As he was about to straighten up he saw two people and what he believed to be a cycle under a lamp post. A witness stated that William had no choice but to mount the footpath and try to swerve around the lamp post. The off-side of the car collided with the lamp post resulting in the lantern section of the lamp falling off and hitting Reginald Morley. Reginald was taken to Birmingham General Hospital unconscious. He died the next day of his injuries. Reginald's wife inherited his share of the business, which in 1926 she cashed in, when the company was reformed as Morley Brothers (1927) Limited, by which time the chain had grown to fifteen shops in Birmingham. The shops continued to be a feature of Birmingham until 1948.

Throughout the turmoil of the Morleys in Birmingham, Louisa continued to run the Malvern shop until her death in 1930. Henry's daughter, Doris, became closely connected with Methodism and gained a reputation as a singer in a choir during the 1940s. She married Arthur Sidwell Johnson, a Wesleyan minister, and together they spent some time in India where Arthur worked as a missionary. Arthur died in 1992. Doris would never have anything to do with Kate or Ellen or talk about her father; she had, after all, lost her father when he eloped with Kate and no doubt felt abandoned. She passed away in 2000.

James Dennis Lester left the Royal Orphanage in Wolverhampton when his mother received an allowance from the Titanic Relief Fund. He remained in the Black Country all his life, marrying Dorothea Cole in Dudley in 1930. Together they had four children: Alan Louis (1931), Christine (1932), Mavis (1935) and Gwyneth (1941). He followed in his father's footsteps working in local industry, becoming a boiler fitter. James passed away on the 18 September 1972 at Sedgley, Dudley.

The Davies family of Richard and Mary, with their children Matilda, Mary and Arthur, propspered after joining their sons William and Richard in Pontiac; although, like all families, there were trials and tribulations. The eldest son, William, had more children with his wife Isabella: Alfred J. (1913), Thomas (1915) and Isabelle (1917). William had not been well for some time and had surgery on a duodenal ulcer in 1913. There were tensions between William and his wife, and in 1917 he went to Canada to join the army and was assigned to the 1st Depot Battalion WOR. On 8 December 1917, William was admitted to the Wolseley Barracks Hospital where the doctors diagnosed 'anemia and general debility in a dying condition as a result of duodenal ulcers'. He died on 13 December 1917 and was buried in the Mount Pleasant Cemetery, London, Ontario. His wife Isabella remarried sometime prior to 1930 to Alfred Deranzo, a watchman at an oil refinery. Isabella changed the surnames of her children from Davies to Deranzo. William's son, Thomas, reverted to his original surname of Davies, and went on to work in the building industry. William's great-grandson, Brent Davies, was living in Oakland, Michigan, in 2002.

The rest of the Davies family continued to do well; by 1920, Richard senior was working in the furnace department in an automotive factory. His son Richard, who had been naturalised in 1919, was a brickmason, Matilde and Mary were both telephone operators and Arthur was studying. All of them lived in a mortgaged house in Royal Oak, Michigan. Richard senior passed away in 1926, and his wife Mary followed in 1954.

Mathilde married Peter Schroff in 1922 and had four children; Richard married Beulah Broomfield in 1923 in Detroit and had a daughter, Dorothy, three years later. Richard passed away in Polk Country, Florida, in 1985. Mary married Charles F. Benedict in 1926, and on his passing she remarried to George M. Stewa. She passed away in 1984.

Arthur, the youngest of the brothers, left school at the age of 14 to support the family by becoming a brickmason. Leaving school at a young age,

Arthur Davies in 1943. (Courtesy of John Willis)

however, did not prevent him from educating himself; he was a voracious reader, even reading the dictionary and Bible cover to cover several times over. He built his first house when he was just 16 – a Tudor-style house in Pleasant Ridge, Michigan. He progressed through the trade, working on prestigious projects such as the Meadowbrook mansion in Rochester Hills, Michigan – the home of Horace and Matilda Dodge, of automobile fame.

During the Second World War, Arthur enlisted in the newly formed US Navy Seabees, serving from June 1942 to October 1945. The Seabees were the United States Navy's Construction Battalions (CB), initially formed with volunteers. To qualify, an emphasis was placed on experience and skill, as they had to adapt their civilian construction skills to military needs. Seabees often formed the spearhead of operations, building landing strips, hospitals and defences. Arthur was stationed in England, Scotland, Ireland and the Philippines. After the war he married Alice Ruth Bazar from Chicago in 1951 and they had two children – Gary Arthur (1952) and Cheryl Lynn (1953). Throughout the 1950s and '60s, he was a brickmason foreman for the Cunningham and Limp General Contractor Company. Arthur retired in 1974 at the age of 68 after putting his daughter through college at the University of Michigan. He spent his retirement years playing a daily round of golf. He had been club captain and champion at Lancaster Hills Golf Club, having at least three holes-in-one during his lifetime.

Arthur passed away in 1995; his children, like all of the Davies family, progressed. The dream of the Davies brothers to better themselves and to provide a more prosperous future for their family had come to fruition even though they never lived to see it. James Lester's family remained in Britain and life continued as it always had. In general, it would take an additional generation for British families to rise to the level of those who had immigrated to the USA.

The story of *Titanic* will be told and retold a million times more as each succeeding generation becomes fascinated with that one voyage. For each individual who explores the story, there is something that particularly appeals to him or her. It may be the engineering, the story of sea power, the social structure of the various classes, or maybe the bravery or otherwise of passengers and crew. There is something in the story for everyone because all of life is in that one voyage. But no matter what appeals to you it is impossible to escape the tragic fact that over 1,500 people never saw land again.

SELECTED BIBLIOGRAPHY

Births, deaths and marriages within the text have been verified by obtaining the relevant certificates. The wills and administrations of the dead have been acquired where available.

Newspaper archives have been consulted at the various archive offices and online at the British Newspaper Archive.

Allen, J.S., *A History of the Horseley Company, 1865-1992* (Landmark Publishing, 1993).

Anon., *Captain E.J. Smith Memorial: A Souvenir of July 29th 1914* (Reprint by 7 C's Press).

Anon., Catalogue of George Field and Company, *c.*1910.

Anon., Historical note in Hoskins and Sewell files, Birmingham Archives.

Anon., *Webley, 1790–1953: A History of Pistols and other Weapons* (Cornell Publications reprint).

Beverage, Bruce et al, *Titanic: the Ship Magnificent*, vols 1 & 2 (The History Press, 2007).

Connelly, W. Phillip, *Pre-Grouping Atlas and RCH Junction Diagrams* (Ian Allen, 2014).

Cooper, G.J., *Titanic Captain: The Life of Edward John Smith* (The History Press, 2011).

Curtis, Bill, *Fleetwood: A Town Is Born* (Terence Dalton Limited, 1986).

Edwards, W.G., 'The Last Surviving Titanic Anchorsmith', in *Blackcountry Bugle*, 1976.

Gale, W.K.V., *Walter Somers Limited: A History, 1866–1986* (Halesowen, Walter Somers, 1987).

Gilchrist, Martyn and Topman, Simon, *Collecting Police Whistles and Similar Types* (Topcrest, 1998).

Godden, Geoffrey A., *Encyclopaedia of British Porcelain Manufacturers* (Barrie & Jenkins, 1988).

Grundy, Michael, 'Love Child of the Titanic', in *Worcester News*, 17 October 1989.

Grundy, Michael, *Worcester's Memory Lane* (Berrows Newspaper Group Ltd, 1987).

Guide Book of the London North Western Railway (1912).

Hiley, Edgar N., *Brass Saga* (Ernest Benn Ltd, 1957).

Hill, William, butler to Tyrell William Cavendish, biographical notes (June, 1913).

Lightoller, Charles H., *Titanic and Other Ships* (Nicholson & Watson, 1935).

Lord, Walter, *A Night To Remember* (Holt & Co., 1955).

Lound, Andrew P.B., *Life In the Balance* (Author House, 2011).

Mallin, Kenneth, *N. Hingley & Sons Limited: A Study of the World's Premier Manufacturer of Ships' Anchors and Cables in the Period 1890-1918* (University of Warwick, 1996).

McGeoch, A.J., *150 Years of Enterprise: William McGeoch and Company* (A.J. McGeoch, 1982).

Mersey, Lord, Loss of the Steamship Titanic Report of the Formal Investigation into the Circumstances Attending the Foundering on April 15, 1912 of the British Steamship 'Titanic', August 20th 1912.

Moss, Ron, *Chain & Anchor Making in the Black Country* (Sutton Publishing, 2006).

Price, John, *The Cutlers Tale* (Arthur Price, 1997).

'Report of the New York Women's Relief Committee for the Survivors of the "Titanic"' (1913).

The Football Association, Minutes of Meeting of the Council held at 42 Russell Square, London, W.C. on Friday 19 April 1912.

The Shipbuilder, vol. VI, Special Number Midsummer, 1911.

'The "Titanic" Relief Fund Scheme of Administration with Schedules', 19 March 1913.

Turner, Steve, *The Band That Played On* (Thomas Nelson, 2011).

Tyo, Bruce A., 'Stanley Fox's Last Service Call', 'The Long Journey Home', *The Titanic Commutator,* vol. 24, no.150, 2000, pp. 96–9.

Upholster Jnr, Russ, *A Look at China Patterns Used on Titanic* (Paper, 2007).

Watt, Quintin, *The Bromsgrove Guild: An Illustrated History* (The Bromsgrove Society, 1999).

Archives and Records

Agreement and Account of Titanic Crew, The National Archives, PRO, BT100/259

Australia marriage records, 1902

Avery Historical Museum

Birmingham Archives and Heritage

Birth, marriage and death indexes and records for England and Scotland, 1837–2009

British Army Boer War records

British Newspaper Archive

Census records for England, 1841–1911

Coventry Archives

Dudley Archives

Ellis Island immigrant passenger records

Ellis Island Immigration Museum

Florida, USA, death records

Grace's Guide to British Industry

Hingley, Peter, 'Notes and documentation of unpublished research relating to the Hingley family and the *Olympic/ Titanic* contract'

Immigrant ships to Canada listing, Government of Canada Migration Records

Institute of Civil Engineers

Institute of Mechanical Engineers

Liverpool Maritime Museum and Archive

LNWR Archive: staff and personnel records, goods traffic records

Lound Archive

Marconi Company Archive

Michigan, USA, birth, death and marriage records

National Football Museum

National Maritime Museum

'Records of Border Crossings', Canada to the United States, 1900–30

'Record of steamer arrivals' at Belfast, held in the National Archives RAIL 405/47

Royal Crown Derby Archives

Royal Navy Registers of Seamen's Services

Royal Orphanage, Wolverhampton, 'Annual Report: 1912'

St Mary De Crypt, Gloucestershire, Banns Register

The National Archives, PRO

Transcripts of the British inquiry into the loss of the *Titanic* (1912)

Transcripts of the US congressional inquiry into the loss of the *Titanic* (1912)

US Federal Census, 1900–40

University of Birmingham, Cadbury Research Library, Special Collections

William Salt Library, Stafford

Interviews

Benton, W.A., 'Documented account of a visit to Stonier and Company as part of a visit by W&T Avery Limited Sales representative', 11 March 1924.

Benton, W.A., 'Documented account of a visit to Noah Hingley & Sons as part of a visit by W&T Avery Limited Sales representative', 18 April 1924.

Benton, W.A., 'Documented account of an interview with Hyla Garrett Elkington', 17 June 1926.

Benton, W.A., 'Documented account of an interview with William Marrian Hoskins', 21 September 1926.

Benton, W.A., 'Documented account of an interview with Cyril Edward Lloyd, Chairman Noah Hingley & Sons', 28 July 1927.

Benton, W.A., 'Documented account of an interview with George Tyler, who was at the time a clerk in the goods-out office at Thomas Webb and Sons', 16 August 1927.

Lound, Andrew P.B., 'Notes of five interviews conducted with Ellen Walker daughter of Kate Phillips', between 1995 and 1997.

Lound, Andrew P.B., 'Notes of interview with Arthur Davies' daughter Cheryl Lynn Lewandowski', 2015.

Pegg, Norman, 'Notebook containing notes of interviews with Worcester people', April 1912.

Principal Newspapers, periodicals and directories

Berrow's Journal (Worcester), 1909–13

Birmingham Daily Mail, 1900–35

Birmingham Daily Post, 1909–35

Birmingham Evening Dispatch, 1909–13

Birmingham Gazette and Express, 1900–13

Birmingham Weekly Mercury, 1909–13

Derbyshire Times, 1909–15

Eastbourne Gazette, 1909–12

Evening Telegraph and Post (Dundee), 1909–12

Express and Star (Wolverhampton), 1909–15

Kelly's Directory of Birmingham, 1895–50

Kelly's Directory of Staffordshire, 1895–12

Kelly's Directory of Warwickshire, 1895–12

Kelly's Directory of Worcestershire, 1895–35

Leicester Chronicle, 1909–16

Liverpool trade directories and musicians directories, 1900–15

London Gazette, 1860–14

Malvern directories, 1909–32

Milwaukee Sentinel, 1912

Montreal Herald, 1910–32

Oakland Press (USA), 2000–02

Records of Magdalen College, Oxford

Sheffield Telegraph, 1909–12

Staffordshire Advertiser, 1902–15

Staffordshire Sentinel, 1904–13

The Engineer, 1900–14

The Times archive, 1900-–2012

Walsall Advertiser, 1900–17

West Bromwich Chronicle, 1909–13

Western Daily Press, 1910–20

Worcester News, 2010–12

Worcester Weekly Messenger, 1908-13

INDEX

Page references in italics indicate illustrations.

RMS *Gigantic* see *Britannic*
RMS *Lusitania* 14–18, 27–8, 31, 34, 59, 79, 85, 87, 120, 140, 144–5, 156, 220
RMS *Mauretania* 15, 27–8, 34, 59, 85, 87, 120, 128, 140, 144
Roberts, Frank John 124, *132*, 205, 207, 211
Royal Crown Derby 98
Royal Navy 13–14, 18, 25, 110, 124, 127
Royal Orphanage Wolverhampton 209–10, 227

Smith, Edward J. 116–21, *131*, 134, 143, 166, 170, 173, 174, 177, 179–80, 182–7, 195, 205, 213–14, *216*
Smith, Helen Melville 119, 214, *217*
Smith, Kate Elizabeth 126, 173, 182, 184, 205, 219
Smith, Silas A.T. 199
Soho Foundry 18, 37, 75, 79, 138, 193, 220, *222*
Spinner, Henry John 153, *158*, 195, 198, 200, 210
Spode, Josiah 96, 99
Stoke-On-Trent 95, 99–100, 116, 120–1, 213
SS *Duke of Albany* 36, 40, *48*
SS *Nomadic* 28
Stonier, John 95–7, 99–100
Stothert and Pitt 34
Stourbridge 57, 96, 195, 204
Stuart and Sons 96–8, *106*–7, 164

Tangye, George 33–4
theatres 128, 189, 201–2, 223

Thomas, Joseph Wakefield 127, 180, 211
Thomas Minton and Sons 100, 143
Thomas Perry and Son 80–1
Thomas Piggott and Company 18–19, *20–1*, 34
Titanic Relief Fund 194, 209, 211, 227
Tonks Limited 56–7
Trotman's anchor 28, 32, *49*
Turkish bath 54, 74–5, *76–7*, 78, 143, 164

US Consulate 153, 155, *162*

Vert and Company 38, 40

W&T Avery Ltd 12, 37, 74–5, 78, 137–8, *142*, 170, 191–4, 220
Walsall 122, 173, 201, 212
Walter Somers & Company 27, 32–4
Ward, Edward 123, 167, 205
Ward, William 123–4, 180, 182–4, 205, 213, 218
Warwick 58, 143–4, 197, 203, 206
Webley & Scott 60, 111–15, *112*, 184
Weikman, Augustus Henry 164, 212
Weisz, Leopold 144, 172, 178, 185, 195, 206–8
Weisz, Mathilde Françoise 144, 172, 175, 177–8, 181, 185, 187–8, 191, 195, 197, 208, 221
West Bromwich 129–30, 154–5, 157, 170, 190–2, 196, 201, 204–5, 220
whistles 108–10, *113*

White Star Line 14–15, 18, 27–30, 32, 34–5, 37–8, 41–2, 53, 74, 78, 83–5, 87, 95, 97, 99, 101–4, 108, 115–23, 125–8, 137, 147, 152–3, 163, 165, 167, 175, 190, 192–3, 195–7, 199, 205, 209, 213, 219

Willard, Constance 140

William Brownfield and Son 99

Wishwood, Samuel 31

Wolverhampton 37–8, 40, 80, 155, 195, 200–2, 206, 209–10, 212, 227

Wood, Henry 123, 163, 180, 205

Woodward, John Wesley 129, *133*, 169–70, 172, 182–3, 185, 205, 211, 219–20

Worcester 98, 145–50, 153–4, 175, 195, 197–201, 203, 207, 209–11, *215*, 223–6

may also be interested in …

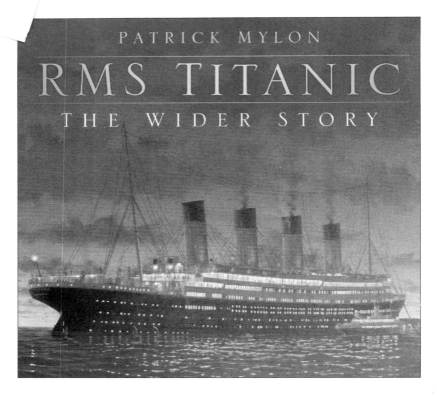

9780 7509 6136 3

Patrick Mylon explores many of the lesser-known aspects of *Titanic*'s legacy, telling the wider story that developed around the disaster. Using rare and previously unpublished images from his collection of White Star memorabilia, he places fresh emphasis on the vessels, events and locations *Titanic* encountered during her short life.